*The Military and Society
in Latin America*

1964

The Military and Society in Latin America

JOHN J. JOHNSON

Stanford University Press
Stanford, California

Stanford University Press
Stanford, California
© 1964 by the Board of Trustees of the
Leland Stanford Junior University
Printed in the United States of America
Cloth ISBN 0–8047–0198–9
Paper ISBN 0–8047–0199–7
First published 1964
Last figure below indicates year of this printing:
79 78 77 76 75 74 73 72 71 70

To my mother

PREFACE

This volume is concerned with the development of the military of Latin America, past, present, and future. More especially, it discusses the role played by the elites of the armed forces when, on their own initiative or at the urging of politicians, they have behaved in an extra-military manner. The study examines the methods available to officers to influence policy decisions, when they are not in direct control of governments as well as when they are. It also treats at length the impact that officers have in the social-economic area. Particular attention is paid to the social-economic background of the officers, because until the services become considerably more professional, officers will often make decisions on the basis of their personal rather than their institutional experiences. Army officers are studied in greater depth than naval and air force officers because armies have ordinarily been more capable of imposing their will upon society, which has given greater potential power to army leaders. This emphasis seemed warranted despite the fact that quite recently the air forces of Ecuador, Venezuela, and Guatemala and the navies of Argentina, Peru, and Venezuela have shown an increasing disposition to challenge army dominance. Also, Spanish America and Brazil and the armed forces in the respective areas have developed in such different ways that it appeared advisable to deal with them separately.

Several concepts and themes emerge from this study. One of the more important ones is that Latin American officers are first and foremost the products of their environments; this should become apparent in those sections of the chapter on Brazil in which the evolution of the military in Spanish and

Portuguese America is compared. Another concept with important implications is that in Latin America officers historically have tended to follow instead of lead, which distinguishes them from their counterparts in the new nations of Africa, the Middle East, and Southeast Asia. But change, constant and profound, both in society and in the military, is the principal theme of the volume. If there is a message, it is that the attitude of the officers toward change and toward emerging groups, rather than toward force and violence and the size of military budgets, will ultimately have the greater effect upon Latin America's position in the world.

The research was carried out and the volume written with several basic propositions in mind. First, the societies of the republics vary so greatly in their individual characteristics, their stage of national development, the strength of their institutions, and their ability to resist political, economic, and military pressures from the outside that it would be impossible to set up categories that would capture all of the important nuances of the existing reality. Second, force and violence, with which the military are always associated in one way or another, are still important parts of the political process in most of the republics, and they must be considered as such. Third, the military cannot be judged simply in terms of being for or against democracy, nor can it be assumed that the armed services are static, with fixed approaches to major political and economic problems. Fourth, an emphasis on the role of the military elites—those higher-ranking officers with the most influence—is still warranted, despite the slowly increasing political effectiveness of non-commissioned officers. Finally, it cannot be assumed that the armed forces will withdraw from politics until civilians evolve stable, organized institutions and provide responsible leadership capable of pursuing solutions to the problems of the republics.

A few words about sources and documentation are in order. The background chapters are based entirely upon printed materials and are meant to be representative of the area as a whole. Those parts of the volume dealing with the contemporary scene are based upon printed documents, manuscript materials, and information collected since mid-1960 from interviews with approximately 500 military men and civilians. The printed materials, as in the case of the background chapters, are representative of the literature for the republics in general. The manuscripts used dealt only with Argentina, Brazil, Chile, Colombia, Ecuador, Honduras, and Venezuela, and the interviews were carried out in Argentina, Brazil, Chile, Ecuador, Honduras, Venezuela, and the United States. Each person interviewed understood that his anonymity would be respected, and I believe I have kept my word on that score. A vast share of the manuscripts were made available to me by agencies in Latin America and the United States to which attribution cannot be made.

I have in places drawn heavily on literature, folklore, and art to illustrate social attitudes. I undertook the examination of a sizable body of material—approximately one hundred selected novels and anthologies and more than five hundred essays, poems, folk songs, and bits of folk verse, plus at least two thousand paintings in a dozen art museums, and dozens of art volumes and journals—not because I felt I had any particular expertise in analyzing such sources, but because I believed they could be used to add a human dimension to a very human problem.

Finally, it seems advisable to indicate briefly what has not been done in this study, or has been done only incidentally. No attempt has been made to recount the story of the hundreds of successful and unsuccessful *coups* that have taken place in Latin America since Independence, much less to recall the names of all those who ruled the people because they ruled the armies. This is not a narrative history, but an interpretation, necessarily generalized, of military-civilian relations. The information I collected on the police and national guards has been excluded because it did not seem to affect in any important way the interpretations offered in this volume. The Cuban militia under Castro was not dealt with for a number of reasons, among which the most compelling is that I had never seriously studied the history of the republic before Castro achieved

power and have no sources on the Castro era that have not
been available to others better qualified to use them. The role
of the various military establishments in the defense of the
Hemisphere is not discussed because that role seems to me
essentially a myth. No attention is given to the policy implications of what emerges from the study, although certain policy
decisions would seem to follow logically from the conclusions
that are offered. This is a study of the internal history of Latin
America, not of foreign relations as they relate to Latin
America.

I wish to express my thanks to Mrs. Carolyn Johnson
Reese, who assisted me with my research when it was getting
under way. I am deeply indebted to Professors Edwin Lieuwen, University of New Mexico, Lyle N. McAlister, University of Florida, Rollie Poppino, University of California at
Davis, and Ronald Schneider, Columbia University, and to
Robert Dean of the State Department, who read the manuscript
and made many valuable suggestions; and also to Professor
Robert Potash, of the University of Massachusetts, who gen-
erously provided me with information on cliques in the armed
forces of Argentina. I especially wish to express my warm
appreciation to the many persons in Latin America and in the
United States who must remain anonymous but without whose
friendly cooperation the volume would have lacked an important dimension.

The Committee on Research in Public Affairs of Stanford
University in 1960 awarded me funds for a research assistant.
Travel and research in Latin America during 1960 and time
off from my regular duties during the academic year 1962–63,
when the manuscript was completed, were made possible by
grants under the program administered by the Joint Committee
on Latin American Studies of the American Council of Learned
Societies and the Social Science Research Council.

                                        JOHN J. JOHNSON
Stanford University
October 7, 1963

CONTENTS

Introduction   3

Part One
THE NINETEENTH CENTURY

I. Militarism and Violence to 1825   13

II. Militarism and Violence in an Age of
    Anarchy, 1825–1850   36

III. Militarism in an Age of Progress, 1850–1914   62

Part Two
THE TWENTIETH CENTURY

IV. Change and Response, 1915–1963: The Soldier
    as Citizen and Bureaucrat   93

V. Change and Response, 1915–1963: The Thinking
    of the Military on Major National Issues   134

VI. The Public Image of the Military since World War I   153

Part Three
THE MILITARY IN BRAZIL

VII. The Political Role of the Brazilian Military   177

VIII. The Public Image of the Brazilian Military   224

IX. Retrospect and Prospect   244

Bibliography   271

Index   299

The Military and Society
in Latin America

INTRODUCTION

MILITARY INTRUSIONS into civilian politics have long been a fact of life in Latin America. The influence of military officers has played a part in virtually all individual and social relationships, and civilians have been unable to devise workable systems for permanently keeping officers in check and military machines subordinate to policy objectives. On occasion, civilians have seemed to triumph over the soldier, but their successes have ordinarily been short-lived; the armed forces, with remarkable regenerative powers, have repeatedly proved too strong for the feeble social, economic, and political institutions of the various countries. Officers are sometimes seen riding the crest of periodic waves of progress; at other times they appear in the backwashes. This situation has existed for a century and a half, and the historical conditions that have accounted for the prominence of officers still remain, in varying degrees, in all of the republics. What officers believe, how they feel, and, at times, even their caprices, probably will continue for sometime to be decisive elements in the formation of national goals and aspirations.

Historically, the nations of Latin America have been best known abroad for their rebels and their rebellions. That rebellions were frequent is not surprising, since most of the republics, for most of the time, have in effect been occupied by their own armies. Spanish America was the first part of the modern world where dictatorship became normal, where it became the practice to tutor democrats with guns, where the military *pronunciamiento* was hallowed by tradition, and where military academies could with good reason be dubbed "schools of presidents." There, more than anywhere else, and for a longer time, ambitious generals, colonels, and majors have used their troops to intimidate civilians as well as their fellow officers. The mobilization of violence for personal and institutional purposes persists today, with only the difference that the armed forces have come to rely more on manipulation and less on terror.

Throughout the 19th century, the activities of the military, often accepted in part by the civilian population, kept the republics in a state of near constant agitation. A few examples, by no means atypical, suggest the extent of this turmoil: Venezuela suffered fifty revolutions during the century following its independence; up to 1903 Colombia had experienced 27 civil wars, one of which claimed 80 thousand, and another 100 thousand lives; between 1830 and 1895 Ecuador lived under eleven constitutions. By 1898 Bolivia had survived more than sixty revolutions and had assassinated six presidents; by 1920 the country had been ruled by seventy-four executives, and by 1952 had undergone a total of 179 revolutions. Altogether, the twenty republics had suffered over one hundred successful revolutions before World War I.

This state of affairs has remained normal for most of Latin America. Throughout the 1920's Mexico teetered on the brink of total anarchy, as self-made generals of the Revolution of 1910 struggled for power and control of the purse strings. Those who were victorious ruled the country with the army and the army with graft. At times it appeared as if they would destroy everything and everybody including themselves. One of the more successful of the lot, the General and President Alvaro Obregón, is reported to have observed, "We can get rid of clericalism and we can get rid of capitalism, but who is going to get rid of us?"[1] In 1930 Argentina returned to military domination after 68 years during which one president succeeded another constitutionally; by 1957 eight officers had headed the government. When Galo Plaza Lasso left the pres-

[1] Hudson Strode, *Timeless Mexico* (New York, 1944), p. 292.

idency in 1952 he was the first popularly elected Ecuadorian chief executive in more than a quarter of a century to complete his term of office. When president-elect Adolfo Ruiz Cortines of Mexico accepted the sash of office from Miguel Alemán in December 1952, the outgoing president was the first civilian since Benito Juárez, in the 1860's, to serve a full term as president. Colombia's officers, who for the first four decades of this century had been largely apolitical, in the 1940's began to play an increasing role in public affairs as politics became intense. With the president and the opposition in a deadlock and tensions so extreme as to preclude negotiations for a truce, the armed forces seized the government in 1953 and made General Gustavo Rojas Pinilla president. Without a coherent philosophy of government and without concrete plans, he promptly submitted the republic to irresponsible military rule. Few countries anywhere have been as disturbed as Honduras, which during the 125 years up to 1950 saw the executive office change hands 115 times, under circumstances that made social and economic progress next to impossible. In 1954 thirteen of the twenty republics were controlled by the military, a high for this century.

Between 1954 and 1960 the pendulum appeared to swing in the other direction. Three military strongmen were assassinated: José Antonio Remón, of Panama (1955), Anastasio Somoza, of Nicaragua (1956), and Carlos Castillo Armas, of Guatemala (1957).[2] Four more were driven into exile: General Juan Domingo Perón, of Argentina (1955); General Gustavo Rojas Pinilla, of Colombia (1957); General Marcos Pérez Jiménez of Venezuela (1958); and General Fulgencio Batista y Zaldívar of Cuba (1959). Meanwhile, General Manuel Odría of Peru, who came to power by military *putsch* in 1948, surrendered the presidency to his popularly elected successor in 1956.

But under the threat or presumed threat of communism,

[2] Remón depended upon a national guard because Panama had disbanded its army.

there has been an accentuation of militarism and a resurgence of revolutionary tendencies since 1960. In 1961 the Brazilian armed services intervened first to prevent a normal succession of office when Jânio Quadros resigned and then largely to dictate the terms under which leftist-leaning João (Jango) Goulart was permitted to be sworn in as president. In 1962 the armed forces removed an elected president in Argentina, and in Peru they voided a presidential election. In April 1963 the military assumed direct control in Guatemala after overthrowing General Ydígoras Fuentes, who although elected to office was in fact a military dictator. In July 1963 officers removed Ecuadorian President Carlos Julio Arosemena and set up a military junta. In September the armed forces ousted Dominican President Juan Bosch, and a few days later the military took over control of Honduras from President Ramón Villeda Morales. Since 1959 Fidel Castro in Cuba has built up the largest and most modern military fighting forces that Latin America has ever seen. The only emphatic setback suffered by the armed forces during the first three and a half years of the decade occurred when the most brutal tyrant of them all, General Rafael Leonidas Trujillo Molina of the Dominican Republic, was machine-gunned to death in June of 1961.

Soldier-presidents have by preference depended upon their military colleagues for administrative work of all kinds. A few recent examples will suffice to illustrate the point. During the regime of Argentine General Pedro Ramírez (1943–44) everyone in his cabinet was a military man; in the Argentine provinces, civil administrators were replaced by military officers, as were the mayors in a majority of the cities. In Peru, General Odría's cabinet at one point was composed entirely of military officers, with a rear admiral conducting foreign relations. By the time that General Rojas Pinilla was ousted in Colombia all governorships but one were in the hands of military personnel and the military also controlled the censorship apparatus. In Guatemala in November 1962, nine of the ten men in the cabinet of General Ydígoras Fuentes were career officers.

But the direct control of government by high-ranking officers or military juntas is only a crude indication of the role that the armed forces may be playing at a given moment, for *influence* • men in uniform have sundry ways of making their will felt. Civilian regimes are constantly inheriting the legacy of military rule. The undercover threat of violence fomented by the military is always present. Few civilian executives are free to staff public offices without considerable deference to spokesmen for the services. Officers reserve the option of supporting or not supporting the group in power; in 1954, for example, the decision of the Guatemalan army not to seek battle with Castillo Armas was what in fact toppled Jacobo Arbenz. When armies make decisions against the wishes of the navies and air forces, the latter often have to be appeased by lavish spending on submarines, aircraft carriers, and jet fighters. Officers can get special appropriations for clubs, such as the ten-million-dollar Círculo Militar in Caracas. In 1959 Argentina was supporting 20,000 *generales de pijamas* (retired officers), and Brazil had 1500 generals and 38 field marshals drawing retirement pay. Officers—particularly in Brazil, but to an important degree in Argentina, Venezuela, and in a number of other republics—influence policy decisions through the positions they hold in numerous state-directed economic and welfare enterprises. Military factories compete with private enterprise in Argentina, Brazil, and Chile, among others. In a dozen republics it has been common practice to "draft" officers for the diplomatic service.

Whether in direct control or operating behind the scenes, the armed forces have placed heavy demands on the financial *cost in. money* resources of a majority of the republics. In the late 1950's the services were costing the nations nearly $1.5 billion annually, or the equivalent of approximately one in six of their national tax dollars, as compared to one in fifteen tax dollars spent for education. Between 1954 and 1959, Brazil spent more on its armed forces than on all public works and development programs combined. In recent years the military's share of the gross domestic product has varied from 3.3 per cent in Peru to 2.8 per cent in Brazil, 2.6 per cent in Chile, 2.2 per cent in Venezuela, 0.8 per cent in Mexico, and 0.5 per cent in Costa Rica; it is 9.8 per cent in the United States.[3]

The area's investment in its armed forces keeps approximately 600,000 men under arms, more than a fifth of whom are in Brazil, which alone provides employment for 600,000 civilians in defense industries. During the past two decades expansion of the armed forces personnel has kept pace with or exceeded the rapid population growth of most of the republics. Because unemployment and underemployment have been so widespread, the social cost of maintaining such large numbers of men in low productive activities has been less than might be expected.

Despite all this, the populations of the various republics are still quick to accept and salute the men in uniform. They line parade routes by the tens of thousands to observe the pomp and pageantry and the gaudy display of the services. In 1960 Ecuador was erecting monuments to those who had fought in defense of the nation against the "Peruvian invaders" of 1941. In the same year Brazilians unveiled in Princess Isabel Park in Saõ Paulo, with considerable fanfare, "the largest equestrian statue in the world"; it was in honor of the Duke of Caxias (Luis Alves de Lima e Silva), "pacifier" during the civil wars of the 1830's and 1840's, hero of the Paraguayan War, and "patron" of the army. Brazil flew two cabinet members to Asunción, Paraguay, to attend the inauguration of the military strongman General Alfredo Stroessner when he began his second term as President in 1958. Earlier, Stroessner had visited Brazil, where President Juscelino Kubitschek, generally respected as a leading civilian administrator and democrat, extended him all State honors and exchanged medals with him.

Such is the general picture, but it must be emphasized that individuality and variety rather than unity and organization

[3] United Nations, Department of Economic and Social Affairs, *Economic and Social Consequences of Disarmament* (New York, 1962), pp. 58–59.

characterize Latin America. Some of the republics have had an occasional officer-statesman who has been imbued with lofty idealism. In some, the tendency has been away from the personal seizure of power by officers. In Uruguay, Costa Rica, and Chile the armed forces have remained in the background throughout most of this century, and militarism as an art has declined significantly in those countries. In Mexico the military have been essentially nonpolitical for a quarter of a century, and the armed services have not overthrown an administration in four decades; furthermore, the number of officers in the Mexican congress, although still impressive, is declining, and in the cabinets only defense posts are held by military men. In 1952 the Bolivian military were defeated by civilian forces and subsequently a people's militia was created which is as strong as or stronger than the regular forces.[4] By any standard, the armed forces of Brazil have a generally commendable record, despite their conduct in 1961; by Latin American standards, they have been remarkable for their reluctance to use terror and bloodshed in pursuit of their objectives. Uruguay has kept military expenditures down since World War I, and more recently Mexico, Bolivia, and Costa Rica have dramatically reduced the military's share of the budget without serious political consequences. As of October 1963, civilian authorities were clearly supreme in Bolivia, Chile, Costa Rica, Mexico, and Uruguay. Colombia's traditionally apolitical officers, after a decade-long foray into politics, appeared content to let civilians again assert their leadership. The longer that President Rómulo Betancourt stayed in office, the more willing the Venezuelan armed forces appeared to see him serve out his term.

All of these activities are pertinent to the social, economic, and political evolution of the Hemisphere, but they hardly portend the approach of a new era in which civilian and military spheres of responsibility will at last be sharply delineated in

[4] In recent years the Bolivian government has been rebuilding the regular armed forces as a counterweight to the politically manipulated militia, which appears to some as a threat to peace and political stability.

Latin America. It is more likely that the quest for progress through construction and the demand for change through violence will create a climate of discussion in which the military will thrive. The armed forces will often control civilian politics and judge civilian authority, and military solutions to social, economic, and political problems will remain a commonplace.

PART ONE

THE NINETEENTH CENTURY

MILITARISM AND VIOLENCE TO 1825

SPAIN held sway over a third of the Western Hemisphere for more than three centuries. The American empire of the Spanish kings was born in violence, matured in violence, and died in violence. But despite the brutality and savagery of the Spanish culture in the New World, Spanish armies did not display praetorian tendencies so long as they served the King; America was remarkably free of militarism for all but a brief period before the colonials set about to break their ties with the mother country. It was only with the Wars of Independence that Spanish America came to feel the full and devastating force of militarism. Militarism, when it came, gave a new dimension to the violence of an earlier period.

The conquest of Spanish America was fashioned by individualistic, haughty, sensitive leaders. They were the heirs of an heroic eight-century-long crusade against the infidel Moor, the remnants of the fighting forces that had driven the last Moorish armies from Spain in the same year that Columbus discovered America. At only fleeting moments during the crusade had the arts of commerce, industry, and agriculture competed with the arts of war. The conquerors, consequently, were neither men of peace nor entrepreneurs, but warriors on horseback who fought with atavistic fervor. Their conquests, which in less than a half century drew a sixth of the earth's inhabitable surface into the Spanish orbit, were conquests by force, slaughter, and terror—victories of the strong and bold over the weak and timid. The conquerors gave little thought to their role as colonizers until the conquest was completed.

The *conquistadores* dominated the Indians by sheer weight

of personality and daring. Far from Spain, the leaders were on their own. Their men were able and adventurous individuals like themselves, and just as convinced that the New World owed them a fortune. They followed only so long as their leaders kept them occupied and did what had to be done more expertly than any one of them could do it. No one knew better than a Hernán Cortés or a Francisco Pizarro that constant movement was one of the keys to success. Once they had taken an objective, they rushed their lieutenants off on new assignments, hoping, but never being sure, that the activity of the march would discourage intrigue. They were not always successful, and almost from the first the Spaniards fell to fighting one another. It took a crisis situation, a conquest or the threat of an attack, to hold such men together in a cooperative enterprise. Once an emergency had passed they were quick to fall back upon their own individual resourcefulness. In the colonies warriors were permanent, but armies were not.

Force and violence became a way of life that endured in Spanish America even after the mother country was expelled. The Indian masses were defenseless against the distempered will of conquerors. Their way of life was not significantly altered with the advent of militarism near the end of the colonial era. At that time privilege and corruption increased but brutality and cruelty did not; the sharing of spoils and privileges that the militarists insisted upon was accomplished at the expense of the privileged groups whose sense of social responsibility was hardly more developed than that of the soldiers. The working people were not driven harder when the soldier became a militarist because they were already being pushed to the limits of their physical capabilities; rather, the group sharing the fruits of Indian labor was expanded.

It is not surprising that force and violence played a more profound role than militarism during the three hundred years that Spain ruled in the New World. The background of the Spanish conquerors, the mentality of the Indians conquered, the remoteness of the colonies, the distribution of a small and primitive population over limitless expanses, and two centuries of isolation from the non-Iberian world—all this led the colonials to favor rugged individualism over institutionalized militarism.

On the battlefield the millions of Indians were no match for the intrepid brigands from Spain. Everywhere, except in the Apache-Comanche country of northern New Spain (Mexico) and in Chile, where the Araucanians held off the Spanish advances until well into the nineteenth century, tribes were cowed into submission. Sometimes they were shocked into a state of inaction by the swiftness of the horses, which gave the invaders a mobility they could not match. The thunder of firearms frightened them, and often they were surprised by the sheer audaciousness and terrorism of their adversaries. Once they were defeated, their families violated, their property usurped, and themselves proclaimed inferior, the Indians quickly became subject to social and economic exploitation. Once the habit of obedience had been instilled in them (and the task was not difficult because the Indian had been taught obedience and respect for authority in his own society), the new masters extended their privileges almost at will.

The oppressed status of the Indians encouraged in them a fatalistic acceptance of their condition, which in turn led them to seek a peaceful adaptation to their environment. Their resistance to their masters was usually silent and passive, if also stubborn and tenacious. After independence from Spain was won, the poet José Santos Chocano wrote of them:

> Mysterious and ancient race
> Your hearts are wholly fathomless
> You witness joy without delight
> And witness pain without distress.[1]

The mestizo, the offspring of the conqueror and the conquered, was restless and unruly at times, but he was no freer

---

[1] Quoted from Mildred E. Johnson, *Swan Cygnets and Owl: An Anthology of Modernist Poetry in Spanish America* (Columbia, Mo., 1956), pp. 110–111.

than the Indian or the Negro or the mulatto to make independent decisions. The total submission of all *gente de color* (people of color) nourished an egregious arrogance among the Spanish overlords.

A class system marked by clear-cut barriers between rulers and ruled was an early and lasting result of the unequal clashes between Spaniard and Indian. The victors claimed the mantle of aristocratic status, and within a generation status and privilege were enthroned. Gone was the sense of equality among the conquerors which had lasted throughout the militant phase of the conquest when personal worth commanded a special value. In its place was forged a chain of dependency relationships, essentially feudal in nature, that bound all levels of the social structure and guaranteed the privileges of the elite groups. This paternalism, which called for obedience from the client in return for benevolence from the patron, was to some degree a humanizing influence in an otherwise savage society. Paternalism was also fostered by the Church, whose local padre, in theory, served as the protector of his community and expected unquestioning submission in return.

The authoritarianism of the civilian and clerical elite was matched by that of the Spanish Crown. The kings were absolute, and in theory at least the system of government they gave to the colonies was highly centralized. In fact, however, the king's authority was felt primarily in the cities, and large areas were left remote from the centers of authority. This condition nourished the growth of local power, from which sprang most of the violence and brutality in the life of the Spanish colonies. A hopelessly inadequate transportation system prompted the *conquistadores*, who in Spain had exalted the *patria chica* (little fatherland) and local institutions, to associate well-being with the family or immediate community rather than a larger, more abstract political unit. Also, by permitting the complete subjugation of the Indians, the Crown encouraged them to separate themselves from even the local community and to give allegiances to their own families and kin-groups, as they had before the Spaniards arrived. These allegiances of the

Spaniard and the Indian, plus the ethnic heterogeneity of the colonies, with their Spaniards, Indians, Negroes, mestizos, and mulattoes, not only discouraged the development of integrated societies and a crystallized system of loyalties, but actually served to align groups against one another. However, in perpetuating the force and violence of the conquest, the major cause was the inability of the Crown to extend its authority over the rural families, who, because of the emphasis on stock raising, tended to scatter over immense areas and fall under the brutalizing influence of life on the plains and pampas, and in the mountains and jungles.

Except in unusual circumstances, the *hacendado* was hardly conscious of the presence of the mother country. He could not look to the Crown for protection against the ever-present dangers of life. He was left to his own resources as long as he fulfilled the loosely defined military obligations of the feudal-like system in which he lived and recognized the ultimate authority of the Spanish Crown. He was free to assume personal responsibility for the welfare of his family and property and, much like a feudal lord, for the care of those who associated themselves in one way or another with the hacienda. The hacienda, consequently, became a social unit whose government was the person of the *hacendado*. He dispensed pay, punishment, and protection. In fulfilling his obligations as provider and guardian he was free to give vent to a bellicose ardor of expression and to clothe himself in the garb of military pre-eminence. He knew that in a society resting mainly on force his prestige was never higher than when he was at the head of his troops. The private army, called into being for a specific undertaking and disbanded once the assignment was carried out, was another manifestation of the force and violence that characterized the age; it was not evidence of militarism, which typically results from the disciplinary breakdown of an institutionalized fighting force.

The cities, meanwhile, were at bottom orderly. There were occasional riots (as for example in Mexico during the seventeenth century) and there were isolated outbursts by individuals who chose to settle their personal grudges by resort to force, but these did not threaten established institutions or Spanish control. Under such conditions a small nucleus of military men from Spain sufficed to maintain internal order even in the largest centers of population. In no case were the troops garrisoned in the cities a determining factor in the political development of the colonies, nor were the privately supported militias like those in Mexico City and Puebla.

With the private armies responsible for the countryside and the cities compliant, defense of the colonies was largely limited to countering the thrust of the latecomers—Great Britain, France, and the Netherlands. Their challenges, except for the Dutch effort between 1625 and 1654, were sporadic and weak until the eighteenth century, and Spain's responses to them were halfhearted. With a continent at stake, attackers and attacked alike seldom committed more than a handful of men. As late as 1758 there were only three thousand regulars in what is now Mexico.

Although the colonists' share in the defense of the empire was important, Spain's forces were for the most part professional soldiers and sailors from the Peninsula who were sent to the New World on regular assignments and who, it was expected, would return to the mother country when their tour of duty terminated.

The French Bourbons, when they came to power in Spain in 1700, held to the policy of their Hapsburg predecessors that limited the colonials' participation in their own defense. With troops from Europe the Spanish rulers withstood the mounting pressure of British smugglers and British merchants that terminated in the indecisive War of Jenkins' Ear (1739–41). Even after defeat at the hands of the British in the Seven Years' War made clear the inadequacy of the overseas military establishments, Madrid continued to think in terms of a colonial army manned by Spaniards. It was only when economic conditions made it impractical to maintain enough regulars in America that the mother country reluctantly approved the creation of colonial militias. Officers and regulars from Spain, however, continued to come to America until the French inva-

sion of the Peninsula in 1808 temporarily suspended the sending of military men to America. Some of those who came to
America during the late eighteenth century served in all-
Spanish contingents and others were placed in the colonial
militias, where they were often favored over the colonials. The
resentment of the colonials over this condition was manifest;
the declaration of independence of the Dominican Republic in
December 1821, for example, took note of the favoritism shown
Spanish officers and the fact that their high salaries had to be
paid from the exhausted revenues of the Province.

The creole elite hailed the formation of the colonial militias.
Deprived for generations of the recognition to which they felt
entitled by their wealth and talent by a system that reserved
most high posts in government and the Church for Spaniards
born on the Peninsula, the creoles, once the opportunity presented itself, took advantage of their social and financial position to gain commissions in the militias. Mounted on their
favorite chargers, dressed in bright uniforms and gold braid,
commanding companies of troops on Sunday parade or marching off to war afforded the prestige and inevitable distinction
accorded the soldier in societies that rest mainly on force. And
the color and bravado offered an exhilarating diversion from
their otherwise humdrum life. More important, both commissioned officers and enlisted men in the militias were entitled
to the privileges of the *fuero militar,* which, according to Lyle
N. McAlister, were interpreted in New Spain (Mexico) to permit officers to "make sport of justice, avoid payment of their
debts, establish gambling houses, and lead a dissolute life under
the protection of their epaulets."[2]

The militias, meanwhile, did not provide formidable fighting forces. Training was often haphazard and troops were often
without arms, uniforms, or equipment. The only impressive
show of force by any creole group before 1810 was that of the
militia that successfully resisted the British invasion of the
port of Buenos Aires in 1806. But that militia was not the

[2] Lyle N. McAlister, *The Fuero Militar in New Spain* (Gainesville,
Fla., 1957). I have relied quite heavily on this study for materials relating to the late colonial period.

well-organized fighting corps that Spain had in mind when it
reconstituted its colonial defense system; rather, it was made
up largely of citizens who spontaneously resisted attacks upon
their homes after the field had been left to the invaders. Once
the British had been expelled, the citizens returned to their
homes with a new-found consciousness of their collective
strength, which a few years later made easier their decision to
break with the motherland. Thomas Jefferson would have approved of the Buenos Aires group. They were his citizens in
arms, natural soldiers who removed the need for regular troops.

Militiamen were often faithless to their neighbors, but they
did not break the faith with the mother country. The militias
did not waver in their support of the Spanish authority until
war broke out in 1810. The attitude of the militiamen was in
tune with the times. Few colonials had cried out loudly enough
against Spain to be heard. Tupac Amaru and his followers in
Peru and Bolivia waged a brief but bloody struggle against
"bad government," but theirs was a class struggle that pitted
Indian against European and as such was doomed to failure
from the beginning. Fanning the small spark of creole discontent provided the Venezuelan-born professional revolutionary
Francisco de Miranda with a good living and an adventurous
life for more than two decades before he ended his days in
Spanish chains. A mob from Socorro, Colombia, anguished
over burdensome taxes levied to stiffen the colonial defense
against the British onslaught, nearly overwhelmed the Colonial
Office in Bogotá, only to be put to flight with their leaders
hunted down like animals soon after apparent victory. Only
the ex-slave Toussaint L'Ouverture succeeded against European colonialism. He fought the French in Haiti for a decade
after 1791, and although at last captured, he was primarily
responsible for Haiti's independence, which was achieved in
1804.

Under these circumstances, the civilians, upon whom fell
the responsibility for initiating and keeping alive the Wars of
Independence, were at first indecisive. Many of them had been

to France, where they witnessed the splendor of that country and were exposed to the exciting ideas of Raynal, Montesquieu, and, especially, Rousseau. But back home the seeds of revolt against legitimacy and the established order that the French thinkers had sown lay fallow long after they had taken root in Anglo-America and France. In Spanish America the seed sprouted only after Napoleon Bonaparte imprisoned the King of Spain and overran the Peninsula. Then the intellectuals, concentrated in a few urban centers, more restless than the affluent merchants and the land-rich country gentry, pulled together their scattered threads of theoretical knowledge to fashion justifications for the dissolution of Spain's empire. The wars that broke out in 1810, therefore, were not the fruition of fervent national sentiment feeding upon accumulated grievances—the kind that the world has witnessed repeatedly since World War II. They were, rather, the manufacture of the fecund minds of a few learned individuals, primarily under the influence of Rousseau, who urged the city fathers of their respective municipalities to emulate the leaders of the French Revolution. Overnight, spirits that had slept were aroused and new energies were stimulated. Uprisings broke out almost simultaneously in such isolated centers as Dolores, Mexico; Caracas, Venezuela; Bogotá, Colombia; Quito, Ecuador; Santiago, Chile; and Buenos Aires, Argentina.

The Wars were a shattering challenge to the political, social, and economic structure. The entire political system and the Catholic Church, the cornerstone of the social system, were weakened and discredited by the overthrow of Spanish control. With the King gone and the Church repudiated by large numbers, there was no person who could command within established limits accepted by all nor any institution to which all could swear allegiance. Congresses were crippled as experienced royalist administrations fled to safety. Economies crumbled. Fields were neglected. Armies lived off the land. Beasts of burden, without which the agricultural economy could not function, were permanently lost in military requisitions and, not unusually, commanding officers failed to leave receipts for the stock they took. War loans drained off capital required by the business community. Repayments were slow in coming, when they came at all. Mines were shut down, some were flooded. The creoles knew that when independence was won they could not depend upon the displaced imperial power, as have many of the recently emergent nations of Africa and Asia. The total effect was to drain the fighting colonials of spiritual and material resources that they would need badly to maintain stability in their fledgling nations.

The Wars were no less a shattering experience to the masses of people. Military service was deeply unpopular. Draft riots were not unusual. Throughout most of the area the ranks of the armies were filled with men of primitive Indian stock, who had to be brought in by forced conscription. Whole villages migrated away from the roads to escape the recruiting officers. Desertions were widespread. The destinations of armies had to be kept secret not only from the enemy but also from the soldiers, in order to diminish incentives for desertion; still, it was not unusual for armies to dwindle by a third or a half during a two-week march.

By the time the struggles had terminated, a generation had grown up inured to battle. Antonio José de Sucre, hero of the Battle of Ayacucho, which broke the back of Spain in the New World, was swept into the contest at the age of sixteen, became a general at the age of twenty-six, and a grand marshal two years later. He died at the age of thirty-five without ever having lived in peace as an adult. Fighting had become a habit to him and to thousands upon thousands of others. Brutality was a commonplace. Bolívar proclaimed a War to the Death against the Spanish soldiers, as had Robespierre against the British and Hanoverian soldiers in 1794. The men who fought so valiantly for independence under José Antonio Páez in Venezuela were the same bloodthirsty lot that in 1814 had served in the name of Spain under the barbaric General José Tomás Boves. In Mexico, Indians killed creoles and creoles killed Indians. Paraguayans fought Argentines and Argentines fought Paraguayans. These internal struggles competed

with the international conflict for the attention of the people
and set municipality against municipality, father against son,
brother against brother. A multitude of warriors had no homes
to which they might return, and tens of thousands of Negro
slaves who became freedmen for having served in the armies
had never possessed homes. Latin America was sick. A decay
spread through the moral fiber of its people. Loyalties to the
idea of freedom and liberty weakened in the face of frustration
and defeat. Faith in the destiny of America became confused
with concern for the destiny of individuals.

The officers of the revolutionary armies experienced a profound mental transformation as the wars dragged on for a
decade and a half. At the beginning, the leaders had been
philosophers in uniform. As the conquerors three centuries
earlier had been inspired by the Catholic faith, so the generals
of the Independence movement at first had found intense inspiration in their prophetic visions of America's future. Like
the philosophers who stayed at home and created the public
opinion that kept the Independence issue alive, the officers
were idealists, and they left their families with a confirmed
belief in liberty and freedom. An exalted conviction of their
providential role encouraged them to believe mistakenly that
they could unite all interests by appealing to quasi-religious
patriotism. By contrast with the *conquistadores*, they were
dilettantes in the art of military science. They had to learn
by doing, because there was in Spanish America no tradition
of military science that they might have studied. Gerhard Masur was correct when he said, "The battles they directed resembled not so much the considered moves of the chess player
as the headlong sallies of gamblers."[3] Only José de San Martín was the kind of disciplined, professional soldier, who, like
the Duke of Wellington before him, could turn men into human
machines on the battlefield.

As the army officers fought with constancy against primi-

[3] Gerhard Masur, *Simón Bolívar* (Albuquerque, N.M., 1948), p.
214.

tive forces, against nature, and against primitive men their idealism broke down and gave way to self-pity and egotism. They suffered hardship, exposure, and sickness and their men went without medicine, uniforms, and pay. Gradually at first, and more rapidly later, the frustrations of the officers were directed against civilians, who were charged with enjoying the comforts of civilization while failing to keep supplies moving to the front. Their swords, the officers believed, destroyed empires while the civilians wrangled over the spoils of victory. Bolívar spoke disdainfully of "those legislators, more ignorant than evil, more presumptuous than ambitious," who "are leading us to anarchy." Soldier Bolívar wrote to soldier–vice president Francisco de Paula Santander of Colombia in 1821 : "the lawyers are acting in such a way that they should be proscribed from the Republic as Plato did with poets in his. Those men think that the will of the people is their opinion, without perceiving that in Colombia the people are the army. . . . All the rest are those who vegetate with more or less malignity or with more or less patriotism without any right other than as passive citizens." So "if the *llaneros* do not complete our extermination the suave philosophers will."[4] Bolívar had improved upon François Joseph Lefèbvre, the commandant of Paris, who, two decades earlier, after being won over by Napoleon, had declared himself ready "to throw the lawyers into the river." Santander differed with his chief on many issues but agreed with him that civilians did not appreciate their indebtedness to the men in uniform. He noted on one occasion that "the liberated, more numerous than the liberators, have possessed themselves of the field." In 1826 he divided the Colombian Congress into two factions, one the enemies of the military, who enjoyed liberty without having to sacrifice anything for it, and the other, those who were for him.[5] The com-

[4] Simón Bolívar, *Cartas del Libertador, corregidas conforme a los originales,* edited by Vicente Lecuna, II (Caracas, 1929–59), 354–55.

[5] Francisco de Paula Santander, *Cartas de Santander,* edited by Vicente Lecuna, II (Caracas, 1942), 137–40. See also José Manuel Restrepo, *Historia de la revolución de la República de Colombia en América Meridional,* III (Besançon, 1858), 143–53.

plaints of the military men were not entirely without foundation. Numerous civilians used or attempted to use the Wars
to enrich themselves, and not a few devoted themselves to
pressing false claims against their governments.

Discontent within the armed forces was the prelude to
insurrection. When the men in uniform lost contact with the
civilians, the stage was set for the total disintegration of all the
moral forces and convictions that had initially supported the
Independence movement. Officers were free to worry about
their place in peacetime society, to take a proprietary interest
in the governments of the states their swords were carving
out of the derelict Spanish empire, and, finally, to challenge
the principle of civilian authority. That stage reached, discipline, which was never strong, deteriorated rapidly. Officers
who had not had formal military training and had risen swiftly
in rank repeatedly demonstrated the inappropriateness of making leaders of men who themselves had never known subordination. Also, as their convictions weakened, the officers found
it easier to see their ideals and aspirations in a *jefe* (leader)
than in a nation, and to exchange national loyalty for personal
loyalty. The familyless, the jobless, the brave, and the mer-
cenary swelled the ranks of the *jefe*, who could provide adventure and the possibility of sudden power or wealth from
plunder.

Once the revolutionary armies turned away from the nations and toward the *jefe*, it was but a short step to militarism,
and militarism made its appearance as a retrograde political
force well before the last Spanish armies were expelled from
the mainland. The liberators turned upon the liberated. Armies became permanent and also the permanent enemies of the
people. Officers grasped opportunities for advancement, material enrichment, and political power. Few swords were
hammered into plowshares, San Martín was one who made
the sacrifice : "I am the instrument of order," he wrote Bolívar.
But he failed to instill his standards in his lieutenants, a dozen
of whom proved to be tyrants or near-tyrants.

As early as 1818 Joel Roberts Poinsett, ex-agent of the

United States to South America, writing to Secretary of State John Quincy Adams, summarized the situation as follows: "Let us look to the actual state of these countries. Can it be said that Stability and Order are established where a corrupt soldiery are accustomed to set up and pull down governments as their Interest or Caprice dictate?"[6]

Although there were early signs that Latin America might become the victim of military ambition, and despite the fact that nearly all military leaders of the Independence movement were eventually assassinated or perished in exile, the articulate civilian sector was slow to react against the perfidious officers. There were some good reasons for civilian reticence. This was not Europe, where standing armies had long been created as offensive forces to threaten, conquer, and dominate, and where the growing commercial bourgeoisie bought exemptions from the military service which they disdained; this was Latin America, where the armies had emerged more or less spontaneously to fight for independence, where officers were first of all volunteers for freedom. The cult of the successful military hero was as strong then as it is now. Also, by the time Spain's defeat was assured, armies had come to be associated with the emerging nations and officers could with considerable justification claim to be the synthesis of nationalism. In actually having fought for nationalism, the independence armies of Latin America went a step beyond the armies of the new states of Asia and Africa, which associate themselves with nationalism but whose nations have generally won their independence without resort to armed force.

All other considerations aside, the fact that the officers could wrap themselves in the mantle of liberty meant that at least for a time their excesses would be accepted with an air of tolerance. But there were other factors. For one thing, the social milieu affected the civilian mentality toward force and violence. By the eighteenth century, when the militias

[6] William Ray Manning, *Diplomatic Correspondence of the United States: Inter-American Affairs, 1831–1860*, I (Washington, 1932–39), 441.

were created, a colonial society, deprived of many advantages and diversions enjoyed by Europe and inured to the use of force, had indicated its readiness to bestow prestige on the wearer of a military uniform.

Following the outbreak of hostilities, matter won quick victories over mind, for the colonials were cut off from their traditional sources of cultural inspiration and learning was badly disrupted. That the colonials were now winning their liberty, arms in hand, accented the prestige of the military. Memories were militarized, for military successes were the only achievements to which the new creole leadership could point with pride. Then, too, since the articulate elements in Latin America retained the Spanish disdain for labor, there was no group to view with contempt the idleness of the soldier, as did the hard-working, money-minded bourgeoisie of England and France, who had small thanks for the soldier who had fought to preserve their way of life.

Finally, by the time ultimate victory was in sight, the social status of the officers was so high that they did not find it hard to think along the same lines as the very narrow elite from which the civilian leadership came. Men like Simón Bolívar, the liberator of Venezuela, Colombia, Ecuador, Peru, and Bolivia, and Bernardo O'Higgins, the liberator of Chile, both of whom were from distinguished colonial families, would probably have been political figures in the new republics whether in uniform or not. José de San Martín, the least politically ambitious of the major leaders, married into one of the most influential families of Argentina, and would have qualified for membership in the inner political circles had he chosen to assert his claim. Officers like José Artigas, recognized as the father of Uruguayan independence and a member of one of the large land-holding families of his nation, might reasonably have expected to become political leaders under normal circumstances. José Antonio Páez of Venezuela, although of humble origin and lacking in formal education, during the course of the Wars acquired certain social refinements, much property and livestock, and he accepted the principle held by all but a few extremists within the political oligarchy, that wealth should be protected at all costs. Páez is also probably the finest representative of a group of officers who, because of sheer personal magnetism and leadership qualities, were welcomed to the ruling coteries. Of all the officers that the Wars produced, the one who unquestionably profited most from wearing a uniform was Augustín Iturbide. Although he was of an undistinguished, if accepted, family and lacked the dynamic personal qualities that made so many officers natural leaders, he rose to become Emperor of Mexico, if only for a brief term.

Patriotic odes and journalistic essays were the typical literary productions of the Independence era. Almost everywhere outside of Lima, the capital of the Viceroyalty of Peru (which remained under the control of Spain until after 1820), the best-known literary men supported the Revolution, and many were eulogists of the soldiery. The Mexican Fernández de Lizardi, generally considered to be the only prose writer of the period to rise above the immediate political situation, gave his stamp of approval to the decorum and discipline of the military when in his *La quijotita y su prima* (1819) he expounded his theories on morals and education, borrowed from Rousseau, through his principal character, an army colonel charged with instructing his daughter in the moral conduct of her life. The national hymns written in the heat of battle were so bombastic that they were soon a source of embarrassment to the new states. The Chilean independence hero Camilo Henríquez was probably as sincerely dedicated to the struggle as anyone who wrote verses to celebrate military victories over Spain. One of Esteban de Luca's best remembered poems hailed the triumph of Chacabuco in Chile. The Argentine Bartolomé Hidalgo told in verse the victories of Argentine armies in far-off Lima. Others focused their attention upon individual military heroes. Wenceslao Alpuche compared Father Miguel Hidalgo, the Mexican revolutionary, to George Washington. Francisco Sánchez immortalized José María Morelos, who carried on when Hidalgo was captured and shot. Juan C. Lafinur wrote eulogies to Argentine General Manuel Belgrano, in whose army he had served. Andrés Quintana Roo, after whom the Mexican state in Yucatan was named, praised Augustín Iturbide; but in one of the few attacks on military heroes before 1825, Francisco Ortega hurled invectives at Iturbide for coveting the title of Emperor when he already held the highest honor his people could bestow, that of Liberator.

As might have been expected, Bolívar was a favorite subject of the poets. His achievements were unequaled, his power to reward nearly unlimited. The Colombian José Fernández Madrid in his poem "Al Libertador," in the space of eleven lines, compared Bolívar to all the great men of antiquity and for good measure included Washington.

But it fell to Ecuadorian José Joaquín de Olmedo, the outstanding poet to emerge from the Independence era, to write the classic in praise of the Liberator. His "Victory of Junín, Hymn to Bolívar," made Bolívar a genius. Olmedo felt that he had adequately honored Antonio José de Sucre, Bolívar's very able lieutenant, by simply mentioning him in a tribute to his commander. In the long shadow of Bolívar and the shorter one of Sucre were the brave young men of Colombia and Peru who had won a hundred cruel battles over the Spanish Lion. Shortly after writing their eulogies, Madrid and Olmedo each received important assignments from Bolívar to represent his government abroad. One is sometimes led to wonder if the art of war was the only art for sale at that time. And it was war as much as patriotism that attracted some: the same Peruvian poets who greeted Spanish victories over the Revolutionaries as long as Spanish forces controlled Lima, praised the Independence forces from Argentina and Colombia as soon as they established their supremacy in the city.

The baseness or "herocracy" of the literati was equaled or exceeded by the General Assembly of Bolivia at the time the "Republic of Bolívar" was established. With both Bolívar and his outstanding lieutenant, Sucre, peering over their shoulders, the gratitude of the Assemblymen was unbounded; they paid greater respect to heroes than to Independence and committed nonexistent funds to the glorification of warriors instead of to the basic social and economic needs of the new nation. They decreed that a portrait of the Liberator be placed in all the tribunals, town halls, universities, *colegios*, schools, and places of instruction. In the capital of each department an equestrian statue—an early indication of the thinking that encouraged the idea of the Man on Horseback—of His Excellency was to be placed on a column. Sucre, being entrusted with the administration of the republic, was charged with having a gold medal struck, studded with brilliants and "of the size he may judge proper," bearing the inscription "The Republic of Bolivia, grateful to the hero whose name it bears." To honor Sucre, the capital city was named after him, a pedestrian statue of him on a column was ordered placed in the capital of each department. Finally, Bolívar was authorized to appoint an agent to arrange a loan of a million dollars to be distributed among the members of the United Liberating Army "as a small reward for their valor and the services they have rendered."

More than a decade earlier, the Paraguayan Assembly that wrote the constitution of 1813 had gone beyond hero worship and had in effect recognized the reality of military violence as part of the political process. They had surrendered the new state to two "Consuls of the Republic of Paraguay," who were given the rank of Brigadier General. All active and effective troops of every grade, as well as all the arms and ammunition, were to be equally divided and put at the disposal of each Consul, and each Consul was assigned separate barracks and magazines, which were to be under his personal command. This arrangement might be called the balance of power at the executive level.

But most public functionaries were far less sanguine about the military than were the literary men and the Bolivian Assemblymen and far less realistic than the Paraguayan Assemblymen. The general tendency was to view the military with trepidation tempered by caution. Although the Argentine constitution of 1813 provided for three representatives of the armed forces in the Congress, the early constitutions ordinarily recognized the armed forces without making an issue of them. Presidents, as a matter of course, were made commanders-in-chief of the armies, navies, and militias. A Minister of War was included in each cabinet. This rather direct approach was warranted, since armies were new and some had hardly been tested. Military service was but one acceptable way of making the sacrifice expected of all. It was not yet considered necessary to look upon the soldier as a member of a group apart or to consider him entitled to special treatment. The idea of a citizen soldier carrying arms in defense of his country ran strong in the thinking of the lawmakers. Few as yet thought seriously of standing armies. It was assumed that when fighting was completed, armies would disband and the soldiers would return to civilian pursuits.

After a generation of fighting, when the time had come to begin disbanding the fighting units, the armed forces could not be taken for granted. They believed, probably rightly, that theirs had been the greater sacrifice, and they wanted something more than heroes' arm bands for their efforts. They wanted pensions, land, cattle, jobs in the government. Widows, younger sons and daughters, as well as parents of the deceased, wanted allowance benefits. A sense of responsibility on the one hand and pressure on the other caused lawmakers to make promises that the nations could not keep simply because they had neither the financial resources nor the bureaucratic machinery to carry out their commitments. Consequently, the "largesse" of the new nations was distributed according to who knew whom, not according to a conception of legal justice. Because he knew the right people, General Páez of Venezuela received property the value of which not only covered arrears in his pay but payments for services to be rendered. There is no question that some other officers, and some civilians as well, came out of the Wars better off financially than when they entered them. But it is not less true that the new states failed to meet their obligations and responsibilities to most officers and most civilians.

The constitutions promulgated in the five years or so before victory was assured in 1825 indicated that four issues involving the military were uppermost in the minds of the political leadership. These were: how to protect civilians from military courts; how to determine the merits of militias as opposed to standing armies; how to distribute control of the armed forces between the executive and legislative branches; and how to prevent interference of the military in the civilian area. The protection of civilians from military jurisdictions was a problem affecting every new republic. During the wars, when extensive regions were under martial law for long periods, military power was unbridled and justice was often arbitrary; the armed forces tried civilians but refused to surrender themselves up for trial by civilian courts for common crimes. The long conflict of interest between the military and civilians in northern South America probably explains why the Colombians were among the first to jump to the defense of the civilian elements. Article 174 of their constitution of 1821 stated that no Colombian, unless employed in the military or navy in active service, could be subject to military laws or suffer any punishment awarded by military courts. Others followed this lead, but Colombia was not successful in regulating the military, nor were her imitators.

The value of a militia as opposed to a standing army was the subject of prolonged argument, with the standing army inexorably grinding to victory. As observed earlier, it was the initial intent of the states to base their defenses on civilians in arms, in the hope of avoiding the unfortunate experience of France under Napoleon. Advocates of the militias insisted that the defense of a republic by arms was the duty of each and every citizen. "All are the nation's defenders" was the way it was stated in the Chilean constitution of 1823. The Mexican constitution in the next year made it the "duty" of every citizen to serve his country. The Central American constitution of 1824, with the rights rather than the duties of citizens in mind, declared that except in cases of tumult, rebellion, or attack with arms upon the constituted authority, the population should not be disarmed nor should any person of whatever rank be deprived of such arms as he may lawfully possess or use. This statement was an obvious paraphrase of the second amendment of the United States Constitution, which reads, "A well-regulated militia being necessary to the security of the free state, the right of the people to keep and bear arms shall not be infringed."

The Peruvians appear to have been the first to accept a standing army. Their constitution of 1823, written under the aegis of Bolívar, retained the militia but declared a permanent armed force a necessity for the defense and security of the republic. The legislators did seek to circumscribe the military by restricting its role to the defense of the nation's borders. After Peru took the lead, standing armies became an accepted and permanent part of the Latin American defense system, although legislators have since then engaged in endless debate on the merits of substituting militias for the armies and navies and, more recently, the air forces.

The constitutions written between 1820 and the end of the Wars gave the executive branches considerable freedom in the control and use of the armed forces. Presidents were accepted without question as commanders-in-chief of the armies and navies. They retained the privilege of naming and removing cabinet officers, including the ministers of war. But with general-presidents already in their midst, legislators sought to establish controls over them before it was too late. The Colombian constitution of 1821, for example, provided that the President could command the armed forces in person only with the previous consent and approval of the Congress. The Central American Federation in its constitution of 1824 reserved to Congress the power to raise and maintain the army and to regulate the armed forces. That constitution, and several others promulgated before 1825, permitted the chief executive to appoint officers under the rank of colonel but reserved to the legislators control of appointments of officers to the top ranks. The Mexican constitution of 1824 reserved to the Congress the power to declare war.

The impulse on the part of the military to challenge the principle of civilian authority quickened as it became apparent that Spain was incapable of launching an effective counter-attack against its former colonials. Nowhere, perhaps, was the fear of civilians to this reaction of the armed forces spelled out more forcefully and succinctly than by the report of the commission that proposed a constitution to the Peruvian constituent congress on June 14, 1823. After pointing out that the wise do not esteem conquerors and prefer officers who are distinguished for uniting moderation with valor and who draw the sword only in the cause of liberty, the commission declared that "A soldier is only a Citizen armed for the defense of his Country, which will reward him with distinctions and honors if, faithful to the laws, he preserves untarnished the national glory; but should he, on the contrary, lend himself, and the power placed in his hands, to the degradation of the Constitution, in order to raise above it the influence of any man who might gain him over to his party, he will be looked upon by his Country and every Citizen as the instrument of tyranny. Wretched is that republic in which the Military cannot distinguish in what true glory consists, and are not inspired by the splendor of the good fame, which exclusively consists in the exercise of virtue, and a strict observance of the sanctity of liberal institutions!"[7] The Peruvians were afraid, and with reason. Their nation was about to be plunged into a prolonged era of extreme violence and anarchy in which officers in the armed forces participated with notable abandon and lack of principle. So disturbed were Colombians over the threat of the military to domestic tranquility that their organic law of the army, prepared as the wars were drawing to a close, cited four different varieties of interference with constitutional legality as technically treasonable, although it failed to mention the act of giving aid to the nation's foreign enemies.[8]

[7] Great Britain, Foreign Office, British and Foreign State Papers, X (1841–), 692–93. The volumes of this set, arranged by year and indexed, provide a handy source of information on the constitutions and public pronouncements of the early period.

[8] David Bushnell, *The Santander Regime in Gran Colombia* (Newark, Del., 1954), p. 268.

The efforts of the Peruvians, Colombians, and their neighbors to check the flow of generals from the field of battle to the offices of government were as understandable as was their failure to achieve that end. Had the armed forces gotten out of hand for only a year or five years and then remained content to live like parasites, that, too, would have been understandable and could have been written off as the price of raising a generation of men to live by the sword. History is replete with examples of rape, pillage, and perversions of justice wrought by soldiers loosed upon society after prolonged submission to the rigors of war. But the liberating generals of Spanish America were not content to be parasites. They energetically converted their institution into a cancer which quickly spread throughout the social body of the already sick new nations. Armies marched and countermarched. Officers affronted the civilians and constitutions with impunity. These men had relatively little professional competence in their own field, no special qualifications as civilian administrators, and represented an institution without deep historical roots in Latin America, but they successfully competed with civilians for political power. The conditions under which this was possible are the subject of the following chapter.

II

MILITARISM AND VIOLENCE IN AN
AGE OF ANARCHY, 1825–1850

THERE is a well-worn phrase in Spanish America to the effect
that the expulsion of the Spaniards in 1825 marked "the last
day of despotism and the first day of the same." There is much
truth in this statement. The young nations—like those of Asia
and Africa today—soon learned what Alexis de Tocqueville
later taught, that there is nothing so hard as the apprenticeship
to freedom. The republics had declared themselves free without having prepared themselves for it. From the day of their
emancipation, the question was not whether they would save
democracy but whether their pervasive traditions would
smother democracy before it was born. Intellectuals could forge
utopias, but they could not make them work. The inhabitants
of the new republics had no traditions and habits of thought
that would propel them along democratic lines. There was no
American tradition to appeal to, and they had not been trained
to respond to national issues. There was an absence of agreement on fundamental ideals and goals. No one institution was
strong enough to command widespread respect, and in absence
of such an institution the clash of interests and passions plunged
the new nations into armed conflicts.

A riotous disorder was added to the social savagery of the
colonial period. Spanish America became a morass of anarchy,
a perpetual theater of civil war. Anarchy and violence became
the universal pattern of political development and force an
accepted political instrument. The "uprising" functioned as
a mechanism comparable to the fall of a cabinet in the par-

liamentary systems of Europe. Acute internal conflict caused ambitious and rebellious men to grow strong; those who emerged victorious could not have stood the kind of regimentation that has been the foundation of the modern totalitarian state. Their lust for personal power prevented the growth of effective political parties.

Those who rose above the anarchical multitude became the arbiters of quarrels. They renounced the *doctores* to whom rhetoric was more important than reality. As an alternative to keeping alive the shibboleths of social and political democracy, these self-appointed arbiters proposed a return to the political orderliness and patriarchal relationships of the past. The laws they made served more to confuse the weak than to confound the strong.

A profound divorce rapidly developed between constitutional theory and practice. The rule of force became more meaningful than the rule of law. The coup became a way to bypass "useless forms." But although usurpers criticized representative government and public liberties, they did not deny the validity of their principles. Given this conflict, it is not surprising that on those occasions when election campaigns were held, violence ordinarily gave the term "campaign" an entirely too literal significance. Transfers in power were confined to transfers in the oligarchies, who conducted a constant intraclass struggle for power but never permitted the formation of a power vacuum, into which the masses might have rushed. The structure of government and the conditions of government were little affected by shifts of power. Under such circumstances social and economic change was in most respects discontinuous.

Liberty, equality, and fraternity gave way to infantry, cavalry, and artillery, as the republics bled themselves in constant warfare. The masses were terrorized into supporting causes in which they had no personal interest. The ranks of public and private armies were filled with grossly uncultured peasants brought in by forced conscription or induced to join up by opportunities to rob and pillage with impunity. The horrors of ruthless destruction were everywhere. Violence and force took on the force of habit.

Battles transformed leaders into heroes, heroes into politicians, and fighting forces into political parties. The land was infested with men of predatory egotism who sought public office only for concrete and personal gain. Once in office they did not have to test their avowed political beliefs, because public opinion did not exist and power, not doctrine, was decisive. Justice was administered without formality or discussion. Control of government made arguments incontrovertible and justified the debauchery, dishonesty, incompetence, and ignorance of a bewildering array of strongmen who tumultuously succeeded one another. The succession of despots was ordinarily broken by interludes of disorder. Under such circumstances the real choice usually was not between constitutionalism and dictatorship, but between dictatorship and anarchy.

The republics were unable to prevent coercion by violence from becoming the ultimate form of power. Once force was elevated to a political principle, violence was rationalized for each new situation. But the ruling elites fought vigorously and successfully against letting violence become the monopoly of any one group. Civilian politicians, sages, tyrants, liberators, and landholders, as well as the armed forces, all resorted to violence at one time or another in order to countermand laws or convert them to special advantage. Liberals used violence against despotism and autocrats used it against demogogues. Violence was also employed by those bent on making a fortune and those determined to preserve one; by those who considered the state weak and by those who considered the state too weak. Sometimes the officers of the armies, which had been created precisely to sustain government, used violence to sustain themselves or to intrude in the realm of civilian government. Sometimes army officers were subverted into taking sides in civilian power struggles. Sometimes disgruntled civilians raised and equipped formidable private armies and then directed their fury indiscriminately against the military and military-backed

constitutional authorities. The power of the victor was unlimited, and it became confused with unlimited prerogatives.

A violence so pervasive cannot be equated with militarism.
Such an equation fails to recognize the essential difference between mobs of men without legal status and the legally constituted but irresponsible forces that scholars ordinarily associate with praetorianism. Nor does it take into consideration
the fact that in the case of the undisciplined mob, the leader
or *caudillo* often was first of all a civilian. In nearly all of the
republics during the Independence era, the military profession
was a hundred years away from becoming a monopoly of the
state. The rebelliousness of the non-military *caudillo* may have
helped to enthrone militarism, but *caudillismo* itself was not
necessarily synonymous with militarism.

The civilian *caudillo* who took up arms and engaged in
violence was usually a sort of "territorial baron." He often
personified the virtues and vices, the culture and savagery, the
arrogance and religiousness of his people, who in the throes
of anarchy looked to him for political salvation. He first appeared when the King of Spain was disavowed and the people
found themselves without an effectively formalized vehicle for
effecting the succession to power. He became institutionalized
when the republic sank into anarchy. He occupied a position
somewhere between the *hacendado* and the central government,
unless, as occurred often enough, he actually became the central
government. Unlike the average *hacendado,* who represented
passive resistance to centralized authority, the *caudillo* was an
activist, a man too ambitious to wait. His political horizons
were most often restricted to his district or province, where
he ruled as an absolute overlord, but they sometimes stretched
to encompass the nation. When he chose to ride out of his
province he was cloaked in some legal authority, perhaps
granted by a municipal council he controlled. With his "legal"
rights he could seize public funds and levy taxes and make
forced loans. Then he fought, and if he won, he was the *jefe
supremo* and he ascended the presidential chair and imposed

the will of the unlettered interior on the capital city. The triumph of the *caudillo* was in essence the victory of the conservative countryside over the liberal cities, which had been the original centers of disaffection against Spain.

Once in control, all power might emanate from the *caudillo*'s will, be exercised by him in an arbitrary manner, be unlimited in scope, and be without regard to the representation of collective interests. Ministers and parliaments became secondary factors in the political life of the territory he ruled.

The varieties of civilian *caudillos* in the nineteenth century were so numerous that it is virtually impossible to find a common denominator for them. A *caudillo* might be extravagant, grotesque, rapacious, and sanguinary, or ascetic and tinged with mysticism. Some were arrogant, hypocritical, repugnant individuals who degraded and debased their subjects. Most were more influenced by their ambitions than restrained by their virtues. Some who felt they did not have enough wealth decided to get more by robbing those who had more, and sometimes by robbing those who had even less. To some, power was a psychological need, to others a means of revenge. Many commanded the rough respect of the responsible members of their communities, and could be compared to the "favorite sons" in the United States. Some sincerely believed that they had exalted missions to perform, and it was these who tended to carry patriotism to the point of chauvinism; they called themselves "liberators," "restorers of the law," "fathers of the people," "pillars of the constitution," and the like. Whereas the aristocrats of Europe, for the most part, sought only honor and adventure, most *caudillos* simultaneously pursued honor, adventure, and profit. Such men were seldom willing to share power, and when two appeared at once, their rivalry heightened the instability of the political process.

Most *caudillos* harvested the seeds of localism and factionalism, but an occasional one, by breaking down and harnessing the power of lesser despots, helped to substitute a larger conception of the state for an agglomeration of personal and local loyalties. Sometimes one and the same person would curtail freedom of speech, show utter disregard for individual rights and contempt for the amenities of life, and give his people the only moments of order and security they had known; but his price for that security was liberty, one of the most basic ideals of the Latin American peoples. The *caudillos* felt obliged to invoke constitutional rights, but this did not keep them from ruling with a minimum of political action and a maximum of administration. They almost invariably discussed issues in personal terms. Their governments were essentially paternalistic, as was society in general; they gave whatever there was to give—roads, tax exemptions, personal favors—to communities or individuals in exchange for loyalties to the government. Without exception, the *caudillos* were content simply to repress views contrary to their own; they never tried to bridge the gap with an ideology, as do modern dictators. Many *caudillos* were international troublemakers who, in their efforts to distract attention from conditions at home, menaced their neighbors. Nonetheless, hostility in the republics was primarily internal rather than external.

Whatever else the *caudillos* may have lacked, they did not lack personality. Personality was their trademark. The *gaucho* (cowboy) who knew only brute force and the sophisticated lawyer alike attached a high value to personal qualities, and the *macho* (literally "male") type was especially admired. The individual who was *macho* was expected to show sexual prowess, zest for action, incredible energy, daring, and absolute self-confidence. Men believed in him because of his rude heroism, because he embodied in his personality most of the qualities they would have liked to manifest in their actions had they talent to do so, and because they were sure that in triumph he would show his friends preferment. The *caudillo,* in short, was often a "charismatic" leader.

In addition to the personalities, ambitions, and elemental knowledge of power politics of the individuals involved, there were basic and lasting economic, social, and political conditions contributing to the pre-eminence of the *caudillo.* The forces of nature—mountains, rivers, deserts, and swamps—combined with a lack of all but the most rudimentary means of communication, encouraged provincial isolation, which helped to conceal the growing power of a would-be leader. Disgruntled by decisions adversely affecting his interests, or simply actuated by personal passions, he could arm his retainers and gallop to the gates of the capital before the government was aware that he had taken to the field.

The *caudillo* flourished in the interior, where to the general isolation from the civilizing capitals was added an isolation derived from the very slight contact between provinces. Each province had its own urban center upon which all the local lines of travel, most of them mere cattle walks, converged. Each of these cities, sure of the fierce loyalties of its inhabitants, was quick to challenge any encroachment on "its territory" by a neighboring city. Isolation and jealousy were intensified when the provincial cities divided along political lines, as in Nicaragua, when León became the center of the Liberals and Granada became the headquarters of the Conservatives. Blind devotion to their own region made rural inhabitants acutely sensitive to any possible threat to their freedom, and their compulsive desire for local autonomy was political capital for any *caudillo* who knew how to use it.

The social system provided the *caudillos* with a servile "mass of illiterates"—Indians, mestizos, Negroes, and mulattoes. Conditioned to unquestioning obedience, they became the pawns needed in the numberless power plays of the strongmen. But the economic and social barriers that the master erected between himself and his men effectively kept them from having any stake in good government; and the psychological barrier that the men erected to shield themselves from the harshness of their master served to isolate them so completely that they knew little and cared less about government of any kind. Although this condition permitted the lower classes to look upon political tyranny with relative serenity (unless by chance they were drafted to fight), it also precluded their participation in politics. Furthermore, the very defects that made them unfit as voters made them fit as soldiers. Between the *caudillos* and these masses there was only a very small middle sector.

The economic structure played into the hands of the *caudillos* from the rural areas. The best and most productive land was controlled by a few great landlords. There was only a small and insignificant landholding group that resembled the embattled farmers of Anglo-America, who were quick to fight in defense of their property. In Spanish America very few had homes or anything else to fight for. Meanwhile, following the close of the struggles for Independence, commerce and trade came to a near standstill, and the business elements of the cities, which had sprung up by trading in war supplies, experienced economic distress after the emancipation, when international trade dried up for want of foreign exchange. Of the businesses that survived, the most vigorous were principally controlled by foreigners. The failure of a domestic commercial class to emerge from the Independence movement meant that a few large landholders continued to be the only ones with well-defined economic interests that could be translated into political action. That was why a landholding group, rather than some other segment of the population, might be expected to react first whenever the status quo was threatened. And the landlord, who wanted strong government, could count on the foreign merchant, who, worried about the legal maneuvers of politicians, preferred to deal directly with despots.

Caudillos were often the benefactors of developments outside their own countries. The numerous occasions when regimes, by harboring political exiles plotting their return to power, gave strongmen in neighboring states the excuse to tighten their controls are well known. Not so well known is the possible contribution that irresponsible foreign investors and lenders made to *caudillismo* in its early stages. When businesses failed, as most did, and the new nations defaulted, as they invariably did, on their loans, foreign capital turned its back on the republics, and this came just at the time when they most desperately needed foreign assistance and skills to revive mining and convert from subsistence to commercial agriculture. Instead of help, the republics were burdened with the reputation of being financially unsound and dishonest. By behaving as they did, the foreign investors indirectly contributed to the economic anarchy which was unquestionably a factor in the rise and growth of *caudillismo*. Perhaps an equally important, if unintentional, outcome of the early availability of foreign capital was that just when potential strongmen should have been forced to go to the public for the financial backing their governments needed, they were often relieved of that necessity by loans from abroad, independent of the will of the public. The loans, and the uses made of them, set a precedent for hazardous borrowing and irresponsible spending as a means of consolidating power, often without respect to public opinion.

What the *caudillos* often saw as unrealistic positions and rabble-rousing propensities made the foreign-educated intellectuals a ready target for them. Many of the intellectuals had in fact spent their formative years abroad, out of touch with their homelands. Much of the abstract idealism they absorbed in France and elsewhere was no more adaptable to Spanish America's environment than were the lessons learned by an earlier group from the French Revolution, but this did not keep them from coming home to expound ideas that repeatedly led to discord.

Most of the above conditions, which encouraged the rise of *caudillos,* rendered the several governments incapable at any given time of commanding the allegiance or respect of more than a very small sector of their total populations. And the weaknesses from which the governments suffered extended beyond those already suggested. Basic constitutional issues like federalism versus centralism and Church versus state remained unresolved, making it extremely difficult for the politically interested to remain passive. As in Southeast Asia today, the ruling class was small and largely overlapped the bureaucracy. The provision in nearly all of the constitutions for strong presidents, and the right of central governments to impose a state of siege and suspend personal guarantees further encouraged dictatorship.

No state possessed anywhere near an adequate number of leaders with practical experience in deliberative government, nor did any state have a bureaucracy capable of efficiently administering even the limited service that the governments pretended to provide. The few officials available were concentrated in the capitals and possibly in a port or two. Civilian representation of centralized authority was seldom seen in the interior, and vast majorities of the rural population were left almost entirely to their own devices. In fact, because of the lack of officials and the crippling problem of communications, the central governments often had to delegate authority to local leaders and in so doing helped to enhance their power position. Even when it was known that a *caudillo* was getting out of hand, the central government often could not or did not act because of the cost that would have been involved. Then it was a case of waiting until the axe fell.

The republics could do little about their grossly inadequate means of transportation and commerce, and without improvement in those areas goods and ideas could not be exchanged on a national basis. Meanwhile, the large coastal cities turned their backs on the interior. Because of the high cost of overland transportation, Buenos Aires found it cheaper to buy foodstuffs from Europe than from the interior provinces of Argentina. A ton of goods could be shipped from the port of Guayaquil, Ecuador, through the Straits of Magellan to New York cheaper than it could be sent through the jungles and over the mountains to Quito, two hundred miles away. With internal trade so limited, there was no merchant class to support a state in suppressing rebellious local *caciques*. Furthermore, life under such conditions was so abject that many people actually preferred war.

There were no national media of communications. Few of the interior towns even had local newspapers. National histories taught in the schools were sometimes written by foreigners and almost invariably printed abroad. Foreign wars were the patriotic concern of no more than the articulate 4 or 5 per cent. When such circumstances are added to the ingrained localism of the people, it becomes completely unrealistic to expect that they should have developed the strong national policies and allegiances needed to overwhelm the *caudillos*.

Nor was a state capable of protecting private property. Law enforcement outside the capitals was usually in name only. Armed bandits roamed the countryside unmolested in most of the states, and especially in Mexico. As late as the 1850's Indians were raiding within six miles of Buenos Aires, Argentina, and carrying off women and children as well as personal property. Under such circumstances the rural property owner, as the colonial landholder before him, was forced to create his own instruments of protection, to make his own rules, and to enforce them the best way he could. It was perhaps not surprising that once he had the means of violence at his command he used them for personal advantage and to back up his "right" to freedom from taxation. Writing of this period, and more particularly of the Mexican War years, José C. Valdes in his *Breve historia de la guerra con los Estados Unidos* (Mexico, 1947) declared that during the war, the government was so weak it could collect taxes from only 5 per cent of the Mexican population—those within reach of the government. Justo Sierra, writing of the same period of Mexican history, said that even as United States troops were entering Mexico no one paid his contributions due the government and the few who gave a peso demanded five in return. Mexican provinces refused to aid the federal government and the ones that contributed the least were those least in danger of invasion by the United States forces. This kind of constant poverty was common to all the Latin American governments, and it kept them from ever becoming wholesale distributors of land and providers of roads, harbors, and other improvements. The United States government, according to historian Walter Webb, came to be looked upon as a great benefactor by the electorate; in Spanish America the only time the government was seen as a benefactor was when a new confiscation of Church holdings made land and buildings available, and then they went mostly to the friends of the incumbent leaders of the regime.

With financial and administrative resources of the centralized authority so strictly limited, the traditional explanation of violence and despotism in Spanish America—the inclination of the Spanish people and the Catholic Church toward authoritarianism—seems almost superfluous. Few people would have behaved differently than did the people of Spanish America under such unstable conditions. Even today, despite the advantages of hindsight and the relatively enlightened colonialism of certain of the twentieth-century imperial powers, the emerging states of Africa and Asia are finding it extremely difficult to avoid similar kinds of violence and despotism.

As perpetrators of violence and transgressors upon human rights the officers of the public forces competed on better than equal terms with the civilian *caudillos.* Just about everything that the civilian *caudillos* did to frustrate political progress and social development the ubiquitous military officers did on a grander scale; under them tyranny, terrorism, and militarism were often maintained at inordinately high levels.

The officers began to intrude seriously in civilian affairs when they used the forces at their command in order to tip the balance of power away from the liberal intellectuals and toward the conservative landed oligarchies, who already had the blessing of the Catholic Church. This occurred before the Wars of Independence terminated, and almost immediately the superiority of the armed forces over the unarmed populace was evident everywhere. Once the generals established their ability to arbitrate civilian disputes, they began converting themselves into *caudillos,* much as the civilian *caudillos* were transforming themselves into generals. Armies took on a peculiarly domestic orientation. Officers became more concerned with internal civil wars, political activities, and the exploitation and oppression of civilians (and of their own soldiers) than with planning their nation's defenses or seeking glory through foreign conquests. Hostility was internal rather than external, and their enemies were their own countrymen rather than foreigners. Their domestic role made the armed forces such valued allies of the landed oligarchs that the one came to lean on the other too much to quarrel seriously, although the representatives of the landholders did find the young officers difficult and uncontrollable allies at times. The interdependence of the military and the landed class remained throughout the nineteeth century.

But not all officers were committed to the Conservative cause. Despite the fact that the Liberals often contradicted themselves by seeking to curtail the liberties of the military men, officers were from time to time found in the Liberal camp. Young officers were often disposed toward the Liberals if for no other reason than that their seniors were associated with the Conservatives. As early as 1828 junior officers were using the Colombian press to attack their seniors.

Regionalism was predominant in the thinking of some officers. Because garrisons near the capital cities fared better than those in the outlying provinces, the officers assigned to the provinces often associated themselves with the regional *caudillos*. Thinking in regional terms also was encouraged by the fact that the officers tended to raise their troops from a single locale. Throughout Latin America squadrons were known by the names of the cities and regions from which they came, as they continue to be in Chile.

The overriding interest of the major share of the officers, however, was not conservatism, or liberalism, or regionalism, but simply power. Although it is true that officers from time to time stepped in to prevent the complete disintegration of established institutions, most often they engaged in politics without principle, pretext, or plan, with nothing except the desire for power and distinction. Such was the intrepid soldier of fortune Antonio López de Santa Anna in Mexico. At times it seemed as if everyone who commanded a garrison, no matter how barbaric, corrupt, dissolute, or disorderly he might be, considered himself capable of holding power.

The armed forces extracted a high price for the dubious services they rendered. Year after year, presidents had to prostrate themselves before the armies they theoretically commanded. The case of Guadalupe Victoria in Mexico offers an excellent example. Upon assuming the presidency in 1824, he felt obliged to speak of the "virtuous army" of the republic and to make a point of promising that he would never fail to pay the soldiers punctually. In the next four years he spoke of "the Mexican army, which has gathered many laurels"; he assured Congress that the army would continue to be well organized and characterized by "brilliant discipline"; and he praised the "exemplary obedience of the army which continues perfectly armed, clothed, and equipped." In fact, by 1830 this army was on its way to becoming the most disreputable legally constituted fighting force in Latin America. Disobedience, insubordination, and demoralization already had become institutionalized in it. Officers had repeatedly shown that they would stoop to the most sordid calculations. Its rank and file, far from being well-clothed and equipped, were a nondescript lot, attired in shreds and patches and often without shoes or socks. For equipment, soldiers had a few rusty flintlocks, but mostly rusty swords and broken pikes. They felt no spirit of loyalty to the nation they served and no attempt was made to create such a loyalty or to give them their rights. A death penalty invoked to discourage desertions was ineffective; thousands of recruits gambled their lives by running off to their villages before their tour of duty ended. In Peru officers prohibited the playing of Indian flutes for fear that the nostalgia invoked by them would be irresistible to the soldier from the highlands.

Statistics are wanting and those that are available are quite unreliable, but it appears safe to say that prior to 1850 allocations to the armed forces repeatedly exceeded 50 per cent of the annual budgets of the new republics. Under such men as López de Santa Anna, in Mexico, the military budget exceeded

total government revenues more than half the time. Soldiers ordinarily had first call on available funds, but even then the states could not always guarantee remuneration of the military. When cash ran low and the salaries of officers fell in arrears, a military revolt became an imminent possibility. It is generally acknowledged that by 1850, except in Chile, where the civilian *caudillo* Diego Portales had struck without mercy at the military, it was politically dangerous if not in fact suicidal to reduce the size of the army or cut its budget.[1] One of the safest moves a politician could make was to support the expansion of the armed forces so that restless junior officers might reasonably expect that their promotions would continue. Restlessness among junior officers was particularly intense just after the Wars of Independence subsided, for the services were then filled with officers of roughly the same age group. Those first in the service were catapulted into the relatively few senior posts and those that came later were assigned the minor ranks and they worried about promotional freezes.

But officer corps grew in size whether civilians wanted them to or not. In Peru, for example, the pressure on the government to keep the officers satisfied was unceasing. The nation's constitution of 1839 stated that there should be no more than one grand marshal, three generals of the division, and six brigadier generals. The constitution of 1856 limited the army to two generals and four brigadier generals. Nonetheless, in 1862 the army register showed six grand marshals, six generals of the division, and twenty-two brigadier generals.

The rise and maintenance of standing armies can be explained on a number of grounds. In practically all emerging nations, including those of the mid-twentieth century, it has

---

[1] Portales used demotions and executions to remove liberal-oriented officers and other "undesirables" from the military and brought the institution under civilian control. In 1831 he created the Guardia Cívica as a counterpoise to the armed forces. Barracks revolts and *coups d'etat,* practically standard tactics elsewhere in Latin America, were ended. Throughout the remainder of the 19th century the Chilean military maintained a tradition of respect for civil authority, but it was also a powerful rampart against social change.

been easier to create armies than to develop such things as modern social institutions, civil administration, and political parties. It is also true that in the absence of an experienced political leadership, the Spanish-American republics needed the great military personalities who had led the Independence effort and whose charismatic qualities were invaluable in binding together certain sectors of the articulate population. In this role the armies served as surrogates for deficiencies in party organization and in traditions of parliamentary work. There was, as pointed out above, considerable instability, and the governments required some means of maintaining internal security and of curbing the excesses of civilian politicians who raised and equipped private armies to oppose established authority. Then there were repeated efforts to upset the tenuous balance of power that existed in certain areas. Brazil and Argentina on a number of occasions infringed upon Uruguay's sovereignty as part of larger plans that were to give one or the other of them hegemony over the entire La Plata area. Haiti, in 1822, successfully moved against the Dominican Republic and in the late 1830's Chile waged victorious war against Peru and Bolivia when those two countries formed a confederation that Chile felt would be dangerous to its sovereignty. Finally, the republics had to have arms to meet the almost constant attacks and threats of attack from the outside. Spain refused to accept in principle the independence of any of its former colonies until the late 1830's, and they consequently had to be prepared to defend themselves, as Mexico was actually called upon to do in 1829, when Spanish forces landed at Tampico. France and Great Britain blockaded the port of Buenos Aires for approximately ten years during the 1830's and 1840's. France engaged Mexico in the short-lived "Pastry War" of 1838, and the United States invaded Mexico by land and sea during the Mexican War (1846–48).

There was a basis for the survival of armies but there is almost no evidence to suggest that the officers had social, economic, or political advantages which made them peculiarly qualified to fulfill the roles they repeatedly usurped from

civilians. Certainly some of the officers from the Wars of Independence, as was observed above, were from well-established
families and as such could have claimed the right to share in
decision making. However, once the Wars ended and the
armed forces quickly earned their reputation for irresponsibility, the social quality of the officers dropped. Essentially
only two types from the landed oligarchy became officers: those
who saw the army as the shortest route to political power
(some officers were permanent candidates for the national
presidencies), and those who were too undisciplined to be of
use in the family business. The sons of intellectuals almost
uniformly avoided entering the services prior to 1850. Thus,
to the extent that the elites failed to supply the personnel to
control the armed forces directly, that control passed to the
lower middle sectors. Consequently, the second generation of
officers, those in the era of the adventurers, came basically
from families—shopkeepers and local officials, for example—
that could barely provide their offspring with minimum education and were anxious that their children not revert to manual
labor. This was a markedly different development than was
taking place in England and France, where the running of the
armed forces remained in the hands of the lower nobility because the bourgeoisie were getting rich too fast to be bothered
with military careers. This meant that in Great Britain and
France the armed forces were led by men seeking to retain their
favored position in society without going into business. In
Spanish America control of the armed forces fell increasingly
to men who, in civilian life, had no position in society and who,
given the stultifying economic atmosphere of their countries,
would have had no future in business had they been inclined
in that direction. The relatively low level of society from
which the officers of Spanish America came makes plain why
the code of honor among fighting men was not as well developed as among civilian politicians, who protected themselves
by generally respecting the right of asylum and granting safe
conduct so that those in disfavor might leave the country.

Officers did not possess technical or managerial skills that were not available in the civilian sector. Although many of the republics founded military academies before mid-century, none of them had an orderly existence. Most officers, consequently, continued to be formed principally on the battlefield and promotions were based on personal, rather than professional, considerations. Officership was not, then, a profession; it was a privilege. Those who attended the military academies received no systematic technical training that could be usefully transferred to civilian spheres.[2] There were two important implications in this situation. In the first place, the alumni of the academies were not prepared to make a living outside the armed forces as were, for example, the pre-Civil War graduates of West Point, whose training was heavily weighted toward engineering and who moved easily into civilian enterprises. In the second place, the unskilled academy graduate who stayed in the service, unlike his counterpart in the United States, was not able to contribute to his country's technical development and expansion as a civil engineer, railroad builder, cartographer, or hydrographer. He could in fact do little more constructive than marching and drilling "potential murderers of his fellow men," and in view of this, it is perhaps not surprising that he often sought to break the humdrum of his existence by conspiring to win political influence.

The academies stressed staff organization. How successful they were in this area is impossible to say, but clearly, the success was limited. Unlike the armies of the new states of Asia and Africa, those of Latin America did not benefit from the tutelage of the colonial power and military missions, at least in their modern sense, were unknown. The officers of the republics, meantime, possessed a bare minimum of knowledge about military science, and there was little they could teach their cadets about it.

But even if the academies had been successful in training

[2] The curriculum of the Colegio Militar of Mexico, founded in 1827, was designed primarily to produce technically trained officers for the artillery and engineer corps. The Colegio, however, functioned only intermittently and turned out only a few competent individuals.

staff officers, as they must have been on occasion, there was little inducement for the officers to maintain any professional expertise they might have acquired. Their armies had no great tradition to look back to, and few military heroes to emulate. The social gulf between them and their soldiers was huge. Their troops were in the service at best because they could not avoid it, and at worst because they were the dregs of society. In this regard, a saying and a quotation are illustrative. The saying runs "if you want more volunteers, send more chains." The quotation is from the dictator Rosas to the Argentine Congress in 1837 : "Recruits are obtained by enlisting vagrants, or such as have been guilty of minor offences. Society, as well as the individuals themselves, derives a positive benefit from this measure. The former sees useful men springing from the lap of sloth to act as its defenders, while the latter, by the habit of subordination, avoid the precipice they were rapidly approaching."[3] Impressed soldiers drawn from the depths of society were hardly the type to incite loyalty and pride in their officers.

The programs of the soldier-statesmen, such as they were, are further evidence that they had no special skills or qualifications as civilian administrators. The record shows that prior to 1850 no politically ambitious officer of any standing ever threatened the elite's basic philosophy of government. On the contrary, the generals, working within the framework of conservatism they had saved, accepted the upper-class program of the conservative oligarchs. They revolted against regimes, not against systems of government. Like the civilians, they felt obliged sooner or later to legalize their administrations and to rule in the name of "liberty and democracy." Politicians in uniform were no more and no less successful than civilian leaders in strengthening the central governments by curtailing the power of the *hacendados* or by reducing the adverse effects of regionalism, both of which were crucial to the resolution of the federalist-centralist issue.

As in government and politics, so in the religious sphere,

[3] British State Papers, XXVII (London, 1856), 866; this volume covers the years 1838–39.

the representatives of the military in high public office permitted the civilians to delineate the issues and determine the grounds on which those issues were fought out. Military men were often non-practicing Catholics, but none challenged the Catholic Church as a religious institution. None of them, moreover, ever made a frontal attack upon the rights and privileges of the family, the basic social institution upon which the Church rested. Nor apparently, did any military president break new ground in the Church-state conflict, which, like the centralist-federalist issue, occupied a pivotal position around which political storms swirled for a century after Independence was won.

Military statesmen were economic traditionalists at least to the extent that civilian leaders were. Nearly all the soldiers who achieved status as politicians had previously amassed wealth and had become landowners themselves, not unusually by padding the payrolls of their companies, buying the notes and land deeds given by the government to the common soldiers in lieu of cash, and by receiving liberal land grants in recognition of their services. Argentina under Rosas awarded huge chunks of its finest pampa lands to officers who served in the Indian Wars of the 1830's. The constitutions, written under the watchful eyes of the military dictators, making the primary responsibility of the state the protection of private property, accurately reflected their interests. They favored tax systems that depended overwhelmingly upon customs duties and levies upon exports for revenues. Such taxes, which could be collected with relative ease, embodied a recognition of the inherent inability of the states to enforce their laws, but they also had the effect of guaranteeing the continuance of the latifundia system, since the production of land, rather than the land itself, was taxed; unworked land, consequently, could be held indefinitely. Following the lead of the landed oligarchy of the nineteenth century, the military politicians were also in favor of free trade.

Thus it may be said that in the chaotic period from Independence to approximately 1850, the military tempered their actions with sufficient discretion to make themselves always appear safe. Each of them stopped short of revolutionizing existing social and economic systems. They showed that they could sweep away governments—between 1849 and 1859 Ecuador had six presidents, four of them army officers active in their military careers at the time they became presidents—but they displayed neither the will nor the capabilities to create new forms of society. Their social and economic conformity and political orthodoxy in effect made them the tools of those landed elements dedicated to the survival of old ideas and old formulas. Because power was in this period based largely on personal magnetism, few were able to consolidate their control sufficiently to hand it on to a chosen successor. Their dictatorships tended to revert to civilian regimes controlled by the landed oligarchs.

That the civilian leaders did not know what to do with the militarism that had sprung up in their midst was evident throughout the 1825–1850 era. Don Manuel Lorenzo de Viduarre, of Peru, had warned at Panama in 1826 that "He to whom the armed forces are confided must be made dependent upon that part of the nation which is unarmed," and his warning was echoed endlessly. But when the military established its ability to negate decisions made by civilians, the voices of those who would limit the power of the men in uniform often went unheeded. One result was that the national constitutions varied widely in the attention they gave to controls over the military and to where the controls should reside.

The Colombian Constitution of 1832 was unique among those charters that sought to circumscribe the armed forces and to limit military interference in civilian matters, for it provided that Congress, rather than the President, should exercise ultimate control over the fighting forces. In an effort to prevent the creation of vested military interests and to make it possible to destroy a military establishment that seemed to threaten the liberties of the people, the charter gave to Congress the power to fix annually the size of the armed forces. The document also provided that the President, who "shall never command them [the armed forces] in person," could declare war only after it had been decreed by the Congress, and required that the President have the prior concurrence of Congress in order to appoint officers above the rank of lieutenant colonel. The constitution further stipulated that the War Ministers be civilians. The armed forces were deprived of any power to deliberate or to grant ranks other than those provided for by law. Strict limits were placed on the use of martial law, and only persons on active duty could be court-martialed. Finally, the armed forces were restrained from appropriating private dwellings for lodgings except by consent of the owners.

But certain national charters, as for example the Paraguayan Constitution of 1844, were written in military terms. That constitution gave the President, who was to "wear the uniform and enjoy all the attributes and prerogatives of a Captain-General," complete control over land and sea forces. He was made "Supreme Chief" and given "the exclusive command" of the services "during peace and war" with the right to command in person and to proclaim war and peace. The President alone was empowered to fix the size of the regular and militia forces, to build and equip war vessels, and to appoint and dismiss all military personnel, as well as to grant retirements and pensions.

The other constitutions fell between the Colombian and Paraguyan extremes, and in most respects reflected the thinking that went into the Constitution of the United States of America. In them the President, a civilian, was made Commander-in-Chief, but Congress had to give its sanction before he could command in person and the concurrence of Congress was required for appointment of officers above certain ranks. Only Congress could declare war or vote funds for military use. The armed forces were deprived of the right to deliberate. In peacetime, only individuals of the army and navy on active duty were made subject to martial law, and, not unusually, civilians were specifically exempted from military tribunals. The constitutions were divided on whether or not men in uniform could hold public office.

The military was not an attractive subject to the men of letters in the 1825–50 period. Although romanticism made itself felt before the end of the era, most writers of the period were under the classicist influence. This influence and a general lack of concern over social problems combined to make the military an unappealing subject except when treated polemically or in adulation. Then, too, few men could qualify as objective interpreters because most had been officers themselves, or had close relatives who were, or alternatively had themselves been driven from power by the military or had relatives who had been.

Taken together, the art and literature produced in this period gave an unfavorable image of violence and militarism, but not as unfavorable as might have been expected, given the realities of the situation. The art of this era that now reposes in major museums suggests a singular disinterest in the armed forces. There is no anti-military art. Except for an occasional epic painting depicting some "great" national triumph and a few portraits of generals and admirals in uniform with their chests plastered with medals, the military goes practically unheeded.

The literature that deals with the military or with military subjects is sometimes friendly, at times unfriendly, and at still other times friendly when referring to the military in the Wars of Independence and unfriendly in reference to it after the movement for freedom. Those who were favorably impressed, as for example the respected Alberto Blest Gana of Chile, recommended, in the fashion of the Mexican Lizardi, that youth emulate the disciplined lives of military officers. It should be noted that Chilean authors had greater justification than other Latin American authors for looking with approval on the armed forces of their country. Their army and navy were early brought under civilian control and during the late 1830's Chile had defeated the combined forces of Peru and Bolivia; the soldiers returning from this triumph in the north had received noisy receptions in the press and from all sectors of Chilean society.

Dr. José María Luis Mora (1794–1854), the great Mexican political thinker, historian, essayist, and educator, was one of the intellectuals most unfavorably impressed with the armed forces. He dwelt at length on the asphyxiating presence of the military in Mexico, and he described in detail the injustices perpetrated on conscripts and the greed, drunkenness, and immoderate appetite for decorations and promotions among officers who kept the nation in tumult. Of all the attacks upon the military by persons of high repute, his was perhaps the most severe.

Don Manuel Ascensio Segura of Peru is believed to have published the first satire upon the military in Spanish America. Writing in 1839, a few months after he left the army, which in alliance with Bolivia had lost a war to Chile, Segura sensed the unpopularity of the Peruvian army and exploited it. In his play *El sargento canuto,* the sergeant is a braggart who proves to be the worst of cowards when confronted by the lover of Jacoba, whom the sergeant hoped to win. Even when exposed, the sergeant persists in claiming that his bravery and friends will soon win him a generalcy.[4]

Three outstanding Spanish American intellectuals of the post-Independence era, Andrés Bello, José Mármol, and José Joaquín de Olmedo, expressed the concern of those who were inclined toward "the cult of the successful hero" but who also felt compelled by the nature of things to pass judgment on violence and military irresponsibility. The Venezuelan Andrés Bello, who lived in self-imposed exile in Chile and there earned himself a reputation as the greatest of Spanish America's men of letters, expressed his ambivalent feelings toward the military on a number of occasions. With considerable pride he paid his respects to the heroes of the battles of Boyacá, Junín, and Maipú, all of which were major steps on the road to victory over Spain, but in his *Silvas americanas* he felt obliged to exhort his people to stop wasting their strength on domestic dis-

[4] See Manuel Ascensio Segura, *Artículos, poesías, y comedias de Manuel Ascensio Segura* (Lima, 1885).

sension and to urge the soldiers to return to the fields, where the fertile soil would close the wounds of strife.

Mármol in his beautiful love story, *Amalia,* first published in 1852 but dealing with the Rosas era, made Colonel Francisco Lynch, a veteran of the War of 1813, a handsome man of culture and high social standing. The author also saluted the common soldier who participated in that war. By contrast, the officers and soldiers of the dictator Rosas were presented as bloodthirsty ruffians and intriguers devoid of principle.

José Joaquín de Olmedo perhaps better than anyone else exemplified the dilemma of the intellectuals. In his *Victory of Junín* he paid homage to the cult of the successful hero by honoring Bolívar. Then in 1835 he wrote *Al General Flores venecedor en Miñarica,* in homage to Juan José Flores, whom Olmedo saw at the time as the only one capable of guiding Ecuador's first steps toward nationhood after its separation from Colombia in 1830. When Flores proved a bitter disappointment as a violent national leader, Olmedo in a letter to Dr. José Fernández Salvador dated November 18, 1840, wrote of "La oda de Miñarica" : "It is not proper to sing of civil wars, for the praise of the conqueror is at the expense of the conquered, and conqueror and conquered are all our brothers." And then, "with all my heart I wish that I could strike out some verses of that composition."[5]

The quarter century from 1825–50 was a lost one for Spanish America. Far from resolving the problems of political infancy, new ones were created when civilians failed to bridle ambitious men on horseback and audacious military officers. Soldiers become politicians proved notoriously inept as civilian administrators, and they were unwilling to compromise with their enemies. By refusing to relinquish the posts of influence they usurped, they kept most of the new nations in constant turmoil and postponed the day of reckoning. That day finally

[5] José Joaquín de Olmedo, *Poesías completas* (Mexico, 1947), pp. lxv–lxvi.

came as the century reached its midway mark. The last of "the marshals" who had earned fame during the Independence movement were about gone. In the words of the Peruvian writer Manuel González Prada at the turn of the century:

> After the Bolívars
> Monteagudos and Sucres
> There were born in America
> Toads and Ostriches.[6]

The new generation of officers generally came from less respected families and did not possess the personal magnetism of the early champions of freedom. Meanwhile, the civilian and military leaders of the new nations that were prostrate from civil disturbances concluded that their countries would not find political solutions to their problems, and that ultimately the key to success would have to be found in economic development. But economic development required order, enough order to make the republics attractive to immigrants from Europe and to draw investment capital and technologists from Europe and the United States. As several of the republics accepted the idea of order, the area began to undergo a massive transformation which continued to gain momentum until the outbreak of World War I. The transformation inevitably altered the role of violence and the military in the political process. The partial transformation and what it meant in terms of force and militarism are examined in the following chapter.

[6] Manuel González Prada, *Grafitos* (Paris, 1937), p. 159.

III

MILITARISM IN AN AGE OF
PROGRESS, 1850–1914

AFTER four decades of militarism and violence the republics
of Spanish America were near the point of collapse. They had
poured vast quantities of physical and mental effort into the
search for means of attaining human liberties through constitutionalism and they had failed. Throughout the remainder of
the century most of the republics either continued their anarchic ways or stumbled forward while looking backward.
Political regimes came and went, but the legacy of the past remained. Politics were still firmly rooted in personal relationships and public office remained a principal means of
social advancement. But a few of the republics—notably Argentina, Chile, and Mexico—envisioned a new order, and
somehow found the resources to launch sustained efforts at
reform, which by World War I had torn them loose from
many of their links to the past and had set them on the road
toward becoming modern, responsible nations. In these more
advanced nations, especially Chile and Argentina, economic,
social, and political developments changed the character of
violence and of the armed forces as well as the public's attitude toward them.

But there was never a direct relationship, and at times not
even a close one, between general progress and achievements
in those spheres of human activities where force is, or may be,
a factor. What has happened repeatedly in the developing
world since World War II, happened in parts of Spanish
America before World War I: nations often "modernized"
their fighting forces faster than they modernized other areas

of their societies. Such was the case, for example, in Venezuela. Mexico, on the other hand, made significant material advances under the Díaz dictatorship (1876–1910) but the modernization was not reflected in the military.

In Argentina, Chile, and Mexico—which comprise approximately half of the total territory of Spanish America and now contain nearly half of the area's total population—progress through economic development and technical change after 1850 became an obsession that produced spectacular results. Enormous acreages were put to the plow for the first time in Argentina, where land under cultivation increased from 373 square miles in 1865 to 95,000 square miles in 1915.[1] Before 1915 Chile and Mexico had completed over 90 per cent, and Argentina over 75 per cent, of their present railroad systems. Railroads through the pampas not only displaced the bullock carts but destroyed the gaucho way of life. Ports were improved, steamships were put on the inland waterways, tens of thousands of miles of telegraph lines were strung, cables were laid down the west coast from the United States, and from the east coast to Europe. Public lighting, water and sewage systems, and public transportation were introduced on an impressive scale in the principal cities. Mining was revived and modernized, notably in Chile and Mexico. In 1913 Chile accounted for 55 per cent of the world's production of fertilizer. Before World War I, Mexico had become the world's third largest producer of petroleum and was a major contributor to the world's supply of zinc and lead.

New manufacturing industries were introduced, old ones were expanded, and new techniques were put to use. Meat processing became "big business" in Argentina and Uruguay; Chile exported wheat flour; chemicals and drugs gained a foothold in Argentina; and electric power began to displace wood and coal. Mexico and Argentina attained self-sufficiency in

---

[1] As the century drew to a close, large-scale banana production gave considerable impetus to the economies of several Central American republics. Costa Rica also laid the foundations for its coffee industry, which is still the backbone of the nation's economy.

coarse textiles. Everywhere manufactures were clearly on their way out of homes and into the factory. Banking, finance, and insurance became vital to the new economies, which needed their services to develop large-scale commercial agriculture, mining, and manufacturing. International trade rose over 100 per cent in Argentina and Mexico during a single decade, according to the averages for the years 1892–96, and 1902–06. The total international trade of all of Latin America more than doubled between the turn of the century and 1913, when total imports and exports by volume actually exceeded those of 1938.

Economic development on such a scale could not have taken place without sustained assistance from abroad. Spanish America needed everything—capital, example, advice, and immigrants. Domestic investment capital was scarce. Technical skills were everywhere at a premium, and Argentina and Uruguay also lacked unskilled laborers. Foreigners willingly filled many of the gaps in the economic structure. Capital poured into the republics from Great Britain, the United States, France, and Germany to build railroads, found factories, and modernize agriculture. Engineers and technicians by the hundreds, mostly from Great Britain and the United States, followed the inflow of capital from abroad. What had been a trickle of immigrants in the 1850's became a torrent by the end of the century. Starting with a total population of less than 1.2 million in 1850, Argentina had a net immigration of over 2.6 million by 1914, the vast majority of them from Italy and Spain. The immigrant impact was no less significant in Uruguay. The uneven pattern of acculturation left some deeply attached to their homelands and their traditional outlook, but others were strongly committed to what they saw as a modern way of life. The latter were in the majority and they often articulated the thoughts of their fellow newcomers and gave some coherence to the wants of native groups. Carlos Pellegrini, the son of an immigrant, became president of Argentina as early as 1890.

Economic development and profound discontent with conditions in the rural areas combined to generate an urbanization movement that after more than a half century continues to gain force. Cities like Montevideo in Uruguay and Buenos Aires, Córdoba, and Bahía Blanca in Argentina more than tripled their population in a score of years. Over 43 per cent of all Chileans were living in cities by 1907. Argentina claimed to be 53 per cent urban, and Uruguay 35 per cent urban by 1914. Recent arrivals and nationals alike contributed to the swelling of the metropolitan areas, and understandably so. Foreign capital tended to concentrate in the urban centers, as did foreign technicians and managers who, although they were often snubbed by the educated upper classes, were quickly accepted by the new rich of commerce and industry and by adventurous public bureaucrats. Wages were higher in the cities and the cities possessed, if they were available at all, the few amenities of life that the workers and their children might hope to share. Finally, to the extent that educational opportunities existed, they were found almost exclusively in the cities, and the immigrants were especially interested in schools for their children.[2]

Agriculture could survive in an atmosphere of anarchy, but industry and commerce could not. Armies might trample crops and drive off livestock, but as long as the owner retained title to his land he could look forward to starting anew. But burned factories and destroyed machines, derailed trains and sunken river boats meant financial disaster. Also, foreign capital and technicians and prospective immigrants ordinarily could not be attracted to areas whose governments were unable to guarantee a reasonable degree of protection. It was largely in response to the demands of these new social-economic elements for order in an age when the seat of power had not yet been fixed that the leadership rejected their historical past before they actually had evolved acceptable substitutes.

The politicians, assisted by the intellectuals, found in the

[2] Argentina, Chile, and Uruguay had good records in the educational field during the quarter century after 1890. For a brief discussion of educational activities in the republics, see John J. Johnson, *Political Change in Latin America* (Stanford, 1958), Chapter 8, and Thomas F. McGann, *Argentina, the United States, and the Inter-American System, 1890–1914* (Cambridge, Mass., 1957), Chapters 1–5.

positivism of Auguste Comte a justification for their decision to cast off their colonial inheritance. As it was modified in Spanish America under the influence of Spencerianism and Social Darwinism, positivism captured the imagination of a great number of leaders of the republics to the south of the Rio Grande, and found a particularly warm acceptance in Mexico, Chile, and Brazil. Such contrasting figures as the writer-philosopher José Victorino Lastarría in Chile, the school-teacher-president Domingo Faustino Sarmiento in Argentina, and the military dictator Porfirio Díaz of Mexico were all impressed by the newly imported philosophy. In those countries where positivism became the dominant philosophy, spontaneous discord gave way to formidable government tutelage and organized society seriously clashed with the individual for the first time, a conflict told so well by the Argentine José Hernández in his poem *Martín Fierro* (1872). But the great historical mission of positivism was to eliminate from Spanish American philosophy its esoteric character, to give it a secular meaning and make it responsive to contemporary issues. The liberal principle of the equality of man was replaced by the theory of the struggle for existence and the survival of the fittest. Inequalities were justified by the science of positivism and that science also justified the rise of emerging commercial-industrial middle sectors and their allies in the government bureaucracies.

Positivism became the syllabus for a new crop of tyrants in whose shadows order was established, wealth evolved, property made more secure, and existence made quieter and more normal. Under the influence of positivism the republics became more "westernized." Westernization led to dependency, and dependency in turn often produced a feeling of inferiority toward Europe and the United States, and at the same time an aggressiveness toward immediate neighbors. Capital was freed from the web of tradition in which a semi-feudal society had held it. Economic activity became more specialized. Powerful interest groups proliferated. Urban labor made its appearance under the influence of anarcho-syndicalism. New middle-sector elements demanded access to the ranks of politics. The ancient oligarchy began to be displaced, its members unable to cope successfully with societies trying to digest the huge doses of materialism being poured into them.

An upsurge of political nationalism was a major by-product of the social-economic transformation that took place between 1850 and 1915.[3] Exhilarated in some cases by the influx of hundreds of thousands of hard-working foreigners, by the construction of tens of thousands of miles of railroads toward their frontiers, and in other cases by the search for and discovery of new minerals and other requirements of modern industry, political leaders began to envisage the day when their countries would teem with productive citizens, when the empty spaces and far corners of their republics would become vital to continued national growth. Far from any longer tolerating the sale of national territory, as had occurred in Mexico under Santa Anna, statesmen now felt impelled not only to guarantee but to expand national boundaries, which with few exceptions still ran through demographic wastelands. When national aspirations clashed, as during the Argentine-Chilean boundary controversies of the late nineteenth century, politicians appealed to the cultural prejudice and pride of their people. To the north the victory of the United States in the Spanish American War, its role in bringing independence to Panama, its insistence upon including the Platt Amendment in the Cuban constitution, and President Theodore Roosevelt's "big stick" diplomacy proved more than sufficient to keep on edge those who feared for the sovereignty of their homelands.

The rise of industry and the enormous growth of international trade around the turn of the century had some generally

---

[3] Cultural nationalism also began to appear among intellectuals at about this time, but it had no significant effect on the character of the armed forces. Economic nationalism was also present, but its full flowering came only after the World War I era; in fact, during the period under discussion politicians, without serious objections from the articulate sectors of society, alienated the public domain and granted long-term monopolies with little thought of the future welfare of their countries.

unforeseen results. They provided the more advanced nations with new and valuable tax sources. Increased revenues in turn permitted the governments to expand their functions and by so doing to multiply the need for the community to communicate with the state. But what proved most important was that the newly found revenues from industry and international trade provided the state with the opportunity to eliminate the traditional oligarchies as the actual repositories of power. Where this transfer of power occurred, the role of the urban elements in government invariably increased and that of the rural elements decreased.

In Spanish America the first social protests, and the first ominous warnings of the class conflicts to come, were heard during the 1850–1915 era. From Europe and the United States came growing evidence that intellectuals, moved by idealism and sympathy, were joining with the workers against laissez-faire policies, which had meant not only "let well enough alone" but also "let ill enough alone." After 1891 intellectuals in Spanish America could not ignore the encyclical *Rerum Novarum* of Pope Leo XIII in favor of the dignity of labor, the undesirability of child labor, and the need for protection of the workers in industry. At home, capital cities filled with new mansions, which imitated Parisian elegance, and the brilliant display of wealth by the new rich of commerce and industry focused attention on the ever-widening gulf separating the scornful rich and the miserable poor. Attention was also directed to the weak position of the wage-earner in the middle sector, who was caught in the squeeze between fixed income and rising prices. In Mexico in 1910, social protest was translated into social violence when an armed peasantry made its revolutionary appearance.

The emergence of nationalism as a political force was the first of these changes to have an obvious impact upon the military as an evolving institution. The disputes that arose from the efforts of the republics to guarantee or extend their boundaries sprang from the influence of the new nationalism; and although most of them were settled by arbitration, peaceful negotiations broke down or threatened to break down from time to time. With the examples before them of Chile, which made war both glorious and profitable by seizing valuable mining territories from Bolivia and Peru, and of Brazil, which used its fighting forces to back up diplomatic efforts that led to the acquisition of territory at the expense of weak neighbors, it was easy for politicians to justify expanded armies and navies in the interests of national sovereignty. Nationalism thus became the ideology on which the military grew. By the end of the century the armed forces had become the agencies for carrying out the spirited international policies of the republics or, alternatively, symbolizing the defense of the national sovereignty. This in turn led to the conviction that the use of the increased revenues from international trade to modernize and professionalize the armed forces could be justified.

The serious beginning of military professionalization in Spanish America, as yet far from complete, is generally dated from the arrival of the German captain (later general) Emil Koerner in Chile in 1886. Prior to his appearance several nations had founded military academies and superior war colleges, and some had given thought to sending officers abroad for training; but only in Chile and in Argentina, where President Sarmiento's crusade against the gaucho society of the interior had brought military reforms, were academies graduating reasonably well-trained, disciplined officers. Elsewhere the military schools were poorly supported and inadequately staffed, and their graduates bore little resemblance to true professionals. Nowhere was there any conception of military science as a unique or specialized branch of knowledge. Consequently, the usual pattern outside of Argentina and Chile was for officers to be first of all leaders without military skills that would distinguish them from their common soldiers. And even in Chile and Argentina the professional officer as a social type was only beginning to appear.

Flushed with victory over Peru and Bolivia in the War of the Pacific (1879–83) and blessed with record-breaking revenues from the nitrate mines of its newly acquired territory, Chile contracted for Koerner's services in the expectation that the Prussianization of its army would guarantee the nation's hegemony on the West Coast. Koerner fulfilled Chile's hopes. By 1890 he had instituted the Prussian system and the Chilean army was equipped with the latest German armament; by 1903, the army was replete with spiked helmets, handlebar mustaches, and monocles. This army guaranteed Chile's power position, but it also initiated a costly arms race throughout most of South America, because once Chile had made its move, other nations felt obliged to follow. Peru, where antagonism against Chile ran high, countered by employing a French mission in 1896. French officers were also called to Ecuador in the late 1890's and to Bolivia in 1905. But Bolivia experimented with German officers even in "the French period" and by 1911 German influence was probably equal to the French influence in that country.

Not only were officers of the Spanish American armies trained by foreign missions but some of them were sent abroad for advanced instruction. Between 1907 and 1913 Chile sent ten officers from its cavalry school to various academies in Europe. In the last years before World War I Argentina was sending thirty to sixty officers a year to Germany, and Paraguay and Uruguay were assigning smaller numbers. Mexican officers trained in Germany taught German military history in the military school of Chapultepec, initiated German methods, and even introduced German marching songs in the Mexican army. Two sons of President Eloy Alfaro of Ecuador attended West Point for short periods.

The Chilean army soon gained such a good reputation that several republics requested Chilean military missions, to which the Chilean government acceded. Chilean Law No. 1610 of September 4, 1903, assigned two officers to El Salvador and three to Ecuador. A law of January 5, 1907, named two captains to work with the Colombian army. It is probable that over the years, and certainly until World War II, the Chileans exercised the greatest single influence upon the Colombian army. In 1913 a Chilean mission was named to assist Venezuela in a reorganization of that country's forces. As early as

1903 Paraguayan, Nicaraguan, and Ecuadorian officers were attending Chile's Escuela Militar.

The reliance upon foreign officers prior to World War I was ironic in at least two respects. First, military reform was intended to help fulfill the objectives of the emergent xenophobic nationalists, but in achieving this end the nations placed themselves in the position of being dependent on the outside for military technicians and war matériel, a situation similar to the one that Sun Yat-sen was discovering in China about this time. Second, General Koerner, the man most responsible for promoting the modernization of armies, took sides in the political dispute that led to the Chilean civil war of 1891 and, by betraying the Balmaceda government that had trusted him, tipped the scales in favor of the rebellious elements. His behavior was a portent of what was to happen often in the future.

The founding of new military schools, the modernization of old ones, and conscription were other results of the urge for larger and more professional armies. Staff schools were founded, and in Chile and Argentina, attendance was normally required for promotion to senior ranks. Dependence upon volunteers to fill the ranks was accepted as a failure in Chile by 1900 and in Argentina by 1901. As an alternative to regular standing armies the nations turned to compulsory military service and it became a prominent, if perhaps inefficient, feature of the shift from amateurism to military professionalism. Universal military service was appealing to the nationalists, who saw it as a means of preventing the rise of a professional soldiery and who argued that the armed forces could perform a major service in making conscripts conscious of the nation in the abstract. But the conscripts themselves served because they had no choice, and they were never consciously or unconsciously patriotic; patriotism was simply foreign to their thinking. Although compulsory military service was general by World War I, and has continued since that time, in practice it was and is applied only to the lower classes. At first the privileged class could provide substitutes, and more recently, enlistment in the reserve corps open to those in institutions of higher learning has served to limit conscription very largely to the members of the poorer classes.

Professionalization and modernization had their advantages and disadvantages. The disadvantages have often been enumerated, but some bear repeating here. The republics derived little immediate good from their efforts to strengthen themselves militarily, since the armed forces seldom were actually called upon to perform defense functions. The revenues they expended on the armed forces—commonly over 20 per cent and not unusually over 30 per cent of the national budgets—might better have been used to promote economic development and social welfare. Once the national armies entrenched themselves, their officer corps often expanded outrageously; everywhere states learned that it was easier to marshal military power than to suppress it. In 1901 the Venezuelan army, for example, had 11,365 active and inactive officers, although the regular army consisted of approximately 4,000 men. In 1910 in Ecuador there were 3,500 men of officer rank in an army that numbered six thousand.[4] On the eve of the 1910 revolution, the Mexican army had an officer for each five enlisted men.

The lack of wars in which officers might display their talents, the lack of any great military tradition to look back to which might have developed pride in the services, and the use of the armed forces for the odious task of suppressing fellow subjects, promised little by way of status for officers except as rank became a symbol of political power. Men in uniform, consequently, were driven into politics despite the fact that even limited military professionalization was encouraging a way of life that tended to divorce officers from the populace and its problems.

Although officers often found it personally advantageous to support liberal groups from time to time, ordinarily when they

[4] Fritz T. Epstein, "European Military Influences in Latin America" (unpublished manuscript, Library of Congress), p. 44. The manuscript was originally prepared during World War II.

turned to politics they did so in support of the reactionary oligarchies. Basically, three considerations dictated this orientation: (1) the oligarchs, who had controlled Latin America since Independence, were still dominant, and any shift in the locus of power would have brought untried groups to the surface; (2) officers, including those in Spanish America, historically have been psychically inclined to sympathize with regimes that live by command instead of persuasion, and the representatives of the oligarchs compared to the representatives of other groups were authoritarian in their approach to government; and (3) professionalization meant bureaucratization. As bureaucrats the new officers, in contrast with the civilian-warriors of an earlier period who moved in and out of uniform frequently and often used rank solely for political ends, had a continuing personal and institutional interest in the services. They were concerned with the attitudes of civilian politicians toward security, salaries, pensions, and privileges, and with armed forces budgets, armaments, and new barracks. The records seem to show that the bureaucratized officers could expect more from landed and Church oligarchies, who tended to place their faith in force, than they could from the emergent, liberal-oriented urban groups. Actually, as it turned out in the post-World War I era, when the urban-oriented groups began to achieve power, their nationalist programs and their desire for prestige, plus the pressures placed upon them by the armed forces, required that they support military programs that were hardly distinguishable from those of the traditional ruling groups.

Trusting in the manifestly superior organizational strength of the army, officers often ordered their men out of the barracks without regard for the interests of any civilian group; their goal was usually no loftier than to overthrow a regime that threatened to curtail military expenditures or sought to bridle those officers who pressed "to sacrifice themselves for their country." On such occasions officers could become the bloody incarnation of the barbarity that had always remained beneath a thin cultural veneer. Then their actions were almost without exception on behalf of an officer ambitious to alter the political pattern, rather than in the name of the military as an institution. This was the military version of personalism and charisma in civilian politics, and it carried with it all the evils of its civilian counterpart. It also called attention to the fundamental weakness of the armed forces: their inability to act as a group in the interests of the group.

By directing against the public the instruments of violence entrusted to them by the nation, the officers put emergent groups, struggling for recognition, in a disadvantageous position. And the armed forces permitted themselves to be used as policemen and strikebreakers by the governments, notably those in power in Mexico and Chile between 1900 and 1910. But quite aside from the antagonism produced by the armed forces in "defense of the state," there were several considerations which, under the best of circumstances, would have made practically impossible the reaching of an easy accommodation of the armed forces with the working groups. Many Spanish American intellectuals were under the influence of the racist Gustave Le Bon in the very period when the worker, who belonged to the "people of color," was making his bid for recognition in the more advanced republics. The officers of the armed forces, on the other hand, were white, or pretended to be, and considered themselves racially superior. Then, too, independent action by workers terrified the military officers accustomed to commanding the masses and made them distrustful of any one from the masses who aspired to command. Furthermore, when the workers appeared on the political scene, at the turn of the century, the nations were not threatened from the outside; consequently, there was no need for the dominant elements to seek homogeneity or to curtail the dissipation of energy on domestic issues, either of which might have forced concessions from the groups that the armed forces supported.

The fact that urban labor groups very early embraced anarcho-syndicalism made them appear more "dangerous" to the armed forces than might otherwise have been the case.

Officers, like the other privileged groups, were unprepared for defiant strikers screaming for the destruction of the very properties that gave them a livelihood. Anarcho-syndicalism, furthermore, stood for direct rather than political action, and the armed forces had arrogated to themselves the right to direct action. But even when the laborers observed the political rules, they registered their convictions first as workers and only secondly (if at all) as citizens. This "all or nothing" attitude of the anarcho-syndicalists was to the armed forces, as it was to the oligarchies, an open invitation to class warfare and was inadmissible. Labor groups, too, contributed directly to keeping their differences with the armed forces alive by waging a running battle against militarism. They referred repeatedly to the armies as "the citadels of ignorance." "The Army is the school of crime" screamed the banners that workers paraded in Chile. In Argentina the anarchist newspaper *La protesta* made almost daily attacks upon the armed forces for their "corruption" and "wastefulness" and for permitting themselves to be used by the privileged groups as "instruments of oppression."

The fact that anarcho-syndicalism was an import from Europe and anarcho-syndicalist unions were often directed by immigrants added to the military's distrust of them. As the repositories of "national honor and tradition" and claiming to be the only governmental institution capable of expressing a truly apolitical will of the nation in time of crisis, the armed forces found abhorrent the foreignisms and internationalisms of the anarcho-syndicalists, many of whom, the officers charged, had left Europe to escape the very type of oppression that their activities in America, if permitted to be carried out, would produce.

Ultimately, however, the professionalization and modernization of armies failed to achieve the goals intended because they came before the nations were prepared for them and before countervailing forces had a chance to develop. First of all, the republics simply were not in a position to shoulder the cost of training and sustaining large numbers of officers or to expend for war matériel their foreign exchange earnings, which were always made uncertain by the vagaries of international trade. Also, the professional armies developed before the growth of property-owning and politically independent middle sectors that might have challenged them. Then, too, civilian politicians—whose irresponsibilities were often at least as great as those of the officers—did little to encourage professionalization. They used the officers in domestic power plays, and once in office they often could not resist engaging in the traditional game of favoritism in appointments and promotions. In such circumstances, officership continued to depend on privilege and patronage, instead of professionalism, and an officer's political loyalties were more important than his level of professional competence. This was demoralizing to those officers who otherwise might have been content to be disinterested servants of the state.

But if it may be assumed, as it was by the positivists, that social order and material progress were high on the list of requirements in Spanish America, a case can be made that professionalization and modernization of the armed forces brought certain real benefits to Spanish America. They did give the states, for the first time, a clear superiority in the control and management of weapons. They made military victories more dependent on organization and armed superiority and less upon individual heroics and surprise. Mechanized armament, the Remington rifle, and later the incendiary bomb put warfare out of the financial reach of the old-time regional *caudillos*. At that point the barricade, the mountain fastness, and the forest began to give way to technical might. This in effect meant the beginning of the end of private armies as makers of presidents.[5] Since incumbents often used the modernized and

[5] Fidel Castro's successful operation in the Sierra Maestra would not appear to disprove this thesis or offer an exception to the rule. At no time when he was in the Sierra Maestra did Castro depend on armed might to achieve his ultimate objective, nor did he dare a frontal attack, as did the *caudillos* of an earlier period. The *caudillos*, with very few exceptions, fought and won or lost with the material available to them at the initiation of hostilities.

professionalized military to keep themselves in power, the means to deprive regional *caudillos* of their ability to seize power did not at the time necessarily enhance democracy, but it was a step that had to be taken before the republics could expect either orderly government or the smooth functioning of democratic processes.

Much the same case can be made for professionalization and modernization in pre-World War I Spanish America as was made after World War II for the militias as a modernizing force in the emerging countries of Africa and Asia. In both cases the armed forces were a part of a scientific vanguard in societies anxious to become technologically advanced but lacking a scientific intelligentsia. The scientific offerings of the new military academies, although admittedly quite limited, were generally at least equal to and often better than those offered in established institutions of higher learning of the period. Victor Alba has suggested that some students attended the military academies solely to gain training in scientific and technical vocations they could use in civilian life.[6]

There are many examples that seem to confirm the contention that because of their training, officers were overwhelmingly on the side of those civilian elements who advocated technological change. The officers of the Argentine and Chilean armies, for example, were in the forefront of national groups who supported the development of modern communications and transportation. The railroad system of Uruguay—along with Argentina's the best in Latin America—was initiated and advanced by generals who became presidents. The military statesman Antonio Guzmán Blanco, president of Venezuela from 1870 to 1888, probably did more to modernize that nation than all other leaders combined in the century following Independence. The Guatemalan statesman Justo Rufino Bar-

---

[6] The weakness in the system of training officers would seem to have lain not so much in the academies as in the fact that the armed forces were so constituted that command posts were more attractive than technical ones. For a discussion of the relatively successful practical application of technology in the military, see the chapters on Brazil.

rios, president of his country from 1871 to 1885, who lived and perished by the sword, is remembered as a symbol of technological progress in the chaotic Central America of the nineteenth century. There are good reasons to doubt that the Mexican Revolution of 1910 would have succeeded had it not been preceded by the great era of building and modernization encouraged by the military dictator Díaz.

Logic as well as available evidence argue in support of the commonly accepted assertion that professionalization led to important changes in the social composition of the officer corps. After the Wars of Independence, when the armies were turned upon the citizenry, certain members of the upper groups continued to seek careers in the military because they viewed them as offering a direct route to political success. And members of the lower middle groups sought officerships because they promised social advancement. Serious-minded young men of the intellectual middle sectors did not associate themselves with the institution because its activities were limited largely to police duties. Professionalism and the rise of nationalism changed this relationship. When professionalism brought bureaucratization and the need for some competence in the pure sciences and an acquaintance with administrative techniques, military careers lost any attraction they still had for the elites, although through favoritism and civilian interference in the armed services members of the elites often received high-level military appointments. Meanwhile, those from the lower middle sectors appear to have been outbid for cadetships in the academies by better educated and less adventurous young men from the provincial towns who were impressed with the prestige the armed forces enjoyed because of their role in nationalistic foreign policies, and the security that professionalism promised in what was often an otherwise unstable environment.

The new generation of cadets was quite different from earlier ones. They came from families that accepted the traditional value systems, but the cadets themselves, by inclination and training, thought more in national and technological terms than did either their parents or their superiors in the armed forces.[7] The thinking of the new cadets made them far better prepared to accommodate themselves to the social-political consequences of economic change than were the landholding elements. This is a consideration of major consequence in explaining the breakdown in military resistance to the shift in the locus of power that came in such countries as Uruguay, Chile, and Argentina during the first two decades of this century, when the new generation of officers had already risen to the decision-making levels of the armed forces. It was in fact the most important development in the evolution of the armed forces between 1850 and 1915.

The concerns of the legislators in the pre-World War I era, as evidenced by the laws they wrote, serve to remind the reader that the civil-military differences of an earlier epoch persisted, while the implied inability of a state to enforce its will recalls the truism that historically the political evolution of the republics has been in response more to cultural realities than to legalistic fictions. The helplessness of the civilian against the military is illustrated by a provision of the Ecuadorian Constitution of 1906: officers were made responsible for their acts against established governments, but nothing was said about who would be held responsible for those officers whose acts against the governments ended in success.

Constitution after constitution delegated to the supposedly civilian national congresses, rather than to the executive branch (which might be, and often was, headed by military or ex-military men) the power to fix the size of the armed forces, to approve armed forces' budgets, and to confirm appointments of all officers above a fixed rank. These provisions were of course ineffective when a congress was a rubber stamp or could be prorogued. The charters of the period, as did those of an earlier epoch, made it illegal for the armed forces to deliberate,

---

[7] It should be emphasized that the support given technology and industry by the armed forces prior to World War I did not result from any expectation that industry would free the armed forces from dependence upon foreign sources for weapons and supplies, one of the reasons that the military in many of the republics support economic nationalism today.

and the Salvadoran Constitution of 1886 went so far as to declare that "the armed forces . . . have not the power to deliberate respecting matters connected with the military service." The Colombian constitution of the same year barred members of the armed forces on active duty from being elected as deputies, senators, or as president—an essentially illiberal action in that it deprived men in uniform of the rights and privileges enjoyed by other citizens.

The *Ley Juárez* of 1855, later incorporated into the Mexican Constitution of 1857 and designed to deprive the armed forces of special privileges (*fueros*), was followed by similar legislation in other republics. Article 1360 of the Colombian Military Code of 1881, for example, denied the armed forces certain *fueros* in time of peace.

The protection of citizens, both in and out of uniform, from military jurisdiction was a major objective of the lawmakers of the period. To defend civilians from the armed forces the Dominicans, in their Constitution of 1858, denied the military any jurisdiction in cases involving both civilian and military personnel. And the Salvadorans in their Constitution of 1886 abolished the *fuero atractivo,* a military jurisdiction granting power to deal with those civilians in any way connected with military parties to a suit or proceeding. The Ecuadorian Congress, meanwhile, went so far in shielding the common soldier from his superiors that President Gabriel García Moreno, in his address on the opening of the Congress in 1864, complained that the legislators had stripped the military of jurisdiction to the point where officers could no longer prevent wholesale desertion of conscripts. In a similar vein, the Colombian Constitution of 1886, while recognizing the courts martial, deprived the military of the right to mete out punishment without trial, except in cases of insubordination and mutiny in the face of the enemy. There is, of course, abundant evidence that the civilians did not always have their way.

Romances, sex, including relations with members of the submerged races, drink, inhuman cruelty, and perverted religion all held greater appeal for the general public in Spanish

America than did militarism during the 1850–1915 era. To the extent that novelists, poets, and those who by verse and song entertained and informed the illiterate masses concerned themselves with the military, disagreement rather than agreement characterized their depiction of the commissioned component of the armed forces. A representative sampling of the literary output and folklore of the period suggests that for every half-dozen anti-military pieces there were about six that were pro-military. If Peruvian men of letters were generally anti-military, those in Chile were generally favorable toward the institution. If poems recited and the songs sung on the Argentine pampas usually pitted the gaucho against the soldier, it was also the gaucho who, once he had served his tour of duty, boasted of his exploits while in the ranks of the army. If after 1910 the *corridos* (popular ballads) of Mexico made Porfirio Díaz a bloody tyrant, for a half century they had acclaimed him the military hero of the French Intervention and the Second Empire.

Unfavorable public comment was directed primarily against individual officers rather than against the military as an institution. This was understandable. Modernization and professionalization of the armed forces had only begun. Many officers were still *generales de dedo* (generals of the finger), a figure of speech used to identify the officers whose superiors during a "campaign" or "battle" had pointed a finger at an individual and said, "You are a general." There was often little about such men to create a favorable public impression. They depended upon individual heroics to distinguish themselves, and the strong tendency among them to accept orders from above only so long as they doubted their ability to rally sufficient support to successfully challenge their superiors tended to make them a disruptive force in society.

Officers were taken to task for all manner of reasons, but certain objections to their behavior were reiterated often enough to make it clear that they were the ones that most disturbed the general public. Among these were grossness and drunkenness, sundry gratuitous brutalities, and taking advantage of women of inferior races and unsuspecting provincial women ; these excesses, at least, were uppermost in the minds of those men of letters who found the officers repugnant. The Argentine, Martín Coronado, for example, in his *Luz de luna y luz de incendio* (1878) portrayed an officer as a drunken brute. In the Argentine folk songs and creole dramas of the late 1800's the young and not so young girls of the pampas were constantly pursued by oversexed officers. The Venezuelan Gonzalo Picón Febres in *El Sargento Felipe* (1899) offered another variation of the female theme when he had Felipe, an industrious small farmer, forced into the army and in his absence his daughter seduced by a wealthy young don. Picón's countryman, Rufino Blanco Fombona, in *El hombre de hierro* (1905), in dealing with the wanton vandalism of officers in the civil wars of Venezuela tells of government troops who, upon leaving the property of a man in the opposition, not only took with them chickens, kitchen utensils, pillows, and the like, but also beat the ripe coffee beans off the trees of the plantation and set fire to the livestock corrals.

Many authors played on the theme of the officers' insensibility to human suffering, but perhaps none did so as effectively as the Argentine Roberto Payró in *Canción trágica* (1900). His captain gave a ball and demanded that the widows of the men he had killed attend it ; *baile o muerte* (dance or die) was the choice he gave them.

Men of letters and balladeers alike tended to take the side of the common soldier against the national army and its irresponsible officers. Verse after verse of José Hernández' classic poem *Martín Fierro* (1872) castigates the officers for their treatment of the common soldier who had been pressed into service. From the Mexican *corridos* brought together by Merle Simmons it is apparent that as far as the armed forces were concerned, the foremost fears of common people were the military draft and the danger that their villages would be converted into arsenals of food, animals, and women for the passing troops.[8]

[8] Merle Edwin Simmons, *The Mexican Corrido as a Source of Interpretive Study of Modern Mexico, 1870–1950* (Bloomington, Ill., 1957).

The Chilean Guillermo Matta, the Argentine Jorge Luís Borges, and the Colombian Carlos Arturo Torres each struck near the heart of the issue. Matta, in the 1850's, accused the *caudillos* of dragging people into the civil wars and then sowing the ground with cadavers; he asked the soldiers if they had not heard their consciences cry out, "This is your brother! What have you done?"[9] Borges in his poem "El General Quiroga va en coche al muere" condemns a *caudillo* to hell escorted by six or seven headless men.[10] Torres, in his *Idola fori* (1908), maintained that the officer was nothing more than a synthesis of the strength and sacrifices of his people, and went on to take serious issue with those who would glorify warriors victorious in the civil struggles that rent his nation.

If the officer was, as Torres maintained, the synthesis of the strength and sacrifices of his people, from the bitter pen of the Peruvian Manuel González Prada came the synthesis of hate and revulsion that the armed forces elicited from some members of a still quite small group of men who at the end of the nineteenth century showed the first symptoms of the awakening social consciousness of Spanish America. González Prada was a man possessed; he could find little good in Peruvian society in general, and nothing favorable in its armed forces. The War of the Pacific (1879–83), in which Peru and Bolivia were defeated by Chile, precipitated González Prada's criticism of his country and its military. He searched for the causes of defeat in the war and concluded that Peru had been humiliated because it had failed to engender a national consciousness in its people. To González Prada the Chilean invaders fought for the fatherland, while the Peruvian soldiers, handicapped by a medieval mentality, fought not for the nation but for *caudillos* intent on personal advancement and the acquisition of wealth and social prestige. He also charged that the military service often turned honest, hard-working men into idle vagrants and social parasites. Complaining of the excessive

[9] *Poesías de Guillermo Matta*, I (Madrid, 1858), 40.

[10] See Hoffman R. Hays, *Twelve Spanish American Poets, an Anthology* (New Haven, 1944), p. 129.

subservience that officers must show before their superiors, González Prada observed, "What insolence has the arrogant colonel before a humble servant . . . but what lowliness does that same colonel display before the general."

About the same time that the Colombian Torres wrote against the glorification of the soldier, González Prada in *Anarquía* (a collection of his writings on social problems) had insisted that a military career did not merit glorification; soldiers, he said, were rather to be condemned as paid assassins of the working man. All carriers of the sword were to the critic equally abhorrent, from the Grand Marshal who cried crocodile tears after his forces had wrought destruction to the corporal raining blows on the humble recruit for not having learned sufficiently the lessons of brutality. González Prada on occasion simultaneously attacked the military and the clergy, as for example when he wrote:

> A soldier and a clergyman hang from a tree!
> How happy and how habitable the world would be
> If from all trees
> Hung such fruit![11]

Favorable recognition of the military ordinarily arose when the subject was the struggles for Independence, including that by Cuba in the second half of the century, or the deeds of the heroes of international conflict. Of the leaders of the Independence movement, Bolívar remained the most revered, and a vertible cult grew up around him, particularly in the five republics he helped to free. As funds were found to import sculptors from Europe, equestrian statues of him began to supplant or be added to the sculptured busts of an earlier period.[12]

The Argentine Independence hero José de San Martín

---

[11] Manuel González Prada, *Libertarias* (Paris, 1938), p. 30.

[12] It is interesting to note that the first statues of the Independence leaders did not show them on horseback, a device used in Latin America to distinguish officers from common soldiers. This is probably because the talents of local sculptors were not up to the task of reproducing a rearing horse. To the best of this author's knowledge, the equestrian statues of the pre-World War II era were done by foreigners.

found an unusually capable biographer in the historian-president Bartolomé Mitre. More carefully and skillfully than any of Bolívar's biographers, Mitre presented San Martín not only as an unusually able soldier but also as a gentleman and a self-sacrificing, disciplined patriot. In his *Historia del Belgrano* (1858–59), Mitre also helped to assure General Belgrano a venerable place in the history of his country. The Chilean Carlos Walker Martínez, in his play *Manuel Rodríguez* (1879), written in honor of the popular Chilean hero of the movement against Spain, went out of his way to commemorate San Martín's daring conquest of the Andes, which led to the independence of Chile.

Guillermo Matta of Chile, although he deplored the civil wars that plagued all of Spanish America, nonetheless called the trouble-making José Miguel Carrera a noble patriot for his exploits during the Independence era. On the other hand, Samuel Lillo in his poem *Rancagua* (1911) found Bernardo O'Higgins, Carrera's principal antagonist, a great leader because he inspired a love of country in his soldiers. In similar fashion, Argentina's schoolteacher-president Domingo Faustino Sarmiento, deplored the barbarism of the provincial *caudillos* but was filled with pride by the deeds of Argentine soldiers, who resisted England's invasion of Argentina in 1806 and then in a hundred pitched battles wrested half a continent from the hands of Spain.

The acclaim that the public of Mexico, Chile, and Cuba showered upon their warriors fighting and defeating foreign troops is strong evidence that the people of Spanish America could quickly forget the irresponsible behavior of their fighting forces. On May 5, 1862, Mexican forces defeated the French invaders at Puebla, and from then until now that victory has been hailed as one of the greatest moments in the life of the Mexican republic. Each year the fifth of May is set aside to commemorate the event, and most if not all major cities of the republic have streets named Cinco de Mayo. The victory at Puebla was followed by bitter defeats and the imposition of Maximilian as Emperor. But the Republican forces refused to surrender, and the Emperor could control only those areas actually occupied by his forces, the backbone of which were French. When the French troops were recalled to Europe, the Republican forces closed in, and at Querétaro, on May 4, 1867, they crushed the Royalist army. The war made national figures of many officers, but probably none caught the fancy of the masses more than the guerrilla fighter Nicolás Romero, whose sterling qualities and patriotism the *corridistas* recited over and over. And the exploits and valor shown by Porfirio Díaz against the French were recalled by the common people long after he had rejected the principles he had stood for during the Intervention period.

The conflict with Spain in 1865–66, in which the tiny Chilean corvette *Esmeralda* surprised and sank the Spanish schooner *Covadonga,* and the War of the Pacific (1879–83) were enough to keep the cult of the hero alive in Chile. Men like Admiral Arturo Pratt and General Manuel Baquedano were, and continue to be, virtually legendary figures. The general public is mindful of lesser heroes, too. During an evening of soccer in Santiago in 1946, at the half-time of the third game (about 12:30 a.m.), several "seventy-niners" (the men who stormed ashore against the Peruvian forces at Antofagasta) with their gold and maroon arm patches conspicuously displayed, were escorted around the playing field on the arms of nurses, while 60 thousand spectators stood and applauded.

The poet Luis Rodríguez Velasco, inspired by Chilean success against Spain, Peru, and Bolivia, kept alive in his poems the martial lyrics of Guillermo Matta. Rodríguez Velasco's poems were filled with passages contrived to inflame the patriotic spirit, for example: "Where is the spirit that urged our fathers to war? Does not Liberty inflame the young souls of this land? Have we lost the noble breast that laughed when it fought?"[13]

Alfred Coester, in the opening page of the chapter on Cuba in his *Literary History of Spanish America* (1941), wrote that Cuban prose "was generally a weapon in the fight for separa-

[13] Luis Rodríguez Velasco, "Achile," in *Obras poéticas* (Santiago, 1909), p. 137.

tion from Spain." So many, including José Martí, the "apostle" of Cuban independence, set their pens to arousing patriotism in the Cuban people and in so doing paid homage to the leaders and to the anonymous soldiers fighting for liberty, that it would be aimless to single out one or a dozen of them.[14] The leaders of the Cuban Independence movement received their share of attention, but a favorite theme was the man who went unsung at home or the Negro slave who became a hero on the battlefield. Meanwhile, the revolutionary writers called frequent attention to the brutalities and devastation of the Spanish forces, without suspecting, or at least not calling attention to the possibility, that the armed forces of a freed Cuba might act, as they actually did, in a similar manner.

Mexico and Peru offer outstanding late-nineteenth century examples of persons seeking to promote patriotism by glorifying the conduct of soldiers in the face of defeat. In Mexico the war with the United States provided many such instances, but two will suffice here. Approximately fifteen years after the war, the purportedly heroic but militarily meaningless attempt of a Mexican soldier to lasso a North American cannon during the battle between Zachary Taylor and Santa Anna at Angostura had been written into textbooks and made into a legend to inspire future generations.[15] And in 1871 Mexico began setting aside September 13 as a day dedicated to the memory of the *Niños Héroes* (child heroes), cadets of the Military Academy, all less than 18 years of age, who, legend has it, flung themselves from the walls of Chapultepec castle rather than surrender to the attacking United States troops under Winfield Scott. To Justo Sierra writing in 1904 they were "child heroes who gave an example to men and whose memory will be guarded eternally by Mexico and adored eternally by Mexican youth."

[14] See, for example, the volume *La poesía revolucionaria en Cuba* and the five volumes of *La prosa en Cuba,* both edited by José Manuel Corbonel y Rivero (1928).

[15] Vicente Riva Palacio, *México a través de los siglos,* IV (Mexico, 1887–1889), 596.

Fighting at Arica during the War of the Pacific provided occasion for two of Peru's outstanding literary figures, José Santos Chocano and Ricardo Palma, to invite their countrymen to emulate the soldiers who sacrificed themselves rather than surrender to the Chilean invaders. Chocana, in *La epopeya del morro* (1900), chose to glorify a body of Peruvian soldiers who, on a bluff and surrounded by a superior number of Chileans, threw themselves into the Pacific rather than be taken prisoner. Ricardo Palma, writing shortly after the conclusion of the war, chose to single out Colonel Francisco Bolognesi, who, when his ammunition was gone, took his own life.[16]

The conditions prior to 1915 which contributed to anti-militarism in Spanish America are by now so generally well known that they will not be repeated here; on the other hand, it will be worthwhile to recall briefly some of the considerations which from time to time induced relatively large sectors of the public to look favorably upon the military. As far as the masses were concerned, their harsh environment had thoroughly conditioned them to the use of force and had developed in them a strong sense of respect for personal valor. Two of the attributes of a good soldier, the efficient use of force and personal bravery, were consequently quite understandable to the masses, and the soldier offering his life in defense of the *patria*, furthermore, could be comfortably fitted into their crudely developed patriotic concepts.

Those men of learning who were pro-military were moved variously by opportunism, realism, and conviction. Many authors, poets, and artists lived by their income as public bureaucrats and diplomats. Opportunism dictated that their literary and artistic productions conform more or less closely to the convictions of the regimes they served, and all but a very few of the regimes were scrupulously careful to see that they not be considered anti-military. Newspapermen whose livelihood depended upon revenues from public notices and government subscriptions to their journals were in much the same

[16] *Tradiciones peruanos,* IV (Madrid, [1923]), 226–33.

position. Novelists wrote for the emerging bourgeoisie, not a few of whom had shot their way to positions of influence or had ridden there on the coat tails of men in uniform. Furthermore, when the bourgeoisie read, they wanted to read of Europe, or at least of things removed from the sea of poverty and illiteracy that beat upon the shores of their tiny islands of ostentatious wealth and learning. Attacks upon the military would hardly have satisfied their escapism, so those writers who addressed themselves to military themes were under strong pressure to show the institution in a favorable light. The artists, meanwhile, knew that the Catholic Church was practically the sole purchaser of the visual arts, and they also knew that the Church could not be anti-military even when it felt called upon to oppose the worst military tyrants. The artists, again like the novelists, had the choice of being either pro-military or ignoring the military as a subject. Finally, a surprisingly large number of men of letters had been, or were, soldiers themselves, or had fathers or close relatives who had been or were soldiers. Under such conditions it is not surprising that when they chose to discuss the military they treated it in a friendly manner.

Several considerations quite aside from those of an opportunistic or realistic nature encouraged a favorable view of the military. It was probably true that, except in Argentina, Chile, and Colombia, civilian politicians were no more worthy of the public's respect and confidence than were the men in uniform. Luis Humberto Delgado faced this particular situation squarely when writing of Peru in the late 19th century, he said, "The *militares* inspired repugnance, and the politicians, hatred."[17]

Positivism was in its ascendancy and the positivists' support of technological progress and abhorrence of disorder strongly inclined many to look with favor on the military. Whenever the armed forces supported technological development or appeared to be on the side of order and stability, they might expect the approval of those positivists who were indifferent to sacrificing political liberties in return for greater

[17] *El militarismo* (Lima, 1930), p. 18.

material progress and order. The contrasting interpretations of military events during the Juárez and Díaz regimes in Mexico offer an excellent example of the effect of positivist thinking. The supporters of the liberal Juárez government, seeking to salvage something from the military disasters of Mexico's war with the United States, dwelt on the individual heroics of certain officers and common soldiers. Much was made of the defiance of officers who knew they faced defeat, and of raw, untrained recruits marching days on end with hardly any food or water, and charging barehanded the "barbaric gringos" after all ammunition had been exhausted. The positivists, on the other hand, chose to acknowledge defeat in the war and to place the responsibility for it on politicians and military leaders, especially Santa Anna, who, they maintained, were undisciplined and hence incapable of organizing and directing an effective fighting force.[18]

Finally, the era was one of individualism and emergent nationalism, both of which played into the hands of the military. In societies that still had not produced either intellectual or scientific celebrities or giants of industry, who better than the valiant, self-sacrificing soldier could rise above the crowd to personify the virtues of individualism? And how meaningful would have been the nationalist outburst of politicians without the soldiers to back them up?

[18] See Homer Chaney, "The Mexican-United States War as Seen by Mexican Intellectuals, 1845–1956," unpublished doctoral dissertation in Stanford University (1959), Chapter III.

PART TWO

THE TWENTIETH CENTURY

IV

CHANGE AND RESPONSE, 1915–1963:

The Soldier as Citizen and Bureaucrat

CASTRO's stunning victory in Cuba placed a challenge before Spanish America: either to find, and quickly, some means of satisfying a reasonable share of the just demands of the desperate masses, or to see those masses turn to political extremists for solutions to their problems. The suddenness with which the working classes made known their age-old discontent was more apparent than real. In fact, for more than four decades the leaders of Spanish America had observed an increasing dissatisfaction among those who had previously accepted ignorance, poverty, and disease as their inevitable heritage. They knew that a new consciousness of social and economic problems was creating demands that strained to the breaking point many time-honored institutions and traditional social and political relationships. They knew this, as did politically enlightened sectors in their nations, and they made their calculations accordingly. And the public was at a disadvantage, for the pulling and hauling, the compromises with the past, the refusals to compromise with the present until it was too late, the successful maneuver and the missed opportunity, have been the essence of Spanish-American history since World War I.

After World War I, the emotional and intellectual commitment to modernization increased rapidly within the privileged groups, which included the politicians. By the mid-1930's, the general public had become fascinated with its economic potential, and by the end of World War II the concerted demands of nearly all groups for rapid economic change had reached a pitch that few governments dared ignore. By that time, four considerations dictated that the republics devote their principal efforts to industry and commerce. First, there were the lessons learned from the breakdown of normal international trade channels during the world-wide depression of the 1930's and World War II. Second, there was the prestige associated with advanced technological capabilities. Third, it seemed that industry was their only hope of escaping the pressure exerted by their exploding populations against their limited agricultural resources. Finally, in the more advanced countries the political and economic leaders were predominantly from the cities that stood to gain most from industrial and commercial expansion. With so many forces working in favor of industry, the more materially developed republics rapidly approached the age of the technician and the producer. First factories and then steel mills became the symbols of developmental aspirations and the showcases of achievement. By 1960 non-agricultural activities were providing more than 50 per cent of the gross national product in several of the republics—Argentina, Brazil, Chile, Venezuela, Mexico, Colombia, Uruguay, and Cuba. And all the republics were determined to try to do more than their experience, skill, and capital would permit.

This industrial expansion, although significant before World War I and in some respects quite impressive since then, has proved satisfying to comparatively few people. For many reasons, including the failure to develop adequate transportation and power systems, the cost of production in general has remained so high that the fruits of industrialization have not been so widespread as its protagonists had predicted. Many are profoundly disturbed because industry, despite the huge sums poured into it, has failed to absorb a large percentage of the hundreds of thousands who enter the labor market each year. Because capital formation has never been large, and also because private capital has tended to flow into real estate rather than into factories, governments have been made the catalysts of industrial development, to the deep dismay of a still well-entrenched core of property owners. Industrial workers know that spiraling prices, eroding wages, and regressive taxation have kept the primary burden of plant expansion on them; they also know that within the economies that they are being called upon to sustain, the gap between wealth and poverty widens rather than narrows. In 1960 the lower 99 per cent of the gainfully employed in Mexico received approximately 40 per cent of the national cash income, 20 per cent less than they received a quarter of a century earlier.

Meanwhile, the agricultural sector, except in Mexico, has been sacrificed to industrial efforts. Since World War II farm production has not kept pace with population growth, and the caloric intake of the area's multiplying millions has been maintained by reverting from commercial to subsistence agriculture, despite the fact that commercial agriculture is the principal source of foreign exchange earnings for all but five of the republics—Bolivia, Chile, Peru, Mexico, and Venezuela. Agricultural inefficiency is now such that farm hands, who constitute about 52 per cent of the total labor force, almost invariably earn less than one-fourth of what industrial workers do. The revolutionary governments of Mexico, Bolivia, and Cuba have seized land and redistributed it with little regard for the claims of the original owners. Elsewhere—except in Venezuela, where the government has had considerable success in obtaining the cooperation of the landholders by paying them good prices for their properties—experts search fruitlessly for a practical legal means of penetrating the closed ranks of the land monopolists, whose power in government has thus far proved sufficient to veto workable agrarian reform programs.

Failures in the agricultural area account in large part for the inability of the republics to diversify their export economies. Figures for 1959 show that nine republics derived more than 50 per cent of their total foreign exchange earnings from a single agricultural commodity: coffee, in Brazil, Colombia, El Salvador, Haiti, and Guatemala; sugar, in Cuba and the Dominican Republic; and bananas, in Ecuador and Panama. Hanging over both the agricultural and mineral economies

(Bolivia, Chile, and Venezuela draw over 50 per cent of their foreign exchange earnings from tin, copper, and petroleum, respectively) is the realization that the republics have not yet found an acceptable way of regulating the world price of their exports.

Sprawling cities pocked with slums are the most strikingly visible monuments to the development of industry and commerce and the neglect of agriculture. These urban agglomerations—of which Montevideo, Buenos Aires, Santiago, and Lima are typical—have acted as magnets in drawing to themselves the brains and learning, the intellectual and managerial skills, and the wealth and income of the several nations. With this monopoly of resources, they have become centers for the diffusion of ideas. Into them have poured, faster than they could be accommodated, the millions fleeing the tensions of the countryside. The consequences have been essentially two. The rural areas have been so completely stripped of their intellectual and economic resources that they can no longer regain viability by their own efforts. The urban centers have been flooded with persons made insecure and restless by the anonymity of the cities, by the uncertainties of competing as individuals for the first time, and by the difficulties arising from dislocations in the social structure; these struggling newcomers can be easily provoked to violence and readily organized by political groups that promise "a place consistent with the heritage of freedom and equality." The maldistribution of wealth is spectacular, making the cities the focal points for internal stresses and strains and the points of encounter with United States influence.

Although the common man in Spanish America still cannot expect, as did the pioneer in 19th-century United States, that his government will provide him with internal improvements, his lot has improved considerably. Society in general no longer regards the urban laborer as an unknown quantity, but accepts him as an individual constantly faced with emergency problems and consequently impatient with the rate of social and economic growth. His chances for advancement, statistically negligible in the past, have been vastly improved, or so he believes, by public education. The clerical issue has been, except in Cuba, at least temporarily resolved; the Church has shown greater concern for the material welfare of the masses, and the anti-clerical element, confronted by the power of the extreme left, has curbed its attack upon the secular influence of the Church. More important, government after government, with Mexico and Chile in the vanguard, has made itself constitutionally responsible for the welfare and security of its citizens.

The recognition by the state of this social responsibility was not only a major achievement of the inter-war years; by vindicating the interests of the masses after four centuries, it gave the era the stamp of greatness. Needless to say, basic laws have ordinarily served as symbols rather than instruments and have not been binding on actual political behavior. Political policies and legislation are still often anticipatory, addressed more to aspirations and hopes than to goals that might practically be achieved. As a consequence, the urban mobs, and still more the rural masses, await with justified concern further concrete evidence of their vindication.

With due regard for the genuine social and humanitarian interests in the working masses generated throughout the Western world by the recognition given them in the Treaty of Versailles and the creation of the International Labor Office (1919), it is apparent that in Spanish America the newly dis-covered concern for the common man was essentially the outgrowth of rapid socio-political change. Following World War I, the power of the rural-based traditional elite began to wane as political leaders came in increasing numbers from the urban middle sectors and came to depend upon urban workers for the hard core of their electoral support.

Once it was established that the urban workers might soon hold the balance of political power in their hands, they became invaluable political pawns to be manipulated at any price. The new urban leaders bid the highest in terms of political alliances, responsiveness to the play of social forces, and constitutional guarantees. At first, the paying off of political debts was almost painless. The number of new voters was small, and they were so miserably paid that their status could be significantly improved without placing a burden on the total economy. The problem of payment was further simplified, or so it seemed, because foreign capital, which tended to dominate those industries from which the newly enfranchised voters came, could simultaneously be made to bear the brunt of "social justice" and to serve as massive targets at which the workers could discharge their anxieties and frustrations.

The urban workers were courted on an unprecedented scale after the area began to recover from the Great Depression. Within a decade, such ideologically diverse leaders as the democratic Pedro Aguirre Cerda in Chile, the leftist-liberal Lázaro Cárdenas in Mexico, the authoritarian Juan Domingo Perón in Argentina, and the politically astute and mildly dictatorial Getulio Vargas in Brazil, alert to every gust of popular opinion, mobilized the working men politically with promises that flattered their dignity and prestige. Before the War's end, however, it was felt in some political circles that in many ways the labor vote had been costly to both society and the worker. Class relations had been embittered and national issues had been distorted. Labor organizations had been made politically dependent upon government. As the number of workers soared and their wages rose without a corresponding increase in their productive capacity, the strains upon the economy became serious. This latter development was particularly unacceptable to the new domestic entrepreneurs who were replacing the foreign capitalists; their representatives in government began to align themselves against leaders who sought political solutions to basically economic problems.

The response of the now entrenched middle-sector politicians to these developments was to broaden the electoral base to include those whose votes could be bought more cheaply. Age requirements were lowered, property and literacy requirements were reduced or discarded, and the unscrubbed, unschooled millions on the farms were enfranchised in the name of democracy. They were swept into the political life of the republics so rapidly that existing parties could not absorb many of them, and they learned little about working within the existing political system. In Chile, the number of registered voters quadrupled between 1937 and 1958. In Mexico, three times as many voted in 1958 as in 1940. In Bolivia, voters cast 956,000 ballots in the presidential election of 1956 compared with only 126,000 in the presidential election five years earlier. In Argentina, 9 million (out of a total population of 21 million) voted in the presidential election of 1958. In the Venezuelan presidential election of the same year, at least two out of every five voters were unable to write their own names.

The victor in the Venezuelan contest, Rómulo Betancourt, who for twenty years had used the traditional appeals of the urban middle sectors, by stressing a moderate land reform plank in his platform won the election not by running well in the cities, as middle-sector candidates had done elsewhere in Spanish America, but by piling up commanding margins in the backward farm states. Urban labor, recognizing immediately that it had been deserted, showed so much discontent through strikes and riots that the extreme left stepped up its political activity; furthermore, some of Betancourt's allies deserted him to create urban-based parties that they hoped would bring them to power by reaffirming the traditional alliance between the middle sectors and urban labor.

In the face of the ever-expanding electorate, which was of course their own creation, leaders of the urban-middle sector were pragmatic and displayed a strong tendency to forsake radicalism in favor of conservatism. In contrast with the communists and more recently the *fidelistas,* who take the position that the individual's quest for identity in a nascent modern society makes him particularly receptive to an ideology that demands his total commitment, the middle-sector leaders had been content to win the voter's sanction without asking him to accept an ideology. In their search for workable formulas, they have ranged across the political spectrum. In Uruguay they have raised respect for democratic processes to unprecedented levels for Spanish America. In Mexico they took over and perpetuated a political party which has monopolized power for more than three decades by controlling the nation's electoral machinery. Elsewhere, they have treated representative government and democracy as luxuries that can readily be priced out of the ideological market, and have not hesitated to make a mockery of democratic principles. Regardless of political orientation, they have depended heavily upon demagogic appeals. Again and again, their speeches, in giving recognition to those whom society has historically refused to recognize, have risen to new peaks of recklessness. They have offered simple answers to complex problems. They have exploited the instincts of chauvinism to develop a xenophobic nationalism, which they have made synonymous with progress, and which they have used not only to attract a wide range of special interest groups but also to help keep alive class grievances. These were dangerous tactics in societies becoming increasingly complex and requiring strength in order to channel their growing demands upon their governments.

But even in their more radical moments, the leaders of the middle sector always kept within the framework of western representative democracy, and the movements they led were distinguished almost as much by what they conserved as by what they introduced. Then, as they increased their stake in society, in some cases by the acquisition of wealth, and in others by job security (as for example by the addition of a civil service to the already bloated public bureaucracies), they tended to alter their philosophy from one of constant change to one of stability. Their declining interest in basic reform, evident immediately after World War II, actually assumed a negative or defensive character when the national leaders chose to qualify for assistance under the terms laid down by the United States as the cold war became hotter.

Numerous intellectuals, including students and some civil servants who had supported the middle-sector leaders but who were in no way pledged to the existing basic political framework, were disenchanted by this "swing to the right." They went over to the opposition, and in giving guidance to the disillusioned workers became the agents of a ceaseless turbulence. Although their skills and talents were particularly appropriate for providing leadership during a period of uncertainty, it was assumed, on the basis of earlier experience, that they would eventually dissipate their energies against the solid wall of middle-sector values that had been erected after 1920. But that did not happen, chiefly because they received sympathy and assistance from the Soviet bloc, whose prestige had soared to an all-time high with the launching of the first satellite in 1957. By providing funds and giving leadership to the outbursts of strongly felt but formally unorganized interests, the communists and *fidelistas* have done much to crystallize and broaden the opposition.

The constant tensions and instability have kept alive the historical difficulties arising from the attempt to maintain a democratic superstructure upon an essentially authoritarian base. Thus today, as for a century and a half, the people of Spanish America are divided between those who favor change within the democratic framework, or at most are willing to tolerate "a little bit of tyranny," and those who feel that the rapidly changing social bases of politics require a strong executive both to restrain the forces of disorder and to institute necessary reforms. Also, as has been the case for a century and a half, there are in every element of society, including the democratic element, those who are prepared to sustain their positions by resorting to violence. It is with an appreciation of this atmosphere of continuing agitational politics and the continuing willingness of civilians to resort to force, or at least to see violence employed, and their persisting unwillingness to commit themselves to a fixed political way of life that the evolution of the armed forces since World War I should be viewed.

The role of the armed forces has not changed basically under the impact of the massive transformation that has taken place since World War I. It has been argued from time to time that they figure in the defense of the Hemisphere and serve as deterrents to aggression from the outside, but it seems apparent that their primary goal, as in the past, is to maintain internal order as a second-line police force. As in the past, they have engaged in politics as the surest way of fulfilling their "obligations to country and self." The depth of involvement varies from country to country (currently it is negligible in Uruguay, Costa Rica, Mexico, Bolivia, Chile, and Colombia), but the fact that they are so involved cannot seriously be disputed. But if the role of the armed forces has not changed, the attitude of the officers has, and how this new attitude came about and what it means in terms of military behavior, especially in the extra-military areas, warrant elaboration.

The substitution of technically trained managers of violence for the heroic leaders of the past has had much to do with the growth of the new military. That substitution is now completed except in Honduras, where some officers entered the services without prior technical training (one high-ranking officer has had only three years of formal education) and the nation's military school did not graduate its first class until 1960. In Argentina, on the other hand, members of the permanent officer corps pass upon all admissions to the military colleges and no reserve or non-career officer can hope to rise to a top rank.

As might be expected, the level of achievement among graduates of the military academies in the several republics varies considerably. Graduates of the academies in Argentina and Chile, for example, have the equivalent of twelve to sixteen years of academic training; in Mexico, Venezuela, and Ecuador ten to twelve years; and in El Salvador and Honduras, six to ten years. All the states provide for postgraduate training in war colleges, command schools, and universities, and by foreign missions. The republics also make some kind of advanced training a requirement for promotion to the higher ranks. Venezuela, for example, sends a relatively large number of officers to colleges and universities in the United States, where they take as much as four years of undergraduate training in engineering, and Honduras proposes to permit approximately one-third of each class graduating from its Escuela

Militar to continue on to the university. Several hundred Argentine officers are in constant attendance at civilian institutions of higher learning; in 1958 there were 514 members of the armed forces registered in the University of Buenos Aires alone.[1] But what is important is that whether the training has been good, bad, or indifferent, the tendency has been for control of the armed forces to pass to "laboratory officers" who in most of the republics have raised the level of military expertise immeasurably.[2]

Better training has not been the only attraction held out to the new generation of officers or the only one shaping their thinking. Their salaries, which compare quite favorably with those of civilians of comparable age and training, are now paid with clock-like regularity. Promotions at the lower levels have been made automatic with the result that officers are free from political pressures for at least the first ten years and ordinarily the first fifteen years of their careers. Chile makes interest-free building loans available to commissioned officers and the government provides housing in many areas, including Santiago, where in 1960 the Commander-in-Chief of the Navy lived in a house that rented for $1,000 per month, paid by the government. In Venezuela, where interest commonly runs to 12 per cent and up, the government makes loans to both commissioned and non-commissioned officers at 4.5 per cent. This author knows of one Venezuelan officer who has received $50,000 under such terms, and it is general knowledge that majors in the Army and lieutenant commanders in the Navy have qualified for loans up to $40,000. President Betancourt said in 1960 that by the time he retired (1964) every commissioned and non-commissioned officer in the Venezuelan

---

[1] Universidad de Buenos Aires, *Censo universitario, 1959*. This census is examined in some detail in K. H. Silvert's contribution in John J. Johnson, ed., *Continuity and Change in Latin America* (Stanford, 1964).

[2] See Victor Alba's articles on the Latin American Military in *Combate,* Nos. 1–6 (San José, Costa Rica, September 1958–June 1959) and in John J. Johnson, ed., *The Role of the Military in Underdeveloped Countries* (Princeton, 1962).

armed forces would have a home of his own if he wanted one.

Furthermore, attractive retirement plans for those who have served out their careers have become commonplace. Argentina retires its officers at full pay after thirty years of service. Chilean officers also retire at full pay after thirty years and in addition can borrow funds for business purposes from the government at favorable interest rates. Upon retirement, Ecuadorian officers receive full pay plus a lump sum (to which they contribute while in the service) of approximately $10,000, which they commonly use to go into business or loan out at rates of 10 to 15 per cent. A Venezuelan officer retires after thirty years at full pay one rank above his last active one. In Colombia an officer can retire voluntarily after twenty years of service and can receive 80 per cent of his basic pay and allowances.

The system does not always work as it is supposed to. Officers are, in general, still a mediocre, if improving, group. They repeatedly violate the military codes. They feel that their services should be requited with more than pension plans. They tincture their greed with vanity and personal grievances. And civilian politicians constantly interfere with the system. At those ranks (general and colonel in the Army and Air Force and captain in the Navy) where congressional approval for promotions becomes necessary, politics rather than technical competence is often decisive. In Venezuela in 1963, for example, certain officers believed strongly that association with the Democratic Action Party was sufficient recommendation for promotion, and the same officers were convinced that President Betancourt was disregarding both seniority regulations and the best interests of the services in order to place officers oriented toward the Democratic Action Party in key positions. And there is no denying that in countries more highly developed than Venezuela promotion by seniority from time to time continues to be tempered by sycophancy and nepotism, with the result that young officers become easily disgruntled.

Despite the failings of the system, recent developments have been highly favorable to the average officer. As a member of a group, he now has a sense of security that he could not have reasonably expected a few years ago. And the armed forces have become institutionalized pressure groups with channels for maintaining close links with the civilian population.

C. Wright Mills once said that "social origins and early background are less important to the character of the professional military man than to any other high social type."[3] This may apply to countries with highly professionalized armed forces, but is not applicable to Spanish America. There, although the situation is changing, a uniform still does not always make an individual first of all a soldier, and at least until that stage is reached the officer's social background will remain one of the keys to his behavior.

One component of this background is racial origin. It is known, for example, that in the armed forces, as in Latin American society as a whole, opportunities have favored men of European ethnic background over the "people of color." Everywhere except in Haiti, which may be considered solidly Negro and mulatto, the percentage of white officers is greater than the percentage of whites to the population as a whole. While observing a military parade in Tegucigalpa, Quito, or Lima, the whitening process beginning with the conscript and proceeding through the various levels to the top ranks can be seen taking place before one's eyes. This is not to suggest that there are not exceptions or that people of color are always kept from becoming officers. As early as 1960 the Peruvian army had at least one general who was a "full-blooded" Indian. In Mexico, El Salvador, and Paraguay, officers are overwhelmingly mestizos, and there is no discrimination against them at any rank. In Venezuela there are a few high-ranking officers who are part Negro. And everywhere except in Colombia, where an undetermined but obviously large percentage of officers still come from upper middle-class and elite families, there is evidence that the white predominance is breaking down

---

[3] C. Wright Mills, *The Power Elite* (New York, 1959), p. 192.

within the armed forces, as it is in the political area; but for what it is worth, "whiteness" will continue, short of revolution, to be a factor for many years.

A major reason why the "whites" will not indefinitely continue to exercise their traditional influence is that everywhere the tendency is to dip deeper into the social strata for officers, and it is in the lower social strata that the mestizos, Indians, Negroes, and mulattoes are most often found. In Ecuador, where both civil and military personnel agree that 5 per cent of all officers are from the working classes (the same percentage as is estimated for the upper middle class and elite), the author was told of a cobbler's son who was making a distinguished record in the military school. Colonel Oscar Osorio, the dictator-president of El Salvador (1950–56), was "strictly peon," having come up from the enlisted ranks. The first class to graduate from the military school of Honduras had three Negro cadets "whose parents were obviously from the lowest middle sectors or working groups." A Venezuelan army officer spoke with considerable pride of the fact that his parents were from the working classes. Examples could be cited endlessly.

There would appear to be two principal reasons why more officers now come from the lower sectors than at any time since the mid-nineteenth century, when the armed forces were in near-total disgrace. First, economic and technological developments and the tremendous expansion of civilian bureaucracies have broadened the opportunities for the best-educated in the non-military areas. Second, public schools have given the lower classes the opportunity to receive the academic training needed to qualify for the military schools. Reasonably accurate figures show that in Ecuador 90 per cent of the cadets enter the military academies from the public schools, and this figure would seem to be reasonably correct for all of the republics. In Mexico, at least theoretically, the government will provide a child of sufficient aptitude with all of his academic and professional training without charge.

In the first half of this century the major source of officer material appears to have been the well-established small town families—professionals, shopkeepers, state and municipal bureaucrats. In El Salvador, for example, very few officers of the present generation came from the capital city; most came from "villages," which in many cases are little more than settlements linked to coffee plantations.[4] In Honduras in 1960, the small towns were especially well represented in the military school and in the officer corps. Because Venezuela throughout nearly all this century has been controlled by a military clique from the farming area of the Andes, bordering on Colombia, perhaps as much as 90 per cent of its officers have come from the non-industrialized states of the republic. The protocol list of officers for Caracas and vicinity published by the Minister of Defense in September of 1954 contained seventy names, for twenty-four of whom biographical information was available. Of that group twenty were from the agricultural and livestock-raising Andean states, including fifteen from the single state of Táchira, whose largest city, San Cristóbal, had a population of 56,000 in 1950. Only one officer was from the populous Federal District. Since 1950 the government has made a conscious and apparently successful effort to break the Andean monopoly over the armed services, and all sections of the country are now reasonably well represented in the military schools. On the basis of considerable reliable evidence, it is apparent that in Colombia the armed forces hold a very strong attraction for young men from the agricultural regions, which provide at least 70 per cent of the officers in the three branches of the service.

Ecuador presents a somewhat different situation. There, one is not so much impressed with the fact that a large percentage of officers come from small towns, which they do, as by the fact that they come in overwhelming numbers from the economically backward highlands with Quito as the hub; the more advanced coastal area, which Guayaquil dominates, is weakly represented, even in the navy. This situation has helped to keep alive the rivalry of the two regions; *guayaquileños* in-

[4] It has been said that the officers in El Salvador today owe their positions to plantation owners who knew them as cadets and recommended them to the military as trustworthy potential officers.

sist that they produce the revenue used to support the national army which is in turn employed to suppress them politically.

In Chile, the small town thesis begins to break down, and in Argentina it simply does not apply. The officers in the Chilean armed forces come from the various states more or less in relation to their share in the total population, and approximately 70 per cent of the Argentine armed forces come from the highly developed Federal District and the province of Buenos Aires.[5] Robert Potash, who has worked extensively upon the Argentine military, holds that in recent years Argentine generals have been big city products.

The potential officers from the small towns appear to be motivated primarily by three factors. First, the military academies offer far better opportunities for education than are ordinarily available locally. Second, a military career affords a chance to break out of the provincial settlements, where economic opportunities are few. Third, military careers provide a chance to improve one's social-economic status. Another consideration, but one not easy to measure, is the "glamor appeal" of the armed forces for young men in hundreds of drab interior towns, cut off from contact with the pageantry and diversions of the cities.

The young man from a provincial settlement takes into his military career attitudes that almost certainly affect his thinking as an officer. In many cases the detachment of six to a dozen officers in his home town provides him with his only direct contact or acquaintance with the national government. The troops and the national flag flying from the presidio thus come to symbolize the nation. The troops, too, command

[5] See the contribution by Lyle McAlister in John J. Johnson, ed., *Continuity and Change in Latin America*. McAlister, drawing upon Potash, also points out that as late as 1951 only 12 per cent of the generals were from Buenos Aires. Two facts go far toward explaining the Argentine situation: there has been a heavy concentration of immigrants in the Federal District and the province of Buenos Aires; and the nation's large army bases and schools are also located in and around the capital city. The military have been swelled by men from this region because immigrants have used the Argentine armed forces as a springboard to social prestige, and because the sons of officers display a strong tendency to follow in their fathers' footsteps and become officers.

youthful respect in a society that places considerable emphasis upon force and violence. And the ready response of enlisted men to the orders of their commander presents an apparent aura of power and influence bound to fascinate an impressionable mind. That mind is also impressed by the fact that the *comandante* is accepted as an equal of the village priest, the *alcalde* (mayor), the president of the Rotary Club, and the large landowners and their daughters. The association of the armed forces with social prestige is consequently strong among village youth.

The boys or young men of the rural towns grow up in an environment far more strongly shaped by Roman Catholicism than is the environment in which their city cousins are reared. Historically, the strength of the Catholic Church has been in the countryside, while the cities have taken the lead in anticlerical movements. It has been the well-established provincial families who have provided the hard core of the narrow and at times almost medieval Catholicism found in the outlying regions. In this regard, it is worth noting that in the Venezuelan presidential election of 1958, the state of Táchira, which in this century has provided an estimated 80 per cent of all army officers, gave over 55 per cent of its vote to the candidate of the Social Christian Party (the most conservative of the four major parties), who obtained only 14 per cent of the total presidential vote.

Finally, the provincial youth ordinarily comes from a non-propertied family or one that associates property with land, if only because its fortunes are closely related to the welfare of the agricultural community. The importance of this economic background is that the provincial youth becomes an officer without a firm understanding of corporate industry and little appreciation of the problems, including labor relations, of technological development which his professional training as a soldier inclines him to support. The agricultural orientation that the cadets from the small towns take into their military careers may be strengthened, and cadets from other social backgrounds made aware of the "agricultural" problem, when as officers they marry into the provincial "aristocracy." This apparently occurs with some frequency, because new officers are often assigned to the least attractive garrisons of the interior and the frontiers soon after they have finished their academy training. In the provinces, their prestige as officers brings them into contact with the socially prominent and marriageable young ladies whose fathers control the countryside, and who, incidentally, are on the lookout for opportunities to escape the boredom of the interior.[6]

A second major source of officers, and one which is becoming increasingly important, is the sons and brothers of officers. Everywhere the academies have a strong contingent of army and navy juniors. A highly placed naval officer in Chile, for example, insisted that 60 per cent of the sons of officers go to the Naval Academy and that 20 to 25 per cent of all officers in the Chilean Navy were navy juniors. Available evidence indicates that a figure of 20 to 25 per cent would hold throughout those republics where the armies and navies are now well established. Thus, there is some truth in the statement that children of officers are born to privilege in Spanish America. The air forces in most of the republics are of such recent origin that it is impossible to determine with any degree of certainty whether or not they will follow the pattern of the armies and navies, but on the other hand, there is no reason to believe that they will not. Military families, meanwhile, are becoming commonplace. In Ecuador, Venezuela, and Mexico research turned up several cases of four or more brothers in the armed forces, and two brothers in a single branch of the service is quite common. When one adds to the sons and brothers the cousins and second-cousins and ties resulting from marriages, the influence of a few families can become decisive, particularly in the smaller forces.

The opportunities for one or a few families to control a

[6] A careful estimate of the frequency with which such marriages take place has not been made, but civilian responses to direct and related questions suggest that the public, at least in the lesser developed republics, is convinced that the rate of such marriages is abnormally high. This point, which must be considered tentative for the moment, deserves more thorough research.

service is illustrated by the situation in the Venezuelan Navy and Marine Corps, and by the Cuban Army under Fulgencio Batista. The Venezuelan Navy in 1962 had six admirals; two of them were the Larrazábal brothers, Carlos and Wolfgang; a third, Sosa Ríos, was married to a sister of the Larrazábal brothers and a second Larrazábal sister was married to a commander in the marines, Oscar Nahmens. Also, the Carúpano and Puerto Cabello revolts of mid-1962, led by the marines, tended to be family affairs. The Carúpano uprising was headed by J. T. Molina, who "jumped the gun" on what was supposed to be a general revolt, when his brother, J. J. Molina, a high-ranking marine officer, was arrested for plotting. The same J. J. Molina is married to one of three Bermúdez sisters, the other two of whom are also married to marine corps officers. Furthermore Lieutenant Commander Morales, who deserted when the revolt broke out in Carúpano but who returned to the barracks the night of the Puerto Cabello outbreak, is a brother-in-law of Lieutenant Commander Francisco Avilan, one of the navy officers who backed the Marine uprising at Puerto Cabello.

In Cuba, dictator Fulgencio Batista was well aware that the Cuban armed forces were essential to his continuance in power, and he accordingly made great efforts to insure the loyalty of the forces. The Tabernilla family played a dominant role in his plans. The leader of this family was Major General Francisco J. Tabernilla y Dolz (with five stars, the only Cuban officer of the rank). A career army man, he was a second lieutenant when Batista staged the "Sergeants' Revolt" in 1933. Tabernilla threw his lot in with Batista and subsequently became one of his closest friends. Promoted to lieutenant colonel in 1934, he made brigadier general in 1942. When Batista forces lost the election in 1944, Tabernilla was promptly "retired." Batista staged his last coup on March 10, 1952, with the active participation of Tabernilla, who was promoted to Major General and made Chief of Staff of the army. In January 1958 he was made Chief of the Joint General Staff and given the rank of General-in-Chief. He fled Cuba with Batista on January 1, 1959.

General Tabernilla had three sons, Francisco, Carlos, and Marcelo. During 1957 and 1958 they held the following positions: Brigadier General Francisco H. Tabernilla y Palermo (two stars) was commanding officer of the Mixed Tank Regiment, which included all the tanks in the Cuban armed forces. Brigadier General Carlos M. Tabernilla y Palermo (one star) was commanding officer of the Cuban Army Air Force which, with the exception of a few antiquated navy planes, contained all the military aircraft Cuba had. Lieutenant Colonel Marcelo Tabernilla y Palermo, "the baby of the family," was commanding officer of the Cuban Army Air Force Bomber Squadron, which included all of the bombers Cuba possessed. In addition, the older Tabernilla's sister was married to Brigadier General Alberto Del Río Chaviano (two stars), who spent most of the crucial years 1957 and 1958 as commanding officer of the Southern Military Zone of Oriente Province, which included the city of Santiago (Cuba's second largest) and the Sierra Maestra mountains, the center and heartland of Fidel Castro's operations.

Like the young men from the small towns, those sons of officers who follow in their father's footsteps doubtless take into their careers certain attitudes and biases that influence their behavior when they step out of their purely professional role. For one thing, their early training has conditioned them to think in essentially bureaucratic terms. Like the youth from the provinces, the son of an officer may have little understanding of the workings of industrial capitalism simply because his parents, if they were typical, would have had very little or no personal experience in that economic area. And the officer's son may well have grown up a superpatriot if only because it was dinned in his ear that the armed forces are the guarantors of the nation's sovereignty and defenders of its dignity, not only against the foreign enemy but also against those who would destroy the nation from within.

The relatively recent arrivals from Europe and their heirs constitute the third and last important source of officers that requires special mention here. The influence of this group has been most pronounced in Chile and Argentina. In Chile, the Germans, who began to come into the republic in the mid-19th century, had begun to infiltrate the armed services by the outbreak of World War I; by World War II their importance in the Chilean army (which had been under German influence for half a century) was of major concern to the Allies. Since World War II a sprinkling of Syrian and Jewish and a rather larger number of Yugoslav names have appeared on the registers of the military academies. But the influence of the newcomers in the Chilean armed forces has been insignificant compared to their influence in Argentina. There, both armed forces personnel and civilians claimed in 1960 that not less than 40 per cent of all officers were first and second generation Argentines, overwhelmingly of Italian and Spanish origin.[7]

The newcomers have looked to careers in the military for several reasons. The services are technical, and submerged social groups see technical training as an avenue to social mobility. The armed forces, because of their strong nationalistic leanings, provide a sanctuary for newcomers who fear being looked upon as anything less than 100 per cent patriotic. And those Argentines only one or two generations removed from Italy and Spain are quite comfortable in an army that apparently enforces an unwritten requirement that all officers be at least nominal Catholics.[8]

We may now ask how institutionalization and increased professionalization on the one hand and the changing social character of officers on the other have been manifested in military-civilian relations since World War II. In terms of the relationships between the armed forces and civilians, the junta

[7] Robert Potash, in a personal communication, reports that in 1961 only 20 per cent of Argentine generals were second-generation Argentines. However, his information indicates that as late as 1951 approximately one half of the generals were sons of immigrants. See Lyle McAlister's contribution in John J. Johnson, ed., *Continuity and Change in Latin America* (Stanford, 1964).

[8] K. H. Silvert, "Political Universes in Latin America," *American Universities Field Staff Reports,* VIII, No. 6 (Dec. 1961), p. 10.

of government has been the most important by-product of institutionalization. In its civilian context the junta goes back to the colonial period, but it has been a regularly employed military device in Spanish America only since the 1920's. In their simplest forms the military juntas are boards or committees that assume power and rule by decree following the removal of a regime by force. They represent joint efforts on the part of dominant groups in the various branches of the military establishment to present a unified front against dissident elements within the services. This is what occurred in Peru in July 1962 when the Manuel Prado government was driven from power: a junta representing a substantial cross-section of the officer corps in each of the branches of the armed services took over the leadership of the republic. The juntas are by definition transitory and several have terminated their rule in favor of civilians but rarely without first laying down the terms under which the successor government is permitted to be selected.

As far as the evolution of the armed forces is concerned, the military junta is a manifestation of the decline of individualism and the growth of an *esprit de corps* or group identification that has accompanied the greater institutionalization of the services. The Venezuelan situation perhaps best illustrates this point. Under the old tyrant Juan Vicente Gómez, the armed forces were used against civilians repeatedly, but at the command and pleasure of the dictator. Their long-range interests were incidental to the immediate interests of Gómez. But under the tyrant the armed forces did take on a national character and did evolve institutional objectives, and when Gómez died in 1935 these developments manifested themselves. Following a number of internal crises that resulted in the younger professionals supplanting the older non-professionals in key positions, the armed forces began to act in the name of the various branches and to claim the role of custodians of the national interests. The juntas of 1945, 1948, and 1958 were the results. Although the junta may now be considered a well-established political device of the armed services throughout Spanish

America, it does not follow that strongmen will not appear from time to time, as in Argentina when Perón emerged supreme two years after the military took over the government in June 1943.

Professionalization has produced officers, who, when they act politically, do so for reasons and in a manner that clearly distinguishes them from their pre-World War I counterparts. First of all professionalization has almost completely destroyed the fluidity that existed when officers moved in and out of the military life at will. Then, too, as Lucian Pye has so ably established in reference to areas other than Latin America, professionalization has created an intellectual atmosphere within the armed forces that makes the leadership acutely sensitive to the advantages of modernization and technical advancement.[9] The new officer's belief in the need to modernize involves him so deeply with the welfare of the nation that he feels obliged to take a position on all major issues. This view can place him in an unusual position at several levels. Although nationalistic, he is, for example, required to obtain his weapons abroad. Also, he can be forced to look outside his own society for models upon which to fashion his own career, which can make him painfully aware of the extent to which his own country is economically and technologically retarded. Or his impatience to see the complete modernization of the armed forces and of the nation may tear him emotionally between those values held over from his youth and those that tend to align him with intellectuals and students and others most anxious to bring about change rapidly. For better or worse, the emotional conflict has held up the playing out of the contest between the military bureaucracies, which have traditionally represented the countryside, and the civilian bureaucracies, historically centered in the cities and inclined to look outward

[9] See his excellent contributions in Gabriel A. Almond and James S. Coleman, eds., *The Politics of the Developing Areas* (Princeton, 1960), and John J. Johnson, ed., *The Role of the Military in Underdeveloped Countries* (Princeton, 1962). Pye's thinking is apparent throughout Max F. Millikan and Donald L. M. Blackmer, editors, *The Emerging Nations; Their Growth and United States Policy* (Boston, 1961).

for guidance. This is why when the cities appear to triumph politically, as they have on many occasions since World War I, there has remained a strong residue of rural-mindedness, which erupts from time to time either at the instigation of or with the collusion of the armed forces, who have held the balance of power more or less continuously in all republics except Uruguay, Costa Rica, Chile, Colombia, Mexico, and Bolivia.

The commitment of the new generation of officers to modernization has also meant that the traditional social-economic gap between the leader and the led has been reinforced by differences in acculturation to modern life. This, plus the fact that in contemporary military establishments there is little or no comradeship between officers and men, has created a void that tends to prevent commissioned officers from being fully aware of the concerns of the non-commissioned officers and troops. Accordingly, non-commissioned officers and troops have been encouraged to look to civilians to fill the vacuum of representation between them, their superiors, and the public. This gap also tends to keep the officers divorced from that part of the populace in which democratic aspirations are nourished. Modernization and its implications, it would seem, weigh so heavily in Spanish America's future that the "pay, promotion, pension" argument—so often used at one and the same time to discredit the armed forces and to account for their participation in politics—loses much of its significance. In the final analysis, the republics will not be made or unmade on the basis of their military expenditures, although their future may well be determined by how important the armed forces consider modernization to be.

In some respects professionalization has made the modern armed forces officer less qualified than his World War I predecessor to run the governments of the republics. The officer of an earlier generation was first of all a civilian who thought as a civilian; he could, if he chose, keep his finger on the pulse of the narrowly based civilian ruling element through direct contact—although in actual practice the military tyrants in the latter stages of their dictatorships often lost all touch with the civilian elite and depended entirely on crudely repressive tactics. And the state, which was charged with little more than defending the national sovereignty and protecting private property, could be managed with only a primitive knowledge of administration. The modern officer-statesman, on the other hand, is never free for more than a brief moment to rule exclusively in the interests of a single sector of society, and government has become extravagantly complex as the state has committed itself to action in many social and economic areas.

The contemporary officer, furthermore, must spend at least twenty years in the service before he can expect to be called by his peers to lead them when they challenge politicians on their own ground. During those twenty years he lives in near-isolation from civilian concerns. Consequently, when he plunges into politics without ethical, moral, or legal support, he must not only speak for the armed services and try to keep them happy; he must also, because of the isolation that the military life imposes, depend for advice on his military friends, who live by the same kind of conventional wisdom that he does. These advisors, like the junta member himself, are usually win-the-war-and-to-hell-with-the-cost men, and as administrators they have been inefficient planners and inclined toward ruinous financial polices, as witness Perón in Argentina and Rojas Pinilla in Colombia. Carlos Ibáñez of Chile is an excellent example of a military man elected to the presidency of a politically sophisticated republic in a free election who by the time he left office had surrounded himself with a disproportionate share of military men because he felt he understood them and they understood him.

During his first twenty years as a soldier, the military ethic teaches the modern officer that man is weak and irrational and must be subordinated to the group, a position which at times has induced officers to disdain the civilians whom they propose to rule. Furthermore, the officer is, for nearly all of his professional career, himself a subordinate, taking orders rather than giving them, carrying out someone else's ideas rather than his own, and fitting himself into the well-defined hierarchical organization of the military. Subordination, and the narrow range of alternatives that subordination in the military permits, make the officer decisive and build up in him a faith in his ability to demand decisive action from others. The professional soldier's ordered and disciplined life has unquestionably made it difficult for him to tolerate the unsettling effects of social change, the "wasted effort" and divisiveness that accompany the workings of the democratic process. Perón, for example, in addressing a class of Argentine cadets before the War's end, accounted for France's military collapse on the grounds of internal disorder resulting from its political system. Above all, it has been the officer-politician's propensity to reject democratic institutions, polemics, and personal rivalry, and to apply military regimentation and modes of thought to all types of civilian situations that has ordinarily kept him in conflict with important elements within the civilian population. In this climate of opposition, he has not been able for extended periods of time to make effective use of his best qualities—self-confidence, experience in taking orders before giving them, the ability to accept rapid modernization, and the disposition to think in national terms.

Finally, the modern officer-politician runs into difficulties never experienced by his predecessor when he insists, as he ordinarily does, on imposing not only his person but a whole system upon the nation. Officers of an earlier generation, assuming control when strains developed, simply "declared for the general will" and were content to exercise personal political power. Despite their apparent ruthlessness, they were haphazard in enforcing their will upon the public, and they invariably proclaimed representative democracy to be their ultimate objective. But the modern officer often enters politics because of ideological differences with the civilian elements in power. When he achieves power as a representative of his branch of the service he feels compelled not only to rule but to define the content of the general will, as did Perón under what he called *justicialismo*. The modern officer may attempt to brainwash his subjects through mass media of communications. He may use the schools and government-controlled labor organizations for the propagation of the ideological position he seeks to impose. He may employ economic sanctions, one of the more easily applied political weapons in a "planned" society. He may lump representative democracy with imperialistic capitalism and reject both as undesirable.

The officer-statesman's confidence in his ability to formulate and implant ideological doctrines arises from two basic causes: contact with officers from other countries, and a conscious effort on the part of the armed forces in the most advanced countries to make officers aware of contemporary developments. Thus, the rise of a totalitarian attitude in the Argentine Army in the 1930's and 1940's can be accounted for in large part by its close connections with the armies of Nazi Germany and Fascist Italy, which at that time must have seemed almost invincible. Today, middle- and senior-grade officers in all the leading countries of Latin America are expected to have instruction in both national and world affairs; as a result, they become convinced that they are qualified to play a leading role in the economics, international relations, and government of their countries. It is still too early to determine how successful these training programs will be. As yet there has not appeared an officer who has publicly displayed a greater grasp of national and world problems than have civilians. But to the consternation of the anti-military elements of the area, the armed forces have won some highly placed individuals over to the military point of view by using them as instructors and extending to them some of the privileges (free air travel, for example) that the armed forces enjoy.

The officers who rush into politics to protect their professional or ideological interests may be no more responsible for prolonging the military interference in politics than are those officers who permit themselves to be used by civilian politicians.

Regardless of which side is more effective, civil-militarism in politics is a reality throughout most of Spanish America. In June of 1959, Rafael Caldera, the presidential candidate of the Social Christian Party in the 1958 elections, formulated the problem well when he said, "Venezuelans are so accustomed to see the army as a factor in their daily lives, so accustomed to make the army the arbiter of their political contests, that at each moment the most varied groups for the most dissimilar ends attempt to involve the army in new adventures to change our political reality."

There is a vast body of evidence to support Caldera's statement. The new political parties that arose in Venezuela after the death of the tyrant Gómez sought support in the armed forces for their demands, and Rómulo Betancourt and his Democratic Action Party first achieved power in 1945 by a military coup. When the armed forces removed his successor, Rómulo Gallegos, who belonged to Democratic Action, and set up a junta, the opposition parties approved—if they did not actually welcome—the role of the junta because of their intense dislike of the party. Then, in one of his campaign speeches during the presidential campaign of 1958, victorious candidate Betancourt listed the names of "soldiers who died in the name of Democratic Action." Betancourt was also charged, probably with considerable justification, with using his office to place officers sympathetic to Democratic Action in key positions in the various branches of the armed forces.

Civil-militarism is unusually pronounced in Venezuela, but it exists everywhere except in Costa Rica and Uruguay. In Honduras, "the army officers belong to the Nationalist Party," according to a prominent figure in that organization, "and we would all be dead if the army did not protect us from the Civil Guard." According to another member of that party, "Everybody praised the military junta for its role in removing Julio Lozana Díaz from office after two years of inept rule and then conducting a free election." Victor Paz Estenssoro, twice president of Bolivia, prior to achieving that high office for the first time in 1952, encouraged young nationalist officers in the army and air force to promote the interests of the Movimiento Nacionalista Revolucionario (MNR) by surreptitiously opposing the "irresponsible older officers." When the MNR achieved power, all officers in what remained of the armed services were MNR Party members. Between 1946 and 1957 the Conservative Party was predominant in Colombia, and it insisted that the majority of students entering the military academy, from which all officers come, be from Conservative Party families. In Mexico the Partido Revolucionario Institucional (PRI) uses armed forces officers as referees at the local level, and the free-wheeling *comandante* is courted if not respected in such modern provincial cities as Guadalajara.

José María Velasco Ibarra, four-time president of Ecuador, who was removed from office by the army in 1962, used to speak of "mi ejército" (my army). He bought the air force a number of jets during his 1952–56 term and, in an excellent display of non-coordination, sent officers to study abroad in at least twelve different countries. In Peru, Fernando Belaúnde Terry, presidential candidate in 1962 (and victor in June 1963) let it be known after the 1962 elections that he would as soon see the armed forces take control of the country as to have the presidency go to either of the leading opposition candidates, and a few days later his alternative to his own election came to pass. At the same time the politically powerful Miro Quesada family, which controls the newspaper *El comercio* in Lima, also urged intervention by the military.

One may dip into the history of Argentina anywhere and expect to find examples of civil-militarism. Hipólito Irigoyen, the first "people's president" of Argentina, during his initial term in office, paid off one debt after another to officers who in the 1890–1916 period had helped to counteract the ruling oligarchy's use of the army as a praetorian guard to manipulate elections. Before 1930 nationalist groups in Argentina found in General José F. Uriburu a possible vehicle for their rise to power, while conservatives, Anti-Personalist Radicals and Independent Socialists gravitated to General Agustín P. Justo.

Marvin Goldwert, in an unpublished manuscript, writes

of a secret Argentine decree dated November 25, 1930, "which seems to have been an out-and-out attempt to bribe the official body of the army."[10] According to Goldwert, the decree called upon all officers to draw up a list of their outstanding debts to be submitted to the government, with the understanding that all approved ones would be paid by the administration headed by General Uriburu. The decree contained provisions for repayment over a ten-year period, but "this never seems to have been done." This decree, it was later recorded, had cost the Argentine people 7 million pesos, and led one historian to call it "perhaps the cleverest wholesale bribery scheme ever witnessed in South America."

On the eve of the 1943 coup in Argentina, Radical Party politicians were in contact with General Pedro Ramírez and other key officers who took part in the ouster of President Castillo. Civil-militarism in Argentina since the overthrow of Perón has been so notorious that only three points of some interest need be recorded here. Admiral Isaac Rojas, who had steadfastly opposed Perón, according to the son of the president of a very staid and conservative club in Buenos Aires, was made an honorary member of the club "in appreciation." Arturo Frondizi wanted the presidency badly enough in 1958 to accept the terms laid down by the armed forces, including the outlawing of the *peronistas,* who apparently constitute at least 30 per cent of the electorate. And although the Popular Radical Party, whose presidential candidate in the 1958 elections ran second to Frondizi, feigned dismay when the armed forces ousted Frondizi in early 1962, high officials of that party in 1960 were said by well-informed sources to have urged a military takeover of the government. To these examples of civil-militarism must be added the actions of all those civilian authorities who rely upon the armed forces to maintain them-

---

[10] "The Argentine Revolution of 1930: The Rise of Modern Militarism and Ultra-Nationalism in Argentina" (Ph.D. dissertation, University of Texas, 1962).

selves in power and in so doing invite military interference in civilian affairs.

Caldera's statement for Venezuela, then, has rather general applicability. From it follows logically the proposition that until the armed forces develop as strong a moral fiber as have the civilians with whom they must deal, civil-militarism will be part of the political reality in large areas of Spanish America. Civilians will probably continue to appeal to the military. for at least three reasons. The first, and obviously most justified one, is that in certain instances the military becomes an important means of removing a group in power. In this sense, the military coup is part of the democratic process, and has been freely acknowledged as such in Latin America.

The second reason that civil-militarism will continue is that violence, although diminishing, remains a definite feature of the political process in most of the republics. In such an environment, the politicians, the parties, and ultimately the people must from time to time choose from among five alternative sources of force: the armed services, the police, the civil guards, armies constituted and supplied by political parties, and forces raised by retired officers. The regular services, under such circumstances, will retain an extremely strong appeal.

The third reason is that the armed forces will continue to be divided by inter-service and intra-service rivalries which can be exploited by civilians in much the same way as they have been historically. Although inter-service differences certainly cannot be discounted, it should be realized that they have not been as important as they might have in view of the fluid situation that has persisted in the republics. This has been true primarily for two reasons. First, in most cases the armies have been so strong vis-à-vis the other military services that they have had the final say. Only on one occasion—the Chilean revolution of 1891—has a Spanish-American navy emerged clearly on top in a showdown with the army. And as yet no air force in Spanish America has attained either the strength or standing that would permit it to meet the corresponding army head-on, unless the Ecuadorian air force action against the army in 1961 may be considered an exception. Second, the political impact of inter-service rivalry has been still further reduced because, unlike in the United States, the armed forces of Spanish America are not pioneering advanced weapons, and their professional futures, therefore, are not constantly at stake.

Intra-service rivalries have had political repercussions more often than have inter-service differences. Such rivalries most often break out into the open in the army, because there the stakes in terms of power are higher than in the other branches of the armed forces, and also because in the navies officers are constantly being broken up into small groups aboard ships, which discourages the formation of cliques.

Differences of a politically important nature often arise between the young officers and their seniors. The reasons for the differences vary widely. Sometimes the younger men feel that as members of the technically trained and "virtuous" generation, they are better qualified than their seniors to represent the services. On some occasions they feel that ranking generals have lost touch with the troops and the field-grade officers are the real representatives of the military consensus. Sometimes they want to involve the armed services more deeply in politics; this is the case particularly with those who have authoritarian leanings. And sometimes they are simply discontented because for one reason or another promotions and privileges have not come to them as expected.

In order to strengthen their position in respect to the senior officers, the younger men are forever forming cliques or secret organizations. Thus a group of junior officers, for example, was responsible for the Venezuelan coup of 1945, and junior army officers, in cooperation with the Venezuelan navy and air force, likewise played an important role in the overthrow of Pérez Jiménez. They were clearly exasperated with Pérez Jiménez because he had consistently followed a policy of showering upon senior officers privileges, political appointments, and opportunities to grow rich by corruption while neglecting junior men.

Secret organizations have been common in the military history of Spanish America. The first known *Logia* (Lodge), which had Masonic connections, was founded as early as 1808 to promote the independence of Spanish America. Since then Masons have with varying success infiltrated the armed services in all of the republics; the Argentine navy had the reputation of being a stronghold of Masonry during the Perón dictatorship. In Argentina the military Logia San Martín dictated key assignments during President Alvear's administration (1922–28) and also won acceptance for an armaments expansion policy during Alvear's tenure.

More recently the secret organizations have taken on a professional or nationalistic coloration. The highly nationalistic, fascist-oriented Grupo de Oficiales Unidos (GOU) in Argentina, of which Perón was a member, is the best known of the secret military organizations that attracted younger officers, but there have been many others that have had some influence since the GOU came into prominence. In Bolivia the Radepa (Razón de Patria) reached its peak of influence during the war years, when it participated in the overthrow of President Enrique Peñaranda in 1943. It was made up of young officers who blamed Bolivia's defeat in the Chaco war on corrupt and greedy politicians, and its leaders reportedly accepted fascist authoritarianism as well as financial assistance from the Perón government of Argentina. In Chile the Pumas (Por un Mañana Auspicioso) and the Línea Recta, two military parties that came out in the open in 1955, were made up of young officers who were impressed with the growing influence of the Argentine army after 1943 and sought to secure the same influence for themselves. They chose to improve their position first by dedicating themselves to the election of Carlos Ibáñez to the presidency in 1952 and, after that was achieved, to giving him dictatorial power to solve the country's problems. In Ecuador, young officers who claimed to be interested only in professional improvement, but who had ties with civilian politicians, created a secret organization known as Forme (Formación de Oficiales Revolucionarios Ecuadorianos), which in 1959 engaged in terrorist activities, but to no avail.[11]

The antagonism and bitterness that have led to inter- and intra-service rivalries and have served to involve the armed forces in politics have at the same time weakened them as cohesive political organizations. When acrimony leads to military executions, as it did in Argentina during the interregnum following Perón's overthrow, it seems unlikely that the armed forces can be expected to act with unity in any given situation; and if this is true, it follows that division in the armed forces will be exploited by civilians for their own purposes.

The police, except perhaps in Argentina and Chile, are not an acceptable alternative to the armed forces when political decisions start to be resolved by force. The police are in general a sorry lot. They often receive only a bare minimum of technical training. Not unusually illiterate and shabbily dressed, they can hardly command civilian respect, except the respect born of fear. They are so poorly paid that they live by various forms of blackmail, and intellectually they are completely unqualified to deal with the abstractions that arise in political life, and thus are subject to innumerable pressures from politicians and political appointees.

The national guards and the armies of political parties are ordinarily the products of revolution or highly unstable conditions. The national guards of Bolivia and Cuba became "permanent" organizations upon the destruction of the national armed forces under revolutionary circumstances, and if

---

[11] Robert Potash, who has made the most thorough study yet of the Argentine army, has come across a number of secret organizations in it: Los Dragones Verdes, Los Gorilas, El Pistón (military engineers), and Los Cuarenta (the forty colonels), to name a few. His tentative conclusion, however, is that in the Argentine case information about the cliques is unreliable, and that more often than not the cliques are short-lived associations set up to advance the personal ambitions of certain officers. Potash also holds that the cliques involve civilians as well as officers.

they become institutionalized they may be expected to assume nearly all the functions ordinarily reserved to the armed forces. And like the armed forces they will be able to influence social and political policies. The civil guard in Honduras arose from a less revolutionary atmosphere than those in Bolivia and Cuba, but for much the same reason : to defend the Liberal Party from possible attack by the predominantly conservative army. The Liberal Party, in effect, caught the Honduran armed forces in a fit of indecision and was able to create what they hoped would be a counterpoise to the army, a situation which the Guatemalan and Argentine armed forces did not permit to arise when Jacobo Arbenz and Juan Perón, in 1954 and 1955, respectively, attempted to arm the proletariat which could then have been converted into a national guard. Only the civil guard of Costa Rica, by and large remaining out of politics and accepting the decisions of four successive presidential administrations on matters directly affecting it, has set an example that one might wish other military establishments to copy.

The armies of the political parties usually have their origins in guerrilla bands, but they may be converted into national guards if their party attains power, as occurred in Cuba and Bolivia. The civil war that raged in Colombia for a decade after 1947, for example, was in part sustained by bands who fought in the name of the Liberal Party, although that party organization did not recognize them publicly (the Conservative Party, of course, had the armed services at its orders). More recently, other bands in Venezuela and Ecuador have been associated with Communist and *fidelista* groups. It was in an effort to provide the armed forces of the republics with better training in anti-guerrilla tactics that President Kennedy in 1961 proposed greater military assistance to Latin America. Thereafter the number of commissioned and non-commissioned officers receiving instruction in anti-guerrilla warfare at U.S. bases in Panama was stepped up significantly.

The quip that when officers retire they conspire seems to

have had almost universal validity for over a century in Spanish America. It still does in those countries (e.g., El Salvador, Guatemala, Argentina, Ecuador, and Venezuela) where officers are continually being retired for political reasons. In order to emphasize the point that officers "driven" into retirement, unless imprisoned and under guard, are a constant threat to political order, one need only recall those Argentine officers who from exile fought Perón throughout his long term in office; or those Guatemalan officers who from a half-dozen countries plotted the overthrow of Arbenz in 1954; or the Venezuelan officers who from the Dominican Republic, Colombia, and perhaps the Dutch West Indies harassed the Betancourt regime during its first months in office.

But officers who retire in the system today seldom remain politically important, and they almost never successfully conspire. A few do run for office; some win elections, particularly if they have "connections" in the rural areas, or in Mexico with the PRI. The institutionalized armed forces have their own interests to serve, and those interests can be represented as well or better by officers on active duty and in a position to keep in touch with the rapidly shifting currents of change. Furthermore, retired officers today receive pensions that enable them to live at approximately the level to which they became accustomed in the service; thus one of the age-old worries of the professional soldier has been removed, and with it one more reason why most retired officers can be expected to avoid conspiracy.

In terms of the evolution of the armed forces a developing tendency for them to withdraw from direct control of the government in favor of exercising indirect influence could become of as great significance as has been the substitution of the junta for the man on horseback. Despite the many cases which seem to prove the contrary, such a trend is discernible. Officers are definitely becoming unwilling to assume direct responsibility for administration at the national level, particularly in the more politically sophisticated republics. There are basically two reasons why the military men are taking this position: the rise of the popular masses, and the many opportunities that modern governments provide for decision-making away from public scrutiny. The emergence of new, politically articulate elements has produced several conditions which have caused the armed forces to re-evaluate the merits of gaining their objectives through direct action. No longer, for example, can they struggle with civilian politicians for power over the neutral masses simply because the masses are no longer neutral. Nor will the newly articulate voters any longer permit power alone to be decisive. This has meant that when soldiers seize power they must test their political conclusions, and this, as we have suggested, they prefer not to do. Also, the armed forces realize that the struggle of the masses against the more privileged sectors will intensify before it subsides. Under such circumstances the suppression of the popular will becomes increasingly difficult. All this means closer and closer relations between the rulers and the ruled. It follows that if the armed forces maintain prolonged and close relations with the people, the working classes will lose the awe and respect which up to now has ordinarily permitted the armed forces to move in and stabilize situations that have gotten out of the hands of the police, whom the public had learned to scorn through day-to-day contact. To the armed forces this is a situation that must be avoided at almost any price.

Meanwhile, attractive alternatives to direct control of government are playing an increasingly greater role in discouraging the armed forces from seizing power. One of the most important alternatives is the ability of the armed forces to act as pressure groups. As in the United States, they can affect budget-making by playing up the danger, real or imaginary, of attack from the outside. A good example of this technique was the development of an Argentine army ski patrol, which supposedly would be advantageous to have in case of war with Chile or against an enemy stationed in Antarctica. Also, many officers—active, inactive, or retired—often hold governorships and seats in the national legislature, where they can be effective on behalf of the military. The *Directorio del Gobierno Federal* of the Mexican Government for the year 1956 showed 16 per cent of all state governorships, 20 per cent of the Senate seats, and 6 per cent of the Chamber of Deputy seats held by men with military titles. Since the PRI controls all elections in Mexico, the selection of officers is not accidental and the opportunity for them to affect decision-making on the national level is considerable. In 1959, during the civilian government of Manuel Prado, there were three officers in the Peruvian Senate, seven in the Chamber of Deputies, as well as an army officer as head of the Atomic Energy Commission. Officer intervention during both military and civil regimes in Argentina is so notorious that it need not be reviewed here.

As the republics have moved prominently into economic and social welfare programs, the opportunities for officers to affect decision-making indirectly have multiplied at a fantastic rate. Officers have moved freely into top-level positions in state-controlled enterprises and autonomous and semi-autonomous agencies that have been created to promote national growth and provide public services. In Argentina in 1958, for example, the General Director of Military Factories ran ten operations, some of which competed directly with private enterprise, and in addition the Argentine navy was engaged in commercial shipbuilding and produced gunpowder in competition with private industry. As of 1963 the army controlled the new iron and steel plant at San Nicolás, which is expected to develop into the largest of its kind in all of Latin America; it has been said that a civilian government "would not dare to oust the military from steel."

The story is much the same in many of the republics. As of October 1962, active and retired officers were known to be serving President Betancourt's civilian administration in Venezuela in the following capacities: Minister of Communications; Director, Merchant Marine; Chief, Technical Division, Merchant Marine; Director, Civil Aviation; Director, Cajigal Observatory; President, Venezuelan Corporation of Guayana; Director, National Institute of Water Resources;

Chief of Production, Venezuelan Navigation Company; Director, National Institute of Railroads; and Director, National Institute of Canals. The post of Director of the Venezuelan Airmail Line was vacant "but normally filled by an Air Force Officer." In addition "about fifteen" officers were serving as ambassadors and consuls. In Chile the army manufactures small arms, agricultural machinery, and hardware. In 1960 an army officer headed the state-controlled railroad of Ecuador. Needless to say, when the armed forces take over direct control of a government, the use of officers in nonmilitary areas is much more widespread than when civilians are in control. In Venezuela under Pérez Jiménez, for example, it was said that "Officers controlled nearly all of the top positions in government at all levels and in all enterprises in which the government had an interest."

The question naturally arises as to why officers hold the key positions they do in non-military areas during periods of civilian rule. There are many reasons, some general and some specific. Three of a more general nature are ordinarily set forth as follows: (1) the influence of the armed forces is so great that they "cannot be overlooked"; (2) civilian politicians use such appointments as a means of paying off past debts; (3) the armed forces' responsibility for the national defense makes them acutely concerned with the development of major areas of the economy, including the heavy industries, all forms of transportation, and power. The particularized reasons, if no more complex, are at least more novel. In the case of the Argentine armed forces, control of the iron and steel industry goes back to 1941, when General Manuel N. Savio determined that the national defense called for an iron and steel plant and since there was no Minister of Commerce and Industry, and since domestic private capital was unavailable and it did not seem advisable to permit foreign capital to come in, the armed forces were put in charge of planning. They have been in control ever since, and if the operation remains unprofitable, as it is expected to, private capital will not be interested in taking over. There was, in 1960, no public disposition to see the industry surrendered to any other agency of the government. "Within the government the military is the best qualified to run it," was the way a professor of economics felt.

In Mexico, military participation in the non-military areas of government is closely associated with the pay officers receive, which is the lowest in Latin America, except possibly in some of the Central American armies. Because of this, it is common in Mexico for officers to hold more than one job. There is a provision for them to be "a disposición" (something between active and inactive status), in which case they can continue to receive full army pay and accrue time credit toward promotion and retirement while holding another appointment with the government or in private industry.

Officers are often called upon by governments because a job is "too hot" for the politicians. The officer, being "above the local battle" and not seeking public office, is a likely candidate to head an almost defunct government-owned railroad or steamship line or to direct an unprofitable enterprise that is about to arouse public indignation. Or, as a Chilean army officer insisted in the course of berating the Ministry of Public Works, "The army is requested to take over government construction that cannot be done with modern machinery." An added consideration is that the armed forces officer may do his job for a small part of what a competent civilian would demand as salary.

By any concept of effective government, ability alone should determine an officer's competence to direct non-military activities, and on that score the soldier-manager in Latin America does not fare well. In every republic there can be found quite responsible citizens who insist that the officers do have qualifications that are not available or are in short supply in the civilian sectors. However, the weight of evidence is overwhelmingly on the side of those who insist that today civilians have equal or greater competence than the officers. Furthermore, there is nowhere in Spanish America a situation comparable to what is found in some of the new nations of Africa, the Middle East, and Southeast Asia, where officers can claim the right to direct government activities on the basis of both acquired skills and moral leadership.

A representative sampling of remarks from notes taken during a tour of the area in mid-1960 indicates the extent to which public opinion downgrades the capabilities of the officers of the armed forces. An Argentine newspaperman observed, "I know many officers, but I would not want a single one of them to head an industry of mine." He added that "officers are excessively free with public funds and the army will produce low-grade steel at the highest prices in the world." An Argentine businessman said angrily, "they will take any damn job, they think they know everything." A Venezuelan newspaperman, asked whether officers in the armed forces were capable administrators, simply replied, "Pooh." An Honduran lawyer was sure that "There is nothing that an army officer can do that a civilian cannot do better." An Ecuadorian banker contended that "They have no systematized training to prepare them for important non-military assignments." And the banker was in effect substantiated by an Ecuadorian officer who said, "Honestly, we have very few skills of use in industry and commerce." A Chilean secretary at the United States Embassy in Santiago disqualified officers for civilian posts on the grounds that "the army and navy are still very old-fashioned." An ex-president of one republic who volunteered to query an acting president of another republic on this subject reported that his friend had said, "I have no faith in men of the armed forces in any post of responsibility." Positions held by retired officers in the business community would seem to bear out the prevailing civilian opinion of them. Except for the unusually capable one, or one with good family connections, those who enter business after they retire do not hold positions of major responsibility.

V

CHANGE AND RESPONSE, 1915–1963:

The Thinking of the Military on Major National Issues

GRANTING that the armed forces, either directly or indirectly, are constantly affecting decision-making at the national level in nearly all of the republics, it becomes essential to determine something else: how institutionalization, professionalization, and the social-regional background of the officers have been reflected in the positions they have taken on such major issues as public education, industrialization, state capitalism, nationalism, communism, and agrarian reform. This can be done by comparing the attitude of the armed forces with that of the currently dominant civilian elements.

Unlike the historian Carl Becker, who considered democracy an economic luxury, the political leaders of Spanish America have almost universally associated working democracy with education. They have publicly proclaimed their faith in public education even when they have had neither the will nor the resources to improve it, and while sending their own children to private schools. Since World War I the new owners of industry and commerce have clamored for public schools that would provide trained personnel needed to operate their plants efficiently. Thousands upon thousands of classrooms have been constructed, thousands upon thousands of teachers have been trained, and the illiteracy rates have dropped to about 55 per cent for the area as a whole; but there are more illiterates than there were in 1950 simply because the spread of education has been unable to keep pace with population growth.

education

The armed forces have caught the spirit of the civilian leadership. Ask any officer what his country's most serious problem is, and seven times out of ten he will say "insufficient education." But on the basis of past experience, there is even less reason to expect a military government to act decisively in the field of education than to expect it from a civilian regime. No military government in Spanish America, unless one chooses to call Lázaro Cárdenas's government in Mexico military, has ever had an outstanding record in the educational field. Perón, it should be noted, built schools and trained teachers first of all to peddle propaganda, not to disseminate learning. In those republics historically dominated by the military, literacy rates are lower than in the republics where civilians have had a greater role in government. Thus in Haiti, Bolivia, and Venezuela, each with a long history of military domination, the literacy rates stood at 10.5 per cent, 30.1 per cent, and 48.9 per cent respectively in 1950; on the other hand, Costa Rica, which has been relatively free from military control for 80 years, had a literacy rate of 78.8 per cent in 1950, and Uruguay, which shook off the incubus of militarism early in this century, had a literacy rate of 80 per cent. Mexico, which was plagued by military government for a century after its independence but which has had reasonably responsible government for four decades, still has not been able to raise its literacy rate above 57 per cent.

In the field of higher education, there is a strong tendency toward regression in military-dominated governments because students are likely to be the leaders of the civilian opposition and, as such, subject to attack by officers. Pérez Jiménez closed institutions of higher learning repeatedly in the hope that he could quell the student opposition to his dictatorship. In Cuba, the National University was in recess a large part of the time under Batista, who ruled with the armed forces at his back.

Military governments have probably been more favorable to Catholic schools than have the civilian regimes, but this is something that is extremely difficult to measure. The revolutionary generals who dominated Mexico from 1920 to 1946 sporadically struck hard at Catholic education, but they did not permanently cripple it. And as of 1963, when Mexico had been under middle-sector leadership for a decade and a half, more children were attending Catholic schools than at any time in the nation's history. Perón broke with the Church at the end of his regime and vented his spleen upon the Catholic schools, but this was to no avail, and the Church's influence on education is as great as it was when he came to power. But under Pérez Jiménez, Catholic educational institutions uniformly were given a relatively free hand, and teachers from various reactionary Spanish Catholic orders flooded the country's cultural institutions. Certainly there was no diminution of Catholic influence in Colombian education under the military dictator Rojas Pinilla. The Catholic Church has also held a strong position in the weak educational system of Peru, where the military has been always close to the center of government; but it has been weak in Costa Rica and Uruguay, where the military men are as nonpolitical as any in Spanish America.

Although the armed forces show relatively little sympathy for education per se, they have made a significant contribution to the civilian sector by providing it with technically trained personnel. Commissioned and non-commissioned officers with technical skills easily move into non-administrative posts in the civilian area. In Argentina, for example, the services have considerable difficulty keeping men trained in electronics and communications from leaving their posts in favor of civilian jobs. Every country in Spanish America with an air force knows, as is known in the United States, that the national air force is the principal, if not practically the sole, source of pilots and navigators for commercial air lines. In republics like Ecuador, where the labor movement is underdeveloped, commissioned officers and non-commissioned officers with technical training move freely into service in the merchant marine. In Venezuela the low level of academic training and the high pay and benefits that military men receive have combined to discourage Venezuelan armed forces personnel from actively seeking civilian employment.

Professionalization and social background appear to be the important determinants in the attitude of officers toward education. They may espouse the ideas of intellectuals regarding public education, but they do not have a clear understanding of what they mean. The army, which is ordinarily the branch most active in the civilian area, is still so nontechnical that the educational requirements of the common soldier are nil. At the present stage of their development, the armies can use an illiterate conscript almost as effectively as they can a literate one. Then, too, the armed forces, despite their declarations to the contrary, have not considered representative democracy a primary objective, so they have not felt the same need as have many civilians for educating the masses.

The attitude of the officers toward Catholic education can be explained in terms of their social environment. As noted above, an important percentage of officers come from "well-established small-town families" and families recently migrated to America, especially from Italy and Spain. These groups are the hard-core Catholic elements in the republics, and the available evidence indicates that the military bureaucracy is at least as Catholic as the civilian bureaucracy or the middle sector as a whole. When we add to these considerations the fact that historically the Catholic Church often has been the only organized group that would readily spring to the support of a military government, the professional soldier's approval of Catholic education is understandable.

The urgent need for greater industrialization is accepted as self-evident in Spanish America. As might be expected, however, there are differences of opinion as to the degree of urgency. These differences exist both between countries and between social-economic groups within a given country. The attitude of the armed forces vis-à-vis that of the civilian elements toward industrialization is determined almost solely by the extent to which military professionalization has been carried out, and the social background of the officers does not seem to be a factor one way or another. In general, it may be said that in the technically lesser-developed countries, and also where professionalization is not advanced, the officers are less concerned with industrialization than are the urban middle sectors. In the more developed countries, like Argentina, the armed forces are in the forefront of those most concerned with the desirability of industrial growth.

The Honduran army does not think in terms of industrial development of the nation. Soldiers' clothes and shoes come almost entirely from abroad, and their officers have no serious interest in changing this situation. "We will buy where we can get the most for our money," was the stand taken by one colonel. Nor are the Honduran armed forces any more concerned than civilians with the development of the country's transportation system. "We do not want easy access to the Nicaraguan border," said one highly placed officer.

The Ecuadorian armed forces take much the same position that the Honduran services do. In the words of a senior air force officer, "We have tried to work with local industry but have been unsuccessful. It is cheaper to import." It was evident that the policy of the armed forces was hurting when in mid-1960 Ecuadorian newspapers carried numerous accounts of the efforts of local business interests to force the military to buy more domestically produced goods, such as clothing and shoes.

The Venezuelan armed forces have moved one step beyond those of Honduras and Ecuador. They buy locally for enlisted men but the officers outfit themselves from abroad. At this time there are only scattered suggestions from the officers that the nation should manufacture anything more than the simplest material requirements of the services.

At the other extreme from Honduras and Ecuador is Argentina. There the armed forces feel that their responsibilities give them every right to be a party to decision-making when industrial development is involved. They strongly favor the expansion of the iron and steel and petroleum industries. They also feel that the nation should manufacture a wide variety of the requirements of a modern military establishment. They have therefore pushed for the manufacture of heavy equipment ;

at one time under Perón's rule they even attempted to produce airplanes. They actively supported Perón's program to develop Argentina's merchant marine and national air lines, and the army has since favored the expansion of land transportation to the south and to the west toward the Chilean border.

In those countries where the armed forces are actively promoting industrialization, the primary area of dispute is the extent to which foreign capital should be permitted to participate. Although since the overthrow of Perón influential elements in the Argentine forces have favored foreign participation in the development of the nation's petroleum industry, the evidence seems to indicate that under normal circumstances they would be as quick to take a stand against foreign participation in basic areas of the economy as would the *peronistas*.

In other of the more sophisticated republics there is a latent opposition to foreign capital, but the armed forces are in general no more opposed to foreign economic penetration than are civilians. The Chilean armed forces, for example, have never seriously challenged foreign control of the nation's copper industry, and in 1963 they were less inclined than a majority of the civilians to advocate expropriation. Under the military dictatorship of Pérez Jiménez, foreign capital was more vigorously solicited than most Venezuelan civilian elements would have preferred. And as of 1960 the Honduran armed forces would have offered foreign capital better terms than would the civilian group in control of the country.

There is a direct link between industrialization and state interventionism in Spanish America. State intervention in the economic sphere first came about as a result of the desire to hasten economic expansion. It is now justified on the basis of three widely held beliefs: (1) Industry cannot survive without protection from outside competition, and only the state can provide that protection; (2) since the accumulation of domestic private capital is slow, the state, with its ability to accumulate capital fairly rapidly through taxation and foreign loans, must intercede in the industrial sphere in order to maintain the highest possible rate of development; (3) solicitude for the working groups requires that the state exercise some control over the prices of necessary commodities.

Although statism is properly associated with middle-sector leadership, there is no doubt that the more professionalized armed forces have for several reasons given the ideology their blessing. Being bureaucrats themselves, officers do not find bureaucratic control of economic resources objectionable. Coming as they do from essentially non-industrial families, they are not disturbed by state rather than private control of industry. The interest of officers in public economic and welfare projects stems also from a desire to manage them, which is a way in which they can exercise financial power of the kind that they could never hope to achieve themselves. Furthermore, state intervention has hastened industrial development, or so it is believed in the area, and the armed forces welcome this. More specifically, the state has assumed responsibility for the development of those basic economic sectors—notably transportation and power—which domestic and foreign private capital has shunned, but which are vital to the armed forces. Finally, state control and regulation of natural resources have the approval of the armed forces, whose future obviously depends on a continuing supply of certain raw materials.

Nationalism·

Throughout Spanish America, nationalism—of a kind that "seeks equality and someone else to blame" but is free of aggressive intentions toward neighboring countries—has been raised to the level of a major ideology. Although it may be given a cultural, economic, or juridical emphasis, depending upon the country and the moment, its essence is always that Spanish American civilization, which is now threatened from all sides, is unique because it was built upon Christian values inherited from Spain and because those values give a primacy of the spiritual against the materialistic. So firmly is this belief held that it may not be going too far to say that it dominates the subconscious Spanish American mind. In more concrete terms, however, nationalism has such political appeal that civilians vie against civilians (and against the state) for the privilege of championing it and the armed forces strive to sharpen their image as its true defenders.

Nationalism in its broadest sense is manifested in such a variety of ways that it would be impossible to determine with certainty whether civilians or the armed forces (which are at all times likely to have militantly nationalistic elements) are the more nationalistic. At a somewhat lower level certain generalizations can be made. Cultural nationalism, for example, is practically a civilian monopoly. Economic nationalism is ordinarily shared by civilians and the armed forces, with the latter, often responding more to emotionalism than reason, becoming particularly concerned when the control or depletion of natural resources is a consideration or when foreign investment is involved in "strategic" areas of the economy. Juridical nationalism, which for our purposes may be taken to mean a concern over direct or indirect threats to the national sovereignty, is in the final analysis the preserve of the armed forces.

As in the case of industrialization, it is generally true that the more institutionalized and professionalized the military establishment is, the greater is the possibility that it will be strongly nationalistic. Thus the Argentine armed forces are the most nationalistic in Spanish America (although others may at times be more chauvinistic). With them it is an article of faith that Argentina has the human and material resources to become a sort of second United States, at least in a Latin American sphere of influence. But even in Argentina, the navy, which has historically had strong ties with Great Britain and the United States, is considerably less nationalistic than the army, whose ties before World War II were with Germany and Italy. And it should be pointed out that Germany and Italy were, in the minds of the Argentine military, "the adversaries of those countries exploiting Argentina." As one Argentine naval officer stated the navy's position, "We spell *nacionalismo* (of the army) with a 'z'" (*nazionalismo*).

In Honduras, which represents the other extreme from Argentina, "officers are by education and profession incapable of thinking in the abstract," and display few nationalistic tendencies. In Venezuela the armed forces feel that they are "the only group to preserve the national heritage," but a priest in Caracas came closer to presenting the civilian consensus when he said, "Officers are strongly nationalistic at first, then corruption takes over." In Quito, Ecuador, a banker stated the prevalent opinion in and out of the armed forces when he said, "There is very little nationalism here; there is a problem with Peru." In Peru there are officers of all ranks who strongly advocate nationalization of oil and mineral properties.

Chilean civilians agree with the armed forces that politicians exploit nationalism more than do the armed forces, who, it is said, "cannot conceive of a situation that would lead to war with a neighboring country." A story illustrating this point was making the rounds of Santiago in mid-1960. It was that Chilean politicians had so incensed the public over Argentine claims to small "Chilean" islands in the straits area that the Chilean navy was obliged to move out of Valparaiso as if to sail south to protect the national interests; in fact, the story ran, the vessels did not have enough fuel to make the trip, so they were simply moved beyond the horizon and kept there until the public calmed down, whereupon they returned to Valparaiso.

When the armed forces do choose to become active spokesmen for nationalism, they have working in their favor three important considerations. First of all, "their swords are consecrated to the national will," and they are charged with the defense of the nation's honor. Second, unlike soldiers of an earlier era whose loyalties were to a *jefe*—and unlike politicians who even today cannot see beyond the borders of their own states or the interests of their parties—officers can claim to react as true national patriots, as Argentines, Chileans, or Mexicans. This image is encouraged by the fact that the armies, navies, and air forces are rapidly replacing the Catholic Church as a symbol of unity on national holidays, a development which took place in the United States at least by 1930, except that in the United States the armed forces replaced the politician who wrapped himself in a religious mantle. This "national" image of the armed forces permits them, on those occasions when they seize power, to maintain that they are interpreting the desires of the people disgruntled with the narrowly conceived if not actually anti-national objectives of the politicians. Third, in several of the republics—such as Argentina, Peru, El Salvador, and Guatemala—the military is the country's best-organized institution and is thus in a better position than political parties or other pressure groups to give objective expression to the national will when the fatherland is confronted with a challenge to its power, position, or prestige. Mexico offers an important exception to this generalization; there, not the armed forces but the PRI is the best organized institution, and the party rather than the armed forces has been the unifying force at the national level.

Anti-communist.

Communism and *fidelismo* have become the principal catalysts that keep the political cauldron boiling in Spanish America. They may be expected to win added support before they decline in favor, if that is their destiny. There is no assurance that they are so destined. Having demonstrated in Cuba that a small group of determined men can take over a government and achieve power by offering a quick way to end "economic imperialism," the communists and *fidelistas* now threaten to fill the power vacuum created by the shift of the middle-sector leadership to the right of the political spectrum, which has occurred in some countries. The communists' potential is enhanced by the fact that despite their successes, the current dominant leadership has refused to take communism seriously. There are four principal reasons for this. First, the leaders are so preoccupied with the internal problems of their countries that they have not developed an emotional involvement in cold war politics. This allows them to feel that the United States is trying to lead them in a great crusade against communism rather than trying to help them meet their real and pressing social-economic problems and political requirements. Second, they are so accustomed to expecting the United States to make the final decisions in the Hemisphere that they are sure, despite what has occurred in Cuba, that if the United States seriously intended to root out communism in the Hemisphere, it could somehow do so. Third, the leaders are convinced that were it not for the evidence of communism in their midst the United States would not be so concerned with the development of the area. Fourth, they feel (for reasons quite difficult to explain) that if communism takes over they would be able to divest it of the worst features of its international connections and mold it to serve the specific requirements of their people.

It can be stated categorically that as a group, armed forces officers are more noisily anti-communist, if not necessarily more effectively anti-communist, than all but a very few civilians. One may say further that without the armed forces, but with all other things being equal, every republic in Spanish America except Uruguay, Costa Rica, and Cuba would stand politically to the left of where it is now; it would only be a question of how much further left. But having said that, much remains unsaid. The military's enmity toward communism often seems more emotional than reasoned; and while sincere, it ordinarily appears not to have been accompanied by a real understanding of communist strategy and tactics on the international or domestic scene. The anti-communism of the armed forces has tended to result in actions that circumscribe communist activities but do not simultaneously effectively combat the conditions that breed more communism.

The communists are untried, and this in itself is enough to cause concern in an institution like the military, which has an inherent distrust of political change. But the communists do not always suffer at the hands of the military. Because the armed forces, when they seize power, must seek civilian support wherever it can be found, they can easily end up in alliance with the communists, whose opportunism and short-range objectives can be served by working with the opposition. It was the search for public approval that drove the Venezuelan military dictator Pérez Jiménez to outlaw the communists and then to work with them so that he might, through them, claim a semblance of support from organized labor and offset Democratic Action influence. And when Batista seized power in 1952 he gave the communists a relatively free hand in the labor movement, and in return the communists kept labor in line until Batista fled before Castro's forces. When the Organization of American States voted sanctions against Rafael Trujillo, who as dictator of the Dominican Republic for a quarter century had represented himself as the principal anti-communist in the Hemisphere, he blandly announced that he might be forced to collaborate with the communists.

More recently, between July 1962 and January 1963, the Peruvian junta (which seized power after a disputed presidential election), favored the communists, who in turn cooperated with the military regime. Communist-controlled unions backed the junta when Aprista Party workers called a strike and in return the communists were given influential positions in government ministries. Communist-controlled labor federations, such as the Civil Construction Federation and the Chauffeurs Federation, were granted official recognition. The government newspaper, *El Peruano,* praised communist union officers as "authentic" leaders of the working class and branded the Apristas as "under political control." A month after taking over the government, junta co-presidents Pérez Godoy and Torres Matos, accompanied by officials of the labor ministry, inaugurated the communist-directed Maritime Congress held at Callao. Finally, in January 1963, the junta began to root out the communists, presumably because of their success in inciting the Indians of the Andes to rebel against the large landholders, who have a long record of irresponsibility and gross mistreatment of the Indians. But as late as April 1963, the junta was unwilling to crack down on communists and intellectuals sympathetic to communism who had found their way into the government.

The Honduran armed forces are probably so completely devoid of ideological bias that it may well be true that they do not distinguish between communist and democratic doctrine. According to one well-placed Honduran, "If you were to ask an officer what his political indoctrination is, he would say 'What's that?' " The Chilean armed forces "know their ideologies," being by Latin American standards quite professionalized, but even they would be reluctant to jeopardize their status by moving against an extreme leftist government that was freely elected and seemed content to work within the framework of the constitution.

Finally, although all the professional armed forces have thus far taken a stand against communism, it should not be concluded that all officers are anti-communist. There may well be a few communists or communist sympathizers in the armed forces of every Spanish American republic. What is more important, however, is that there are some who ignore communism or who might opt for communism if it appears to be the winning side in national politics. These elements do not appear to constitute a serious threat at the moment, but they may be dangerous in the near future, when officers drawn from the working sectors of society and from the cities choose to compete for power with their seniors in the military hierarchy.

Agrarian reform.

Agrarian reform has been given top priority in a number of republics and has been made one of the major objectives of the Alliance for Progress, but so far achievements have not been impressive. Vastly more complex than simple land redistribution, agrarian reform impinges upon every major area of Spanish American civilization. In the social sphere, agrarian reform cannot ignore the fact that almost everywhere family, clan, and village ties discourage large-scale relocation of the landless peasants to isolated frontier regions where public lands are often available. Thus the Indians of Ecuador will not willingly go in large numbers to the tropical Amazon drainage basin unless conditions are made far more attractive than they are at present. In the economic area agrarian reform involves creating incentives to production, granting credits, training technicians by the hundreds, developing hybrid seeds, improving livestock strains, and importing farm machinery, to mention only a few of the more important tasks. In the political sphere, the problem is to satisfy the deserving and restless but economically and politically unsophisticated peasants without disturbing unduly the economies of the countryside or driving into militant opposition the reactionary landholding element, which, through family ties, often shares many interests with the urban financial elites.

Like the current middle-sector leadership, the armed forces have been ambivalent in respect to agrarian reform. The question "what is the single most serious problem your country faces?" was put to several dozen officers interviewed in Honduras, Ecuador, Chile, Argentina, Brazil, and Venezuela; not one mentioned land reform. In pursuing this subject with them, it was obvious that they are only passively favorable to agrarian reform. A Venezuelan colonel might have been speaking for a vast majority of them when he said, "I support orderly agrarian reform," which in effect meant reform, including land distribution, that would proceed only as rapidly as the state could or would allocate scarce resources to agrarian reform rather than to alternative and competing needs. As late as 1963, nowhere in Latin America except in Venezuela had an agrarian reform program predicated upon such a premise given more than a glimmer of hope that the over-all agricultural problem might be resolved in the foreseeable future, to say nothing of satisfying the impoverished peasants' demands for "land now."

The armed forces' stand on agrarian reform, including land redistribution, derives from a complex of circumstances, some with historical roots and some of recent origin. The historical ones are the military-landholding-Church alliances and the personal interests of officers with family ties linking them to the landholding elite. These circumstances have relevance, but they do not seem to be controlling. In the first place, the old military-landholding-Church alliance is no longer meaningful in several of the republics (Chile, Venezuela, and Argentina, for example), yet in those countries the armed forces would as quickly look askance at revolutionary agrarian reform as they would in Colombia, where the alliance still persists. In the second place, as we have said, at no time since the Independence period have a significant share of officers come directly from the landholding elites.

More recent and more relevant developments determining the attitude of the armed forces toward agrarian reform include the effects of institutionalization and professionalization, the officers' economic views, and above all their growing political ties with the urban middle sectors. Institutionalization has made bureaucrats of officers, and as the Mexican novelist Mariano Azuela has remarked, "The bureaucrat represents the force of inertia." Officers simply do not see what they have to gain from rapid change, particularly when all the evidence they have indicates that rapid agrarian reform probably would be accompanied by decreases in foreign exchange earnings, which are desperately needed for modernization. And to officers, modernization has become synonymous with technological modernization; they support the building of smokestacks rather than haystacks. Their professionalization makes them gradualists and thus distrustful of disorder and social ferment, which are inherent in any revolutionary movement.

To the extent that officers have had a comprehension of the workings of private capital, it has ordinarily come through having invested private capital in real estate. They can associate a farm with family ownership much more quickly and meaningfully than they can an impersonal factory, and their sympathies, consequently, may be easily enlisted by the embattled landholder but not by the industrialist or man of finance. Retired Ecuadorian officers, for instance, have shown great interest in possessing their own banana plantations, no matter how small the plantations may be; it is tempting to speculate that for them the landholder, astride his horse and issuing orders which are accepted without question, combines at a rather primitive level the individualism they were deprived of in the service and the discipline and respect they were trained to expect during their professional careers.

Historically, land meant power in Latin America; today, it is associated with affluence and security. The urge to own a plot of land and a home on the outskirts of the overcrowded cities is shared by civilians and military men alike. And as long as officers can look forward to satisfying their desires "to get away from it all," they will be inclined to share with the more financially secure civilian elements the distrust of legislation designed to circumscribe the landholder's freedom of action.

Army + elite of Caudameo

One of the most persistent and widely held misconceptions regarding the armed forces is that they remain aligned with the landholding elite. The conception is not only untrue but pernicious, for it often leads to dangerously wrong conclusions. The military no longer reflects the thinking of the landed elites in Mexico, Cuba, Costa Rica, El Salvador, Venezuela, Bolivia, Chile, Argentina, and Uruguay; in several of those countries, the historical alliances were dissolved decades ago. That group of countries not only contains approximately 70 per cent of the area and 69 per cent of the population of Spanish America, but it includes the five best-developed countries of the area—Mexico, Costa Rica, Chile, Argentina, and Uruguay. In Portuguese Brazil, which must be ranked with the five more highly developed Spanish American republics, the alliance between the military and the landed elite collapsed before the end of World War II; when we add Brazil to the others, it is apparent that at least 80 per cent of all of Latin America by area and 72 per cent of the region's population is not subject to rule by landholders and officers. The remaining countries, Colombia excepted, constitute the most backward and least influential part of the Hemisphere.

This is not to say that since World War I the armed forces have not fought to keep the old elite in power; they have done so on several occasions, as in Peru, where officers have seldom reflected the interests of the groups from which they come. It is to say rather that the armed forces are sufficiently flexible and opportunistic to accept change once it occurs. Thus when middle-sector leadership took over in Uruguay (1903), Argentina (1916), Chile (1920), Mexico (1946), and Costa Rica[1]

---

[1] Authorities differ on when the middle sectors, in this case a rural middle sector, achieved control in Costa Rica, but most would agree that the shift took place sometime before 1920.

the armed forces joined them, except that in Argentina the military returned the landed elite to power in 1930 and kept them there by force for thirteen years, when an anti-landed elite element within the officers corps seized control of the government. The military coup of 1945 gave the Venezuelan middle sectors their first opportunity to govern, and while the coup of 1948 negated all the gains made by the civilians, the armed forces after 1958 provided President Betancourt with the strength he needed to maintain his precarious control of the nation.

The attitude of the officers is more explicable than is the reasoning of those who refuse to see what has happened to the military. In the first place the armed forces up to now have come from essentially the same economic groups as have the middle-sector leaders — from that small but growing class standing between the very rich and the miserably poor. It was thus understandable that as soon as the middle sectors established their political capabilities the armed forces might, as they actually did, align with them. Middle-sector government is bureaucratic and modernizing, as are the armed forces. Furthermore, officers' families are well represented in the civilian bureaucracies. Middle-sector governments have expanded public spending enormously, and this has meant larger budgets for the armed forces. Finally, the middle sectors and the armed forces are in basic agreement on most major issues—industrialization, state capitalism, nationalism, and agrarian reform. It bears repeating at this point that the military ordinarily would broaden the political base more slowly than the middle sectors have found expedient, and that the officers would take a tougher stand on communism than the civilian politicians have been willing to take thus far.

If the civilians and the armed forces can work together harmoniously, the question naturally arises, "Why have the civilian sectors rather than the armed forces seemed to be innovators?" To begin with, the civilians have not always been the innovators, as witness the transformation that took place under Carlos Ibáñez in Chile during the late 1920's and in

Argentina under Perón in the 1940's. But in the vast majority of cases in which civilians have been innovators it is probably because the various military establishments have been saddled with seniority systems. Seniority, whether in an African tribe or a Spanish American military establishment, is an inescapable recipe for extreme conservatism.[2] As long as the seniority system remains, military decisions will be made by men in their late fifties, their sixties, and their seventies, men who have theoretically had a minimum of contact with civilians. At the same time, three out of four civilians are under 35 years of age, the average voter is 36 years of age, and a large share of those elected to high public office are in their thirties and forties. Therefore, serious differences of opinion will inevitably arise between civilians and the military as to what should be altered and how rapidly the alteration should take place. This assumes that officers are going to remain involved in politics and decision-making, a warranted assumption as long as officers think like the Venezuelan colonel who said in August 1960, "Since 1958 we have given civilians all the authority they need to run the country."

One cannot be sure what the outcome would be if it were decided to retire all officers in Spanish America promptly at age 45 (and the increased cost of retirement benefits would be negligible) ; but it is generally agreed that majors and lieutenant colonels have been on the side of those civilians anxious for "progress" more often than have full colonels and generals. Furthermore, since the tendency in the armed forces is toward ever greater technical preparation, early retirement would serve to narrow the gap between the technically more competent junior officers and their superiors.

The point, again, is simply that officers from middle-class families have been able to cooperate successfully with the civilian urban middle sectors once those groups have beaten the traditional landed elite at the polls. Today in several of the republics the officers have come to support the interests and

[2] Ibáñez and Perón, it should be noted, were middle-ranking officers when they achieved power.

aspirations of the urban propertied groups; the conservatism
of the officers is of the same nature as that found in the urban
middle sectors, and not, as is sometimes contended, the conservatism of the rural, landholding elite. From this two important conclusions may be reached: (1) now that officers are
coming increasingly from the lower middle sectors and the
working masses, the armed forces may be expected to be more
inclined than formerly to gravitate toward positions identified
with popular aspirations and to work with the representatives
of the popular elements, such as the Frente de Acción Popular
(FRAP) in Chile, on those occasions when they attain power
legally; and (2) any Latin American politician who compla-
cently expects the armed forces to hold off the mob power of
the left for an indefinite period faces not only a rude awakening
but risks an irreparable loss in influence.

VI

THE PUBLIC IMAGE OF THE MILITARY
SINCE WORLD WAR I

THE ARMED FORCES of Spanish America have been as controversial since World War I as they were in the century following the political emancipation of the colonies. Most intellectuals appear to recognize the impact that professionalization and rising nationalism have had upon the armed forces; but whether as detractors or defenders, they have argued throughout much of the period from basically the same positions that their predecessors did in the nineteenth century. Evidence derived from a sampling of current literature, newspapers, art, and personal opinion permits these generalizations; more could be advanced, but they would lack the support of adequate records.[1] Even these general findings, however, provide sufficient material for a worthwhile discussion of the range of arguments put forth for and against the military, and for an attempt to establish the general reactions of the public toward the services in several of the republics. Given the fact that in Spanish America the intellectuals historically have provided the hard core of opposition to the military, it should not be surprising that they have treated both military men and the military as an institution unfavorably more often than favorably.

Especially in the lesser-developed countries and those in the throes of civil conflict, anti-military novelists have tended

---

[1] One would have to know, for example, how many volumes of a given work were sold, what the circulation of each of the many newspapers was, and whether the frequent absence of military art was due to censorship or apathy or some other reason; furthermore, the opinions of thousands rather than dozens of civilians would have to be polled.

since World War I to concern themselves with the generally low quality of the officers and the treatment meted out to conscripts, who are drawn almost exclusively from the "people of color." No one has taken the officers to task in more biting terms than the Mexican Revolutionary novelist Mariano Azuela, who wrote during and immediately following the decade of civil war that his nation entered in 1910. In a splendid little satire, *Las moscas* (1918), he depicted officers in all their grossness. He made them disgustingly debauched and gave them an infinite capacity for immorality; he wrote of them as "red-eyed and filthy" and he described a general lying on his back between his women (who were the worse for wear) "his neck expanding and contracting like an accordion" until he sounded like "a whole pigsty." Time and again, Azuela portrayed officers as opportunists and cowards. On one occasion he had an officer say, "Let's eat, drink, and be merry, for tomorrow we run." On another occasion an officer transforms himself into the chief of police of his small home town by taking a commission (which he carried for emergencies) out of his wallet; and still another officer, confronted by the enemy, yanks the identifying marks from his uniform so furiously that he tears off a piece of felt, after which he completely disassociates himself from the battle by tossing his rifle into a mud hole. Azuela's Mexican contemporaries added to the list of charges against officers. Gregorio López y Fuentes in his *Campamento* (1931) insisted that soldiers "never respect a woman," especially a woman of color. "They live off the villagers, evict them from their homes, and rob and kill them," he wrote. Nellie Campobello in *Cartuche, relatos de la lucha en el norte de México* (1931) portrays one general as a drunk who entertains himself by shooting holes through sombreros, and another officer, an expert at cutting off ears, who lets his enemies die slowly rather than waste bullets on them.

South American novelists lend support to the charges of baseness brought by the Mexicans. The Peruvian Ciro Alegría, in *El mundo es ancho y ajeno* (1941) has troops sow terror as they advance. One of his leading characters is the bastard son of a soldier who came to an Indian village and "was stronger than the girls' protests."[2] The internationally known Venezuelan novelist Rómulo Gallegos, in *Doña Bárbara* (1941), described a civil magistrate as possessing neither more nor less than the necessary qualifications for his post in a provincial village: "absolute ignorance, a despotic character, and a military rank." The Ecuadorian Enrique Terán in *El cojo Navarètte* (1940) makes much the same point when he draws a comparison between an officer who was interested in learning and his cohorts, whose hours away from the barracks were aimless and empty. Terán also has a colonel declare that he feels his beliefs rather than reasoning them.

The treatment of the common soldier has been a major concern of numerous authors in Spanish America. None has dealt with the problem at a more human level than the Ecuadorian Jorge Icaza. His *En las calles* (1935) returns to the subject time and again. According to Icaza, the conscripts, without any idea of what they are fighting about, are made to fire upon their families and friends, and the author's reformer dies begging the soldiers to cease being the tools of their oppressors. Icaza's countryman Humberto Salvador, in *Noviembre* (1939), uses a variation of the Icaza theme when he has representatives of the poor elements comment that in Ecuador the army, which once represented the heroes of history, has become a mob of demons who shoot the masses down. The Peruvian writer Alegría had much to say regarding the conscript and his officers. In one place he states that armies on the march meant Indians on the march because officers, wearing shining swords as symbols of their authority, invariably rode. In another passage Alegría wrote: "It is told of Marshal Castillo that whenever he heard an Indian soldier humming to himself, he said, 'An Indian who sings a song of his region

[2] Manuel Gálvez of Argentina, in *Los caminos de la muerte* (1928), which deals with the Paraguayan War, portrays the officer Jerónimo del Cerro as uncultured, sexually promiscuous, and boastful of his conquests. It is true that in the more ethnically homogeneous countries, young officers either seduce or promise to marry provincial girls of social status and then leave them.

is a sure deserter; give him forty lashes.' " The sensitive Alegría pushes the point of inequality and cruelty a step further when he has an Indian become a corporal only to mete out the same brutal punishment to those of his class that he had received as a conscript. In much the same vein the Mexican José Mancisidor in his *El sargento* (1932) has a sergeant turn upon his class in return for rewards from his superiors.

But authors in nearly all the countries have dealt with the military on higher or more sophisticated levels than this. The Argentine Luis Reissig in his satire *La campaña del General Bulele* (1928) and the Chilean Carlos Cariola Villagrán in *Entre gallos y media noche* (1919) attacked the egotism and stupidity of the officers by showing their marital lives. One of Reissig's generals, a notorious coward who thoroughly dislikes everything about the army and war, permits himself to be driven to seek the rank of marshal in order to satisfy his exceedingly ambitious wife, who feels that he should attain a marshal's rank because generals are so common. The egocentric wife of Cariola's officer will not permit the maid to call her husband "caballero" because he is not just a caballero but a colonel; the colonel himself is a stupid, presumptuous fool, so completely dominated by his spouse that he can hardly complete a sentence without prompting from her.

Contributions of the Chilean Guillermo Labarca and Gonzalo Drago, the Mexicans Martín Luis Guzmán and José Vasconcelos, the Venezuelan Gallegos, the Colombian Luis Enrique Osorio, the Argentine Reissig and the Cuban Carlos Loveira are representative of the intellectual reaction to the military as an institution. Labarca in *Mirando al océano* (1953) compares a young officer trained in Germany with one trained in Chile. The German-trained officer had a finely developed sense of technical awareness but also a disturbing faith in the ability of the military to cleanse the country. The Chilean-trained officer lacked both technical and cultural competence and was without political awareness. Drago in *El purgatorio* (1951) examines the psychological impact upon an individual of military discipline and of learning the art of killing. One of his interesting conclusions is that a boy from the street might be content with the army because it has clothed and fed him, and a hungry man does not philosophize; and a boy raised in a Chilean-German home might adjust to barracks life because at home he had been taught duty and respect for higher authority. But military discipline, he suggests, would be disastrous for a sensitive, individualistically inclined Latin youth reared in the intellectual milieu of Chile.

The Mexican Guzmán is representative of dozens of novelists who have directed their attention to the military in politics. In his *La sombra del caudillo* (1929) and *La querella de México* (1915) the conflict between military ambition and civil authority was made a cardinal source of danger to Mexico, and the author was not hopeful of a satisfactory solution because the military had force on its side; the actions of the officers were based upon pure opportunism, and the generals consequently would always end up on the winning side. The Venezuelan Gallegos struck at the heart of the problem of the military by portraying a strong brutal general who "sinks into the psychological weakness of the Venezuelans like a wedge into soft wood."

Osorio in *El iluminado* (1929) deals with the plight of a liberal who cannot win power without military support and who must, upon achieving power, become a tyrant in order to divest himself in any way of military dominance. To suggest the basic conservatism of the armed forces, Osorio has a general, opposed to everything foreign, who objects to a request to permit a French cultural mission to be established in the country. Reissig in his satire and Loveira in *Generales y doctores* (1920) both express concern over the readiness of the public to admire medals without bothering to inquire how they were obtained, and Vasconcelos in his *Breve historia de México* (1937) strongly objected to a type of nationalism that glorifies such unsavory characters as General Santa Anna.

Mexican mural painters during the inter-war years contributed significantly to the stream of civilian criticism of the armed forces. Diego Rivera, José Clemente Orozco, and David

Alfaro Siqueiros, to mention only three of the best known of the large school of revolutionary artists of the era, attacked the military unmercifully while on the national payroll and with the walls and ceilings of numerous public buildings at their disposal. Only Orozco made any effort at subtlety. Their "murals for the masses" depicted officers alternately as oversexed, brutal oppressors of the common people, and as enemies of the Revolution, who in alliance with the Catholic Church and foreign capitalists engaged in peculation, to the serious detriment of the country.

After approximately a decade and a half of revolutionary art a number of circumstances contributed to a new climate of thought in which the military did not figure. Under President Cárdenas (1934–40) the last of the military *caudillos* were brought under control. The military sector of the Partido Revolucionario Institucional (PRI) was dissolved in 1940. Shortly thereafter President Avila Camacho called for the end of class warfare and for national unity in the face of the fascist threat. And by the end of World War II, when the middle sectors had obtained control of the government, public support of revolutionary art came to an end, and an economic class with resources to give support to a middle class tradition in Mexican art emerged. With the new rich on the one hand and expanding business on the other providing the market for Mexican paintings, the military was all but eliminated as an art subject.[3]

Elsewhere in Spanish America the military has been a subject of almost no interest to artists, except for the newspaper and magazine caricaturists, and museums of modern art simply do not show military art, either favorable or unfavorable. There are several reasons for this. In some countries—Honduras for example—very little local art is of better than low quality, and so it is not displayed in public places. In countries like Chile, the military has not been controversial for a long time, and so military art ordinarily would not command public attention. And in countries such as Peru, Para-

[3] Virginia B. Derr, "The Rise of a Middle-Class Tradition in Mexican Art," *Journal of Inter-American Studies,* III (July 1961), 385–409.

guay, and Venezuela, where the military have exercised so much influence in civilian areas, artists throughout most of the period since World War I would have found it inadvisable to take an anti-military position. A highly respected editor of a Caracas newspaper told the author, "Venezuelan artists have dealt with all subjects, the military excepted." On the other hand, the armed forces have not engaged in campaigns that have produced heroes who might have invited spontaneous approbation by artists and public. Also, unlike their predecessors, officers today, except for those rare ones like Perón and Trujillo, know that ostentatious display of their "achievements" invites public criticism and blurs rather than sharpens their public image. But whatever the cause, the important point is that except in Mexico, where much of the anti-military art was produced under military presidents, at no time since World War I has the man in uniform been a popular theme for Spanish American artists.

Once the commissioned eulogies and the literary contributions of officers and their immediate families are disqualified, the favorable image of the military is visible but unimpressive. The armed forces have derived some reflected glory from a rising nationalism, which has discouraged objective analysis of Independence heroes. The statues of Bolívar, San Martín, and Sucre, for example, continue to rise. It will be recalled that when Perón established his military dictatorship, he associated his actions as best he could with those of San Martín. At least until the outbreak of World War II the Cuban military profited somewhat from the reverence—which resembled the attitude prevalent a century earlier in such newly freed republics as Chile, Argentina, and Colombia—that was still accorded the heroes of the Cuban Independence movement that culminated with the defeat of Spain in 1898. Many Mexican publicists agree with Francisco Bulnes that the Mexican army did credit to itself and defended the national honor by frustrating the efforts of the Pershing expedition to Mexico in 1916. Mexicans were quick to pay respect to General Obregón, who lost an arm in battle and emerged from the Revolution of 1910 as Mexico's outstanding officer. Governments born of the Mexican Revolution, with their accent on nationalism and youth, made the story of the Niños Héroes one of Mexico's national legends.[4]

In circumstances involving the use of force for political ends, many newspapers have been ready to lend their support to the armed forces. The example of the highly respected liberal newpaper *El Tiempo* of Bogotá serves admirably to illustrate this point. When the Conservative Laureano Gómez was ousted in a military coup led by General Gustavo Rojas Pinilla in 1953, *El Tiempo* in its June 14 issue proclaimed that the army "has always been Colombia's maximum expression of democracy."

Individual authors in the various republics have found a number of reasons for presenting the armed forces in a favorable light. Alberto Cabero in his *Chile y chilenos* (1926) maintained that while the Chilean people repudiated militarism they loved the army for what it had done for the country and added that the Chilean character served to make unusually good soldiers. Luis Humberto Delgado in *El militarismo en el Perú, 1821–1930* (1930) made two observations that retain a certain pertinence today. At that early date he saw the army as a bulwark against communism, and he concluded that when armed forces officers were compared with civilian politicians the officers often had a great deal in their favor. Thirty years later a young Argentine novelist, David Viñas, also used comparisons to the advantage of the military; he is credited with having said, "If I have to choose between priests and soldiers, I'll stick with the soldiers."[5]

---

[4] Legend has it that the Niños Héroes (little heroes), cadets of the military college of Chapultepec, took their own lives rather than surrender to the invading forces during the United States–Mexican War. The Niños Héroes were made to exemplify honor, dignity, and inspired patriotism, while their seniors, both in and out of the services, were made to represent corruption and the sacrifice of national well-being for personal gain. (See Homer C. Chaney, "The Mexican–United States War as Seen by Mexican Intellectuals, 1846–1956," unpublished doctoral dissertation, Stanford University, 1959.)

[5] See Héctor Gross, "Angry Young Argentine," *Americas,* January 1960, pp. 14–17.

Democratic ex-President Galo Plaza (1949–52) of Ecuador, widely respected in the United States as one of Latin America's foremost contemporary statesmen, after completing his term in office wrote a warm defense of the armed forces in *The Problems of Democracy in Latin America* (1955). Señor Plaza insisted that the armed forces, far from always serving the cause of despotism, have been responsible for deterring "the providential type" of ruler from perpetuating himself in office. He then added, "It must be fairly stated that in most cases the armed forces have not divorced themselves from the people by serving as instruments for oppression: they have been the guardians of peace and national dignity as well as the sentinels of continental unity. . . . While in countries dominated by dictators there is always a growing reaction of hate and fear against the armed forces that have strayed from their sacred mission, in the democracies the army is considered an enlightened institution, deeply respected and loved, constantly contributing to the welfare of the country through many useful activities."[6]

After one hundred years of political independence and legislating, Spanish American lawmakers are still seeking the elusive formula that will permit a nation to have an armed force whose actions can be regulated. Building on the experience of the past, legislators in this century have concentrated on preventing the man in uniform from running for public office, particularly at the national level. Thus today the constitutions of eleven countries prohibit military men in active service from being candidates for legislative posts. Six constitutions forbid their running for the presidency. Four constitutions, including that of Brazil, put limits on the eligibility of men in uniform for elective office at the state, provincial, departmental, and local levels. However, the Argentine constitution of 1853, restored after the overthrow of Perón, did not place any restrictions on the political activities of the army or on military personnel.[7]

[6] Galo Plaza Lasso, *The Problems of Democracy in Latin America* (Chapel Hill, N.C., 1955), p. 70.
[7] William S. Stokes, *Latin American Politics* (New York, 1959), pp. 132–33.

But the constitutional status of the armed forces in Ecuador and Honduras is eloquent testimony to the inability of most of the republics to curb their armed forces effectively. The Ecuadorian constitution of 1929 allotted to the military one of fifteen senate seats assigned to "functional representatives." And that country's constitution of 1945 granted special privileges [*fueros*] to members of the armed forces, provisions which protect them from being sued in civil courts and from being deprived of their ranks, honors, or pensions, except in a form and under circumstances to be determined by law. The constitution then went ahead to make it clear that the armed forces enjoyed a special status by declaring that the military *fuero* did not apply in any way to members of the police force.

Even more impressive is the Honduran constitution of 1957, which gives the armed forces more freedom of action than any document since Paraguay's constitution of 1844, which was written under the direction of an avowed military dictatorship. The Honduran constitution places the armed forces under the direct control of the Chief of the Armed Forces, to be named by the National Congress from a list of three persons proposed by the Superior Council of National Defense and who "will remain in office for six years and who may only be removed from office by the National Congress when he has been impeached and found guilty by two thirds of its members, and in such cases as may be provided for in the Constituent Law of the Armed Forces." Article 319 of the Charter provides that when any difference arises between the Chief of the Armed Forces and the national President, it will be submitted to the consideration of Congress, which will resolve it by majority vote. Thus the armed forces are for all intents and purposes free of any control by the executive branch of the government. Given their freedom from restraint, the oath required of the armed forces by Article 321 becomes largely meaningless. It reads, "In my name and in the name of the Armed Forces of Honduras, I solemnly swear that we will not be instruments of oppression; that even if they come from superiors in rank we will not carry out orders that violate the letter or spirit of the Constitution: that we will defend the national sovereignty and integrity of our land; that we will respect the rights and liberties of the people, that we will maintain the apolitical and professional dignity of the Armed Forces, and that we will defend the suffrage of citizens and the alternation of the exercise of the presidency of the republic."

Military codes are another device for protecting members of the armed forces. Those in Ecuador and Chile, for example, shield officers from arrest for civil crimes until after they have been tried by military courts and found guilty. And in Chile, military courts have jurisdiction over civilians who abuse (*desacato*) the military as an institution, or abuse individuals because they are members of the military, or insult the national flag; they also have jurisdiction over crimes against the military that involve both military and civilian personnel.[8]

If my findings are valid, the general public in Spanish America does not share the profound concern of the majority of the intellectuals who have gone on record regarding the armed forces. Nor are they deeply distressed that the legislators have not touched upon a sure means of channeling, in the best interests of society, the urges of impatient officers. It is fairly easy to find persons, particularly intellectuals, who welcome the opportunity to cite long lists of charges against the military, but it is just as easy to find individuals, even among the working groups, who are pro-military. But neither the pro- nor the anti-military elements are nearly as numerous as those who simply accept the armed forces as a fact of life, and will often argue, in a ten-minute conversation, both for and against the man in uniform.

Since the responses of the anti- and the pro-military elements are well-known, it becomes important to try to describe the convictions of that vast share of the population which has

---

[8] It should be noted that in Chile even military cases can be appealed to the Supreme Court, so that curbs on the responsibility of the armed forces do exist.

not yet taken, and may never take, an unequivocal position on the military problem. These are people from all social classes, people ordinarily swayed more by emotion than by reason and more by personal interest than by national goals.

Given the prominent role that the military has played in their republics, it is appalling how little the average person in Spanish America knows about the armed forces of his country. Since it is commonly argued that the financial burden of maintaining modern military establishments has been a major factor in forcing the postponement of industrial, commercial, and educational development in the republics, one might expect that the public would have certain factual data on the armed forces at its collective fingertip, but such is not the case. Neither the man in the office nor the man in the street ordinarily knows how many men are in uniform or even whether the military establishment is being reduced or expanded. The average person of some education, wealth, and status is befuddled when he is asked what share of the national income goes to the armed forces, and he has probably never heard a discussion of a question that would seem of great importance to him—which branch of the service places the heaviest burden on the limited foreign exchange that is ordinarily available to his nation. Nor, in all probability, has it ever occurred to more than a very few men, that given the army's present state of technological development, the farmer is in most cases the greatest legitimate benefactor of budgetary allotments to the armed forces. Even among intellectuals, a surprisingly few have explored the economics of militarism thoroughly enough to have reasoned opinions as to whether commerce, industry, and agriculture have any need for the skills and labor presently assigned to the armed forces. But it does not follow that simply because they do not know the answers to vital economic questions that they do not have opinions. There is a widespread feeling that the military establishment represents an uneconomic allocation of resources. An Ecuadorian professor at first insisted that his nation could not afford a military establishment at all, and then qualified this by saying, "Well, we can afford a small one to defend us aganist Peru." But if it is true that few individuals are qualified to discuss the economics of militarism intelligently, a large number of persons have accurate economic information which they can and often do use to demonstrate the privileged position of officers. It is almost unanimously held in Spanish America that officers enjoy greater economic advantages than civilians of comparable age and training. But only in Venezuela, where "the officers are the best-paid in the world," does the public feel that the base pay of the armed services personnel is out of line with civilian salaries.

It has been "fringe benefits" and outright corruption which has aroused the ire of the public. Kickbacks from military purchases, particularly military purchases abroad, have been a common means for officers to enrich themselves. The list of fringe benefits is long. Post exchange and commissary privileges—which, in Chile, for example, often include the right to buy foodstuffs at approximately one-half the retail price—and free membership in officers' clubs are commonplace, and they serve as one of the inducements to young men to enter the services. Post exchange privileges are often extended to include exemption from customs duties and in certain instances where naval vessels are used, from freightage on "personal effects" brought in by armed forces personnel returning from overseas posts. In 1960 many Ecuadorian officers had a second income from the surreptitious sale of such duty-free items as canned goods, whiskey, watches, and household appliances. So widespread was this bootlegging that Quito and Guayaquil retail merchants felt obliged to take their case to Congress and, through the press, to the public. Venezuelan officers returning from assignments abroad, including university study, with expensive automobiles, camera equipment, record players, TV sets, and all manner of electrical appliances, have made Caracas famous, according to a Venezuelan university professor, for being "the most materialistic city in the world."

The extras go far beyond post exchange privileges, which

are in fact a minor item, although the public does not seem to appreciate this fact. Medical and dental care and drugs either free or at reduced prices afford officers valued opportunities to stretch their paychecks. Free or low-rent housing, automobiles, and assistants and servants at government expense are widely available, particularly away from major cities. Loans at rates considerably below those available to the general public or even businesses, and "free" education for officers' children, have already been mentioned. Next to the low-interest loans the surest legal way for the officer to enhance his economic position is to be assigned as an attaché overseas, preferably in the United States or Western Europe. These positions are widely sought, and it is generally accepted that those who receive them are ordinarily successful because of their connections rather than because of their professional qualifications. Highly responsible Argentines and foreigners in Buenos Aires estimate that benefits such as those named above add 60 per cent and upwards, depending on rank, to the income of the officers; Chileans and Mexicans appear to feel that such extras add approximately 40 per cent to the income of officers in their countries.

Of all the benefits available to officers, the retirement systems (discussed in Chapter IV) are the most resented by the public, especially by members of the civilian middle sectors, who generally speaking are poorly cared for in their old age. In reference to the large number of wives, children, and grandchildren of deceased officers who draw pensions from the state, a research economist in the Banco Central del Ecuador remarked, "They [the officers] are the only animals in Ecuador who continue to earn money after they die." In response, Ecuadorian officers concede that they have a better retirement system than other public employees and most private employees, but they argue that without it officers would be inclined to leave the services in favor of private employment because they cannot save on what they earn while on active duty. But several Chilean professors, interviewed separately, unanimously agreed that an officer, despite the fact that he has considerably less academic training than a university professor, could expect to retire fifteen years earlier at 25 per cent more pay than a professor. One Chilean civilian bureaucrat noted that Chile had more generals in retirement than had Mexico. And a well-informed Argentine businessman observed, "We have two armies, one on duty and one in retirement."

Despite public disapproval of the considerable economic advantages that accrue to armed forces officers, the military as an institution can attain and retain public approbation if its representatives exercise restraint in the political area. This is quite apparent from the good will enjoyed by the armed forces of Ecuador and Chile as compared with the feeling against the Argentine armed forces that prevailed as recently as 1961. In Argentina the anti-Perón faction within the armed forces probably had the support of at least 60 per cent of the total population when they overthrew the dictator, and they probably retained that support during the return to "democracy" under General Aramburu; but after Arturo Frondizi took the presidential oath, the prestige of the armed forces declined rapidly and by early 1962 they were, it appears, in disfavor with the general public. There were several reasons for this. The military had prevented any serious attempt to integrate the *peronistas* into the political life of the republic. They had supported the austerity program which Frondizi felt obliged to undertake in order to qualify for vitally needed economic assistance from the United States, and over the short range austerity bore heavily upon the working men and the civilian bureaucracy while benefiting a relatively few within the business community. Officers also insisted on meddling in state-operated economic enterprises. But the public loss of faith came primarily because the armed forces would not permit Frondizi to run his own government or to formulate his own foreign policy, particularly in regard to Castro. Thus was added to the discontent of large sectors of labor that remained loyal to Perón the disfavor of the vital middle-sector elements who felt that Argentina could not respond energetically in the economic sphere until it had attained political stability under civilian leadership.

Under such circumstances the best that the defenders could say for the services was that "they are necessary evils" and that "the people are hostile because they know that the officers can take over by force at any time they choose." The height of oversimplification regarding the army came from an Argentine businessman (speaking in English) who called the officers "goddamned bandits pretending to be apolitical. Anyone who talks to them is suspect of plotting with them."

In Ecuador, on the other hand, the armed forces had studiously avoided direct interference in civilian affairs from the 1940's until 1961, when they forced President Velasco Ibarra from office. After the repeated forays in civilian politics during the thirties, the armed forces' new posture had by 1960 won them widespread commendation. The citizens of Ecuador, particularly in Quito, were quite ready to forget the past and the financial burden of the armed forces and to accept them as being apolitical, responsible, and representing the national will. Former army conscripts agreed that they had come out of the service better prepared to cope with problems of making a living than when they had begun their tour of duty. A taxi driver who had never served in the army was impressed with the learning that was expected of soldiers. According to him, "Even corporals must know many things." The editor of a Quito daily, a man with communist connections, declared that "For nearly thirty years the soldier of Ecuador has been very respectful of civilian authority. Everyone is convinced that the soldier now understands his role in society." But as if to sound a word of warning, he added, "They [the military] have no chance and they know it." Another editor of a "moderate" newspaper asserted that "In a showdown between the army and the police the public would support the army." Still another newspaperman declared that "Our armed forces are absolutely not militaristic." A university professor, defending the armed forces, insisted that historically "Ecuador's worst dictators have been civilians," and that "between the Church and the army, the army has been the more liberal." Another professor, while avowing that the army has behaved "very well," observed that "what the military does in the future will be determined

by developments in other countries." A nationally famous artist could not understand why anyone should study the armed
forces, since "they have no importance." A young Ecuadorian
secretary in the United States Embassy in Quito said that "The
army is enchanted with democratic government." It seems
safe to say by way of conclusion that practically all well-informed Ecuadorians, as of 1960, were prepared to credit the
armed forces rather than the political parties with guaranteeing the electoral process after so many years of political
turbulence. It is not known how the public reacted to the overthrow of President Julio Arosemena in July 1963.

The Chileans had all the confidence in their armed forces
that the Ecuadorians had in theirs, and probably with considerably more justification. Three years earlier (April 1957) the
military, "to the relief of a badly embarrassed public," had
moved in and restored order soon after the police had lost control of the crowds and the national capital was given over to
spontaneous rioting of the type that citizens of Santiago had
been sure "could not happen here." But a Social Christian representative to the National Congress and a learned Jesuit priest
stated the more basic case for the military; the congressman
observed that "since 1853 we have been occupied by our armed
forces for only three years (1927–31)"; the priest pointed out
that the military "have never played a role and the people are
indifferent to them." A professor at the University of Chile,
with considerable assurance, stated categorically that "Chile
has been less militaristic than any other country in Latin
America" and one of his colleagues provided a historical justification for his conviction that the armed forces did not pose
a threat to the political stability of the nation. He began by
observing that "they are symbolic, they represent the soul of
the nation," and from there went on to insist that during the
Ibáñez dictatorship (1927–31) the people were opposed to the
dictator but not to the military as an institution. A professor at
Catholic University in Santiago believed (in 1960) that "currently there is no problem of the military in politics. They can
guarantee public order but they are not powerful enough to
take over." The wife of a former Minister of War was sure

that "the military is different here. They are a sickly profession and we will keep them that way." And a young engineer-businessman felt that only the army was saving Chile from "communist aggression." A very young and alert librarian in the Biblioteca Nacional in Santiago noted that "When cadets are shown in the newsreels we clap and squeal. We like them better than we do high-school boys." Her observation was confirmed by a male graduate student in history at the University of Chile, who believed that girls were influenced by the colorful cadet uniforms and by the fact that they associated job security and early marriage with the armed forces. Already in his mid-twenties, the graduate student explained that he would not be in a financial position to marry for several years. Variations on these themes could be related, but they would be superfluous.

Civilians consider the navy the "aristocratic" service and the army the "democratic" service, although there is no longer much basis for the labels. A generation ago naval officers did have to have greater technical skills than army officers, and therefore they probably appealed to a somewhat "higher social type." Probably a more important consideration in establishing the public image has been the political role that the two services have played. The navies, except in Chile, have not been able to compete with the armies in decision-making at the national level and so have tended to remain out of the public eye. The very fact that they have been unknown to the public has given them something of an Olympian status, which may not have been warranted in the past and certainly is not today. Meanwhile, army officers have staged their battles in public, and in the process sergeants have occasionally become generals and presidents. In societies in which opportunities for the lower classes to succeed politically are strictly limited, the relative ease with which army officers can still achieve political influence at least suggests that social democracy is at work.

Knowing what they do of the economic advantages that armed forces officers have won for themselves, and of their long record of interference in politics, civilians have remained remarkably realistic and objective in their analysis of officers as social beings. Largely depending upon the social position of the individual making the judgment, officers are fitted into the social hierarchy "some place between the Indian and the elite." The laborer, firmly implanted on the bottom rung of the social ladder, and with little precise knowledge of where those above him belong in the social hierarchy, tends to consider junior officers as solidly middle sector and those senior officers who appear at public functions alongside high civilian officers as having entered "high society." The civilian elite, seeing the officers from atop the social ladder, consider them as definite inferiors with whom social contacts ordinarily should be limited to official or semi-official functions. The civilian middle sectors consider officers a group apart, but enjoying most of the privileges and advantages accorded middle sectors, including living in middle-sector and upper-middle-sector residential areas. But this does not necessarily make them socially acceptable. Intellectuals — who are middle sector by almost every conceivable measurement—more than any other group pointedly avoid social contacts with officers. Businessmen, while less averse than intellectuals to social contact with the armed forces officers, do not seem to seek them out, and it is apparent that many social contacts are based on commercial considerations.

Those middle-sector elements who reject the military socially are inclined to be harsher on the wives of officers than they are on the officers themselves. The official explanation of women belonging to the middle sectors is "we have our own circle of friends and we are not interested in bringing others into it." This suggests rather strongly that the basic objection to wives of officers is that they do not make the transition into higher levels of society as easily as do their husbands, who are in more or less constant contact with individuals who are generally considered to be of somewhat higher status. Thus one often hears statements to the effect that "army wives in the provinces are high local society," with the implication that they are not necessarily acceptable in the cities. Alternatively, one hears that army wives are considered "very unsophisticated" or "notoriously inept" or of "a pretty low type." The wife of Pérez Jiménez, for example, was called "the illegitimate daughter of a well-known Venezuelan" and was shunned because of her adjudged inability to fulfill the role of the nation's first lady.

In Chile the supreme rebuff is to refer to wives of armed forces officers as *siúticas,* which is more or less the equivalent of "dressed-up doll" in English. Closely related to this attitude is the problem raised by a former high official in Ecuador. He contended that one of the chief reasons his nation felt obliged to suspend the practice of permitting able non-commissioned officers to win regular commissions was that their wives simply could not make the social transition; this made them unacceptable to the wives of the regular commissioned officers and an embarrassment to their own husbands, all of which often led to family difficulties. An objective evaluation would seem to be that quite often wives do not come from backgrounds that give them experience in social skills, and consequently they are often unable to contribute much to the social prestige of their husbands.

But if private groups tend to align themselves against "social climbers" among the officers and their wives, they offer little or no resistance to progress by the sons and daughters of officers. Those sons of officers who do not enter the armed forces appear to compete on equal terms in the universities and are accepted as equals in law, medicine, and teaching, as well as in the civilian bureaucracy, and they marry into "solid middle-sector families." Likewise, daughters of officers with considerable frequency become stenographers and marry into "good families" or "the professions." The conclusion at this time must be that the armed forces provide an exceptionally good springboard for upward social mobility for the children of officers.

Meanwhile, officers are in general satisfied with their lot. Most of them in fact feel that they are able to maintain sufficient contacts with the privileged sectors to satisfy their own social objectives. If they feel resentment against those who refuse to accept them as social equals, they conceal it quite well. They appreciate the opportunities open to their children and express satisfaction in the expectation that their offspring will enjoy greater social status than they do. An apparent majority of officers want their daughters to marry "outside the services." Nonetheless, officers do sense their unfavorable social position at times. The ten-million-dollar Círculo Militar in Caracas is Latin America's most expensive monument to the inferiority complex of officers; it is generally agreed that Pérez Jiménez built it to appease the high-ranking officers of the Venezuelan army, who could not "crash" the aristocratic country clubs.

PART THREE

THE MILITARY IN BRAZIL

VII

THE POLITICAL ROLE OF THE
BRAZILIAN MILITARY

A SEEMINGLY ENDLESS parade of military officers seeking to
impose their will upon an often unwilling and rebellious people
has kept large parts of Spanish America in almost constant
turmoil ever since Independence. Portuguese Brazil, on the
other hand, was relatively free of violence and militarism from
1822, when it won its independence, until 1889. And since
then, although the Brazilian military has repeatedly encroached
upon the civilian preserve and played a decisive role in the political life of the nation, it has done so without creating turmoil or arousing public wrath. It is worth inquiring at some
length into the reasons why the Brazilian armed forces have
been able to maintain decisive political influence while avoiding the kind of difficult military-civilian relations that have
long plagued Brazil's neighbors.

The military historian Liddell Hart has noted that "the
nature of armies is determined by the nature of civilizations
in which they exist." The American historian Clarence H.
Haring has observed that "the Brazilians were not a military-
minded people, not as martial, perhaps, as their Spanish neighbors." And the Brazilian sociologist Gilberto Freyre has written that "No viceroy of Brazil, no king, no emperor, no president, no bishop, has been assassinated in the history of the
country." These statements by recognized experts would suggest that the Brazilian military, representing a basically moderate people, have been essentially nonviolent. By projection,
the statements would also seem to support the conclusion that
military-civilian political relations in Brazil have been essen-

tially nonviolent. Whether or not for the reasons that may be adduced from Hart, Haring, and Freyre, this has actually been the case. And the peaceful nature of the Brazilian people probably helps explain why Brazil has been relatively free from violent political moves by officers while certain of its neighbors have been sub-nations dominated by their own armies. But it does not explain everything. The full explanation must also include interpretations of political, social, and economic developments that in some cases date back to the end of the colonial era.

Up to the moment that the armies of Napoleon overran the Iberian Peninsula there was little in the contrasting evolution of Portugal's and Spain's American colonies to explain why the Brazilian people, for the most part, have lived at peace with their armed forces while the people of Spanish America in general have warred with theirs. Both Portugal and Spain fought their international wars in America—Portugal along the Brazilian seaboard and in La Plata, and Spain in the Caribbean—with officers and troops mainly from the home country, although there were colonials who held commissions in the armed forces of both nations. Also, the largest landholders in both Spanish and Portuguese America were made responsible for defending themselves and their property against Indian incursions, slave uprisings, and attacks from neighboring proprietors. Thus, nearly every plantation in Brazil had its well-trained "army," which might be counted in the tens or hundreds and on occasion in the thousands, particularly if the landholder was also a slave-hunter. And, although Portuguese administrators in Brazil theoretically controlled the private armies, they did not in fact exercise that control, which left the landholders relatively free to convert their forces into instruments of attack. By the end of the colonial period Brazil had a cadre of men who formed the basis of a "colonel type" not unlike that found at the head of militia columns throughout much of Spanish America. Meanwhile Portugal's loose control over Brazil —in contrast to Spain's centralized and firm administration of its colonies—might reasonably have been expected to encourage federalist tendencies of the nature that developed in Spanish America, tendencies that led simultaneously to the violent breakup of Spain's New World empire and to bitter struggles for local autonomy in the states that emerged from the wreckage. But this did not occur.

If in terms of violence and militarism Portuguese and Spanish America developed along similar lines during the three centuries prior to 1800, they followed sharply divergent paths during the next three decades. Between 1800 and 1830 prolonged and bitter wars with the mother country, punctuated by numerous internecine struggles, gave Spanish America its independence, but they left the emergent republics many unresolved problems which civilian *caudillos* and armed forces officers exploited throughout the remainder of the century.[1] Brazil, meanwhile, won its freedom from Portugal without indebting itself to a generation of military heroes, and even without developing a military spirit. It then passed through its first years of independence without confronting its ruling oligarchy with the choices that might have unduly magnified the differences that existed among them.

Brazil's peculiar role in the Portuguese empire and, after Independence, its relationships with the royal house of Portugal, the Braganzas, largely determined that first the colony and then the sovereign empire should avoid the violence and anarchy that crippled Spanish America during and immediately after its struggle for freedom. When the royal family of Portugal, fleeing the forces of Napoleon, reached Bahia early in 1808, Brazil was in effect emancipated from the mother country and became the center of the shrinking but still impressive Portuguese empire. Prince John, in the name of his demented mother, Queen María, was already opening Brazil to the trade of the world, encouraging industry, and creating sundry financial, scientific, and cultural institutions when revolution burst upon Spain's American empire in 1810.

In December 1815, when Brazil was raised to dominion

---

[1] The major unresolved problems included the federalist-centralist and Church-state issues, recognition by the mother country, general economic stagnation, and the lack of communication, education, and experienced political leadership. For a fuller discussion see Chapter II.

status in the empire, the Spanish king, Ferdinand VII, was blindly refusing concessions to his already battle-weary but still determined subjects. Some Brazilians objected to efforts to push Braganza claims and those of John's wife, Carlota Joaquina, sister of Ferdinand VII, in the Plata area; and creole resentment against Portuguese haughtiness and extravagance flared up occasionally, as in Pernambuco in 1817. But when the time arrived for John (king since 1816) to return to Portugal in early 1821, the prompt separation of Brazil from Portugal was not a certainty. However, that step was taken on September 7, 1822, by John's son Pedro, who from São Paulo declared for "independence or death."

Independence came to Brazil almost, but not quite, without bloodshed, when Pedro was crowned in December 1822. By contrast, it was not until 1824, after a full fifteen years of fighting and the loss of hundreds of thousands of lives and enormous destruction of property, that Spain was finally expelled from the mainland of the Hemisphere. In defeat, Spain stubbornly withheld recognition from its colonies until the late 1830's, and for three decades thereafter its threats of reconquest encouraged military buildups in countries already overburdened with "defense spending" and overrun with ambitious officers. In Brazil, the easily won independence was followed by early recognition from the mother country, which came chiefly because Great Britain prevailed upon Portugal, its old ally, first to acknowledge the loss of its New World empire and then to maintain amicable relations with Brazil. Pedro, secure in the knowledge that Great Britain would protect him from overseas attack, chose to divert attention from the internal problems of the emerging empire by seeking, as had his father, to advance the claims of his house in the Plata region.

The Plata venture, unpopular from the first and a failure in the end, was the last of three decisions under John and Pedro which served in a significant way to make the role of the Brazilian military quite distinct from that of its counterparts in Spanish America. The first decision directly involved the troops and their command. By retaining companies made up entirely of men from the home country, and by relying upon troops sent directly from Portugal to suppress the Pernambuco uprising of 1817, Prince John left little doubt about his distrust of the colonials. Subsequently, more than once, he was advised to keep his soldiers and sailors under the command of Portuguese officers, and although this apparently did not become official policy, the highest posts in the armed forces were in fact conferred almost exclusively upon men from the Peninsula. And when John returned to Portugal, the legislature in Lisbon by decree excluded Brazilians from military offices. The presence of Portuguese troops and officers thus became the first basis for the creation of a permanent and stable military organization in Brazil. It was not a firm foundation; it aroused the hostility of creole officers and the oligarchy, who were being taxed heavily to support what was in a real sense an army of occupation. Creole hostility heightened when Pedro used his predominantly Portuguese troops to disperse legislative deputies in November 1823. When, during the following two years, the young emperor employed armed forces to quell federalist uprisings, bitter personal encounters between Portuguese and creole officers increased. Differences between the two groups of officers had the salutary effect of discouraging creole officers from following in the steps of their Spanish American counterparts, who were already beginning to act on their own behalf.

More decisive than the attitude toward Portuguese officers and troops in the shaping of the Brazilian military mind was the winning of independence without a major sacrifice of lives or property. This achievement was the work of the distinguished scholar and statesman José Bonifácio de Andrada e Silva, one of Pedro's first trusted advisers. A conservative, if not a reactionary by temperament, Andrada e Silva for a decade watched closely the consequences upon Spanish America of revolution based on the tenets of Rousseau and the radical thought of the French Revolution. He deplored the loss of life, the growing bitterness among the ruling groups, the appeals to the lower classes, and the destruction of property that he saw. When it was time for Brazil to strike out on its own, his counsel against violent revolution and in favor of political evolution was adopted. He reasoned that the installation of Pedro, the heir to the Portuguese throne, as Emperor of Brazil would guarantee a rapid and easy break with the mother country, preserve Portuguese America from demagoguery and tumult, attract maximum support from the resurgent monarchies in Europe, and assure national unity. Basically, all these expectations were fulfilled. Portuguese troops either swore allegiance to Pedro or offered only token resistance to his takeover before returning to Portugal. Creole officers were deprived of the opportunity to become heroes and claim a share in the government on the grounds that they had carved the emergent empire out of Portuguese holdings. Victory was achieved before opposing views on vital issues became battle-hardened. The economy was spared the ravages of war, which could have been as costly in the highly industrialized sugar zone as it was in some mining regions of Mexico and Peru.

Pedro's intervention in the Plata, which turned into a three-year war with Argentina, was the third and last of the major developments prior to 1830 that significantly affected Brazilian thinking on military matters. The intervention was unpopular because it was generally believed that Pedro's ultimate objective was to promote not Brazil's but Portugal's interest in the area. When this feeling, plus resentment against serving under Portuguese officers, caused young Brazilians to openly refuse to serve in the army, Pedro brought in German and Irish mercenaries. The Germans and the Irish did not prove to be the answer to Pedro's dilemma, but their presence did serve to help destroy the image of the armed forces as a patriotic, national institution. When the disasters of the war —8,000 lives were finally lost—struck home, young men fled into the woods and the plains to avoid service and their elders lost any vestige of the martial spirit they might have had at the beginning of the conflict. Brazil lost the war, but she was spared the price of evolving in a direction that might have made military service more attractive than civilian careers.

Charged by his subjects with full responsibility for the Plata fiasco and with continuing to be pro-Portuguese, and with the last remnants of his popular following fast disintegrating, early in 1831 Pedro sailed for Portugal after abdicating in favor of his five-year-old son, the future Pedro II. There followed a decade of extreme agitation during which Brazil threatened repeatedly to lapse into the anarchical ways of Spanish America. A succession of uprisings rent the Brazilian empire from one end to the other.[2] The rebellions that broke out immediately after the abdication of Pedro I tended to be nativistic or alternatively monarchist or republican. However, when it became apparent that the Regencies, ruling in the name of the future Pedro II, were unable to exercise firm centralized control, localism and federalism soon superseded all other motives for revolt. Thus, as early as 1833 the disturbances in Brazil came to resemble those going on simultaneously in Colombia and Mexico, except for the important difference that in Brazil antagonisms were not compounded by the injection of the Church-state issue into the federalist-centralist issue, as occurred periodically in many parts of Spanish America. Finally, imperial arms were succeeding everywhere except in the south, when moderate minds prevailed, and in 1840 the young Pedro, at that time fourteen years of age, was declared to have reached his majority. A year later he was crowned Pedro II, and Brazil returned quickly to tranquility under civilian leadership.

Force and violence reached their peak intensity in modern Brazil during the interregnum period. Troops who had joined the revolt against Pedro I threatened to impose their will upon the government. They and their officers from time to time deserted to the revolutionaries, notably in the case of the Farrapos Revolt in Rio Grande do Sul. Revolutions were fought largely by armies raised by levies on the plantations.

---

[2] The principal revolts were as follows: Ceará, 1832–38; Pernambuco, 1831–35; Minas Gerais, 1833; Mato Grosso, 1834–41; and Rio Grande do Sul, 1835–45. Other revolts took place in Minas Gerais and São Paulo in 1842 at the time Pedro II was crowned.

Each landowner with a private army was a potential threat to the central government. The *fazendeiros* (landholders) formed "national guards" to protect themselves from the central authority. The Regents countered by creating municipal guards, the control of which was shared by the central government and the local citizenry.

Had there been a latent bellicose spirit in Brazil at the beginning of the interregnum, disturbances undoubtedly would have awakened it, but it did not exist. The Brazilian navy remained largely on the sidelines during the hectic days immediately before and after Pedro's resignation. Armed forces officers accepted without a serious struggle the decree of January 17, 1832, which deprived the military of their privileged status in the case of political crimes. And despite a decade of turbulence, the decision to declare Pedro's majority was a civilian one, although it is true that the decision was made in large part on the basis of the calculation of armed forces officers that they could not check the tendency to national disintegration as long as the interregnum persisted.

For the purposes of this study, Pedro's reign of nearly fifty years divides into two well-defined periods. During the first one, dating from his coronation until approximately 1870, the Emperor and his close advisers were in complete command once the agitations of civil war subsided. First in peace and then in a prolonged war with Paraguay, a robust rural element, centered in the sugar-producing "Hump" of Brazil, and the Catholic Church gave to Pedro all the support he needed to exercise the moderating power granted him by the constitution.

During the second period, which ended with Pedro's overthrow in 1889, a combination of circumstances destroyed both the monolithic nature of the Emperor's government and the personal influence which had previously enabled him to balance antagonisms before they got out of hand. Monarchy became increasingly anachronistic in the Hemisphere. Pedro, ill and unable to appreciate the urge for rapid technological and economic change, lost touch with his people. The Church-state issue, which lingered on after attaining disruptive proportions in the 1870's, and the slavery issue, which was re-solved by the Abolition Act of 1888, cost Pedro the staunch backing of the Catholic Church and the landholding aristocracy of the north, two of the principal pillars upon which the mon-archy had rested. Finally, emergent economic and political groups—the new coffee barons, the aggressive capitalists of Rio de Janeiro, São Paulo, and Minas Gerais—and republi-cans and positivists drawn from a cross section of the articu-late population—took advantage of the personal and political freedoms that Pedro's lofty idealism had guaranteed and began to promote their own interests and to downgrade both the monarchical system and the Emperor.

Conditions prior to 1870 encouraged Brazil to sustain an effective military establishment but also discouraged the armed forces from openly aspiring to a civilian role of the nature that had become commonplace in most of Spanish America. Brazil's foreign relations were the principal condition favoring the maintenance of a representative army and navy. Its differ-ences with Great Britain over the termination of the slave trade threatened to lead to armed conflict during the mid-1840's. In 1851–52 Brazil interfered in Argentina to help overthrow the dictator Juan Manuel de Rosas, and in 1864 it sent troops to Uruguay in support of the Colorado Party. Throughout the period the Imperial Navy was charged with keeping open the Paraná River route to Mato Grosso. Im-perial military engineers assisted in the construction of the defense system along the Paraná River, which was supposed to protect Paraguay from Argentine encroachments but which in fact was later used to defend Paraguay against Brazil. When the Paraguayan War broke out in 1864 Brazil had an army of approximately 17,000; before victory came in 1870, Brazil had put over 100,000 men into the field and had supplied more sol-diers, sailors, ships, and armament than its two allies, Argen-tina and Uruguay, combined.

Brazil managed to avoid the normal Spanish American ex-perience of military meddling in civilian affairs prior to 1870 primarily because of five considerations. First, Pedro could not be attacked on personal grounds, as could many of his contemporaries in neighboring republics; his family life was above reproach. He was widely respected for his honesty in financial matters, his genuine, if paternalistic, concern for the welfare of his subjects, and his conscientiousness in honoring commonly accepted democratic practices. Pedro, thus, did not need armed support, and use of force against him would not have received the approbation of any responsible sector of society. Second, because of the monarchical system, Brazil was relieved of the periodic electoral campaigns which in Spanish America were supposed to conclude with the popular selection of the next president, but which in fact often ended up with the armies in the field and the victorious forces imposing the new chief executive upon a reluctant public. Third, the Emperor, who was expected to be, and for the most part was, above factional disputes, possessed the constitutional power to dissolve the Imperial Assembly. Pedro used this power on eleven occasions in all and provided a method of rotation in office which in Spanish America could often be supplied only by an armed uprising. Fourth, the Paraguayan War was unpopular from the first among certain highly placed elements. And when the conflict proved inordinately costly in money and lives—casualties are given variously between 33,000 and 50,000—many politicians directed the criticism indiscriminately against the Emperor and the commanders in the field. Their criticism increased as material progress came to a halt at home and it became apparent that the Empire would end the war with a huge debt and little of a tangible nature to show for it. In this respect, the Paraguayan venture was a repetition of the Plata involvement under Pedro I; in similar fashion, it did little to evoke enthusiasm for a military with offensive capabilities, which seemed especially unnecessary in view of the fact that Brazil already had a vast undeveloped hinterland and was surrounded by weak, warring neighbors.

Fifth, the Duque de Caxias (Luiz Alves de Lima y Silva), Brazil's outstanding armed forces figure of all time and hero of the Paraguayan conflict, was throughout his long public career a firm defender of Pedro and the established political system. After building his reputation as a military strategist in the civil wars of the 1830's and 1840's, Caxias entered the government in the 1850's as a conservative partisan and sponsor of the armed forces. But he steadfastly resisted employing the military to obtain his or his party's political objectives. On the contrary, he used his influence to keep the young officers in line, and in this he was supported by nearly all senior officers in both the army and navy, who, like Caxias, had served Pedro since his infancy and who had been rewarded during the Paraguayan conflict with the Emperor's unswerving support. The degree to which Caxias was responsible for restraining his fellow officers is suggested by the fact that immediately following his death, in 1880, Brazil was confronted with a serious "military" problem for the first time since Pedro II was crowned.

The discontent within the armed forces that Caxias had been so instrumental in containing burst forth after his death. Brazilian officers quickly acquired many, though by no means all, of the characteristics of their contemporaries in Spanish America.[3] Officers complained that they were not and could not be appreciated by civilians. They were irreverent toward Pedro and they sowed disrespect for high civilian officials, whom they professed to hate for their lack of realism. Contrary to military regulations, officers took positions before public assemblies and in the press on such basic national issues as slavery. The armed forces in general opposed slavery, and some officers, on the ground that it was beneath their dignity, refused to use their men to pursue runaway slaves. Although there was no legal basis for their action, there was considerable precedent on their side in the Western world, and furthermore their position on the matter of slavery tended to place them on the side of the rapidly growing anti-slavery elements. And when, after a decade of irresponsibility and insubordination, the armed forces decided to overthrow the empire and terminate the monarchy in 1889, their action was sanctioned

---

[3] The Brazilians, for example, showed very little disposition to resort to widespread violence, which their counterparts in neighboring states employed indiscriminately in order to gain their ends.

by practically all social groups and was applauded, either openly or secretly, by what was probably an overwhelming proportion of the articulate population.

After half a century of Pedro, the people were ready for a change, and for good reasons. With 80 per cent of its population illiterate, Brazil lagged well behind Argentina and Chile in that regard. The nation was still living in a manorial tradition, its plantations forming archipelagoes of economic nodules, its towns the satellites of neighboring plantations. Industrial establishments provided employment for less than 55,000 workers. Many responsible, progressive leaders, unable to achieve their ends in a landholder-controlled parliament, were quite willing to see the military assume the vacuum-filling function that it did. Thus, while the armies in most of Latin America were staunchly defending the status quo, dominant elements in the Brazilian forces, in favoring the abolition of slavery and overthrowing Pedro twice in a decade, had broken with the past and supported change.

Officers became deeply embroiled in civilian affairs during the 1880's for much the same reasons and under the same conditions that officers in Spanish America traditionally had. Like officers in neighboring republics, who returned from the struggles for independence feeling that they had been inadequately supported and that their personal sacrifices and achievements were not comprehended by the civilians, some Brazilian officers returned from the Paraguayan war dissatisfied with the recognition accorded them and the institution they represented. And there was justification for this feeling. Some civilian officials, disturbed by the expenses incurred during the war and fearful of fanning any sparks of military fervor that remained from the war, had dispersed the "expectant heroes" without fanfare. The armed forces also feared the National Guard, which was controlled by the landholders and which might at any time be converted into a militia that the royal family could rely upon. Moreover, Pedro, who had thrown all of his influence behind the war effort, and who freely acknowledged his debt to Caxias, increasingly depended upon civilians to assist him in his government, as is shown in the case of his selections for the Ministry of War and the presidency of the province of Bahia. In his cabinets between July 1871 and November 1889, eighteen civilians and only four military men occupied the position of Minister of War. During the first thirty years of his reign, officers had outnumbered civilians fifteen to three in that position. Meanwhile, the highly important office of president of the sugar-producing province of Bahia went exclusively to civilians from 1865 until the fall of the empire.

Of a more serious nature to the officers was the Emperor's practice of neglecting the army and navy in favor of programs of a more personal interest to him. Appropriations, consequently, were invariably so low that they did not allow for expansion, and as a consequence the opportunities for promotions were strictly limited. Because troops were permitted to go badly organized, badly instructed, and badly paid, the ranks were filled overwhelmingly with Negroes for whom alternative choices of employment were practically nonexistent. Units were broken up and distributed about the interior of the country in small garrisons, often of twenty men or less. This dull, commonplace duty was not conducive either to good discipline or to high officer morale. This consideration, plus the low prestige that went with commanding ex-slaves, and added to an unsatisfactory recruitment policy, had the effect of bringing into the services, especially the army, a generation of officers whose families, belonging as they did to the emergent bourgeoisie, lacked traditional attachments to the Empire. The new group of junior officers was particularly susceptible to the blandishments of the positivists.

Positivism, as developed by Comte and later by Spencer, and modified by the local scene, found considerable acceptance in Brazil after 1870. Its stress upon progress and responsible social authority made it particularly attractive to the new generation of Brazilian officers. They came from homes that had little patience with metaphysical credos, such as the need for a personal sovereign, and they would with confidence undermine the rudiments of Brazil's traditional culture. Also, the Brazilian armed forces, like the forces of certain of the Spanish

American republics (see Chapter III), were entering an age of greater professionalization and technology. This made the officers conscious both of the scientific revolution that Western Europe and the United States were undergoing and of the backwardness of their own fatherland, for which Pedro could be held accountable. It also conditioned them to the acceptance of order over individual liberalism, which was one of the principal ingredients of the aging Emperor's political philosophy.

Within the Brazilian military, positivism found its most enthusiastic reception in the Escola Militar in Rio de Janeiro, where it was forcefully taught by Benjamin Constant, republican, mathematics professor, and tutor of Pedro's grandchildren. By the mid-1880's positivism was the "gospel of the military academy," which had become a beehive of agitators who knew political doctrines better than theories of warfare. As a logical projection of their positivist indoctrination, the cadets became convinced that they had a moral responsibility to regenerate the nation, and on at least one occasion prior to Pedro's overthrow, they indicated their willingness to follow Constant in such a crusade. Thus, when senior officers moved against Pedro they not surprisingly had the ideological support of the cadets. And when the republic was created the new ship of state was launched upon a positivist course, albeit an ill-defined one, with a flag that bore the positivist motto, "Ordem e Progresso."

But had the civilian defenders of the empire remained firm and united and had the Emperor's health permitted him to give his attention to the pressing problems of his regime, the armed forces might well have been restrained despite the developments discussed above.[4] But in fact, Pedro's supporters did not remain firm and united, and his health deteriorated rapidly during the last years of his rule. The Catholic hierarchy remained largely indifferent to the welfare of the empire after the Church-state squabbles of the 1870's. And the slaveholding aristocracy, anticipating the loss of their chattels without com-

---

[4] Such a position is at least arguable on the basis of the Spanish American experience, which seems to indicate that military intervention in civilian affairs is mostly likely to occur under weak administrations.

pensation, and resentful when that step was actually taken in 1888, exhibited an increasing receptiveness to republican slogans as the empire headed toward collapse.

Everywhere there was evidence that Pedro's poor health (he suffered from diabetes and died from that illness in 1891) was sapping him of the energy he needed to give proper direction to his government. But nowhere was his withdrawal from public life more evident than in the behavior of the traditional political parties. Liberals and Conservatives no longer displayed the political sagacity that they had earlier. Both parties gravitated so far toward the center that there was little to distinguish the program of one from the other, and the country was left to drift. One party would propose legislation only to see it voted down by "statesmen" who would sponsor the same legislation when they attained power. Party leaders were truly "wine from the same cask, flour from the same sack." Irresponsible parties, cabinet crises, and the resulting disorganization of civilian agencies might have provided sufficient cause for military intervention. But civilians practically guaranteed intervention when the monarchical parties, in cynical bids for power, solicited military backing by encouraging high-ranking officers to engage in partisan politics, and republicans chose to profit from the breach between the army and the Imperial government.[5]

[5] It has been contended that the insubordination of the Brazilian army can be traced back to the Paraguayan war, when (1) the Brazilian officers got the idea from the armed forces officers of Spanish America, with whom they cooperated during the struggle and who were notorious for intervening in civilian affairs, and (2) Brazilian officers during the course of commanding Negro troops developed an understanding of them and became interested in the abolition of Negro slavery, an interest that they later translated into political action. It is the feeling of this author that any carryover from the Paraguayan war, if such was actually the case, was of little or no importance in determining the behavior of the Brazilian armed forces in the 1880's. Also, rumors, as for example the one that Pedro proposed to exile the highest army officials and form an all-Negro army, which circulated widely immediately before the monarchy was toppled, are not examined in the text because they were not of the same level of importance as those that are discussed. The most that could be said for the rumors is that they may have prompted a decision toward which the Brazilians had been moving inextricably for at least a decade.

Those who were optimistic that a major transformation would result from the shift to republicanism were disappointed. It was almost immediately apparent that the republic had been born deeply permeated by the past, and the next forty years established repeatedly the lasting qualities of the system that had developed under the monarchy. Pedro's had been a patrician society, and under the republic Brazil continued in the genteel tradition of the plantation economy. The rich, as they had during the empire, sent their products abroad to be consumed and their sons abroad to be educated, while their wants were satisfied by importers of luxuries. Although the "one thousand publicly devoted men of the empire" were gone, the new leaders came from the same social-economic classes, albeit in somewhat different proportions. They were not radicals. Ruy Barbosa, the early republic's most distinguished statesman, for example, was a Liberal of the English stripe, and was much preoccupied with sympathy for the emerging bourgeoisie and the conservative tradition. The new leadership proved to be quite barren of fresh ideas, as was made readily apparent during the campaigns preceding the elections necessitated by the substitution of republicanism for monarchism. As it turned out, republican government was a monotonous repetition of the monarchy, with all the virtues and vices of a monocultural agriculture based upon cheap labor. Public opinion remained rudimentary or in a dormant state. The literati continued to be primarily interested in the picturesque. The technical intelligentsia was small and poorly trained. Technological development was largely in the hands of foreigners. The Brazilian people were only beginning to look to their national roots.

But as far as the armed forces, especially the army, were concerned, there was a world of difference between the monarchy and the republic. In the monarchy they had played a secondary role until practically the last moment. In the republic they assumed a primary role from the outset. Marshal Manoel Deodoro da Fonseca, who led the units that deposed Pedro and who later became the first president of the republic, instituted a frankly military regime that was continued by his immediate successor in office, Marshal Floriano Peixoto. Officers' salaries were increased and their privileges extended. Promotions were made promiscuously. The Naval Club was given valuable property in the heart of Rio de Janeiro. Military personnel summarily displaced civilians in key administration posts, senior officers were named to cabinet positions and young officers, some of whom had just completed military school, were appointed interventors in the provinces. Deodoro dissolved Congress and prepared to rule as a dictator. As a consequence wars broke out in the north and south and carried over into the Floriano regime. Until 1895 disorder was compounded by rivalries between the monarchist-inclined navy, which considered itself aristocratic and ethnically pure, and the republican, democratically inclined army, whose officers were of more modest social origin, some of them having Indian and Negro blood in their veins.

A civilian, Prudente de Moraes Barros, assumed the presidency in 1894, and civilians retained control of the executive branch of the government until 1910. Insubordination, however, was general and in 1897 an attempt, directed by senior officers, was made upon the president's life. The army, moreover, considering itself the "backbone of the nationality," refused to be isolated from politics, and army officers, still strongly under the influence of positivism, were in part responsible for the preoccupation with material progress that was one of the unmistakable characteristics of the era. Cooperation, such as it was, did little to alleviate the military's distrust of civilians and vice versa. And at the end of the fifteen-year civilian rule, civil-military tensions persisted, as officers felt that their patriotism and technical training made them superior to the "bachelors" who claimed the right to rule despite their personal antagonisms and regional ambitions.

The presidential election of 1910 was contested by General Hermes da Fonseca, nephew of Deodoro, who called for a "regeneration by the sword," and Ruy Barbosa, who called "renascent militarism the primary problem of the nation," and charged that "the army is supported, feared, and adulated, but does not inspire confidence." The military won, according to the electoral judges, and General Fonseca went on to head what is generally conceded to be the most inept, corrupt, and extravagant government that modern Brazil has known.

The presidency was returned to the civilians in 1914 when Hermes da Fonseca completed his term of office. Thereafter until 1922, the military, although always reserving the right to arbitrate political disputes between civilians, a role it had been carefully nurturing since 1894, avoided any serious confrontation with the civilian leadership. This did not prevent officers from letting their displeasure be known when President Epitacio da Silva Pessôa broke with republican tradition by naming civilians to head the War Ministry and again when he made the navy, which had been neglected since the uprising against Peixoto, his special care. And when another civilian, Arthur Bernardes, succeeded Epitacio Pessôa in the presidency in 1922, senior officers were pushed to open revolt in defense of their privileges. The Bernardes regime, however, was sustained, although shakily, by loyal forces. After displaying their ineptness in dealing with the *tenente* revolt of 1924–26, the armed forces went into eclipse, only to reappear in 1930, when in the midst of a civil war senior officers quartered in Rio de Janeiro overthrew President Washington Luiz Pereira de Souza and turned the government over to Getulio Vargas, who launched a fifteen-year-long civilian dictatorship. By this act the armed forces once again reaffirmed their assumed "right" to fill any vacuum even temporarily created by a struggle for power between the established ruling groups.

But there was also a favorable side to Brazilian military relations between 1889 and 1930. That side showed not only that the excesses commonly associated with Spanish America were ordinarily avoided, but that the Brazilian armed forces played a generally constructive role in the Republic's critical early years. Take the case of Deodoro da Fonseca. He had turned against Pedro only after considerable soul-searching, and when he acted he did so on the urging of highly placed and generally responsible civilians rather than those of his fellow

officers. Furthermore, many army officers, influenced by the
Imperial tradition, objected to the army becoming involved in
politics and as it turned out only a few units actively participated in the "revolt." The navy, moreover, even after the coup
tended to favor the Emperor and the monarchical system. This
meant that when Deodoro became provisional president he was
obliged to solicit the support of capable civilians who were not
yet ready to barter the republic's welfare in return for power.
Under the influence of these counselors, Deodoro's hand-picked
Assembly wrote a civilian constitution that the General-Presi-
dent swore to uphold. But Deodoro's contribution went beyond
that. During his short regime there was established the institutional framework under which the republic functioned for
nearly forty years. And when his civilian advisers and military
comrades, still somewhat under the influence of Imperial indoctrination, it would seem, refused to approve his decision
to rule without Congress, Deodoro resigned the presidency
rather than chance civil war by attempting to impose his will
by force.

Marshal Floriano Peixoto's administration was also crucial
to Brazil's peaceful political evolution. Peixoto, like Deodoro,
had authoritarian tendencies, but unlike Deodoro, he energetically stood his ground in the face of widespread overt opposition and in so doing made two significant contributions in
the political area. By effectively crushing the civilian revolts
and navy and army uprisings that plagued his regime, Peixoto
put to rest once and for all the monarchical issue which, had it
survived, could have served as a rallying point for all manner
of malcontents. And when he concluded his term of office and
surrendered the presidency to his legally elected civilian successor, he not only demonstrated that the army could have
power in its hands and return it to the people, but he set a precedent for the orderly rotation of the presidency which was honored until Vargas, a civilian, instituted his dictatorship thirty-
six years later.

Above and beyond those steps taken in the direction of
orderly political processes that can be attributed to Marshals

Deodoro and Peixoto, the military as an institution performed an added function by serving as an agency of national unification. When Pedro, who had symbolized Brazilian cohesion, was overthrown and the plantation system, which had served to knit together the civilian elite, began to disintegrate following the abolition of slavery, the armed forces and the Catholic Church remained as the only two traditional institutions that might have provided sufficient unity at the national level to withstand the ravages of regionalism, which enjoyed a resurgence after the fall of the empire. Between the military and the Church, the military mentality was nearer to that of the newly dominant civilian groups than was the Church's. This is particularly true of the regular army, whose officers, like the republican leaders, were generally of modest background and eager for new and improved status. The military was more liberal and democratic than was the Church, although the Brazilian Church was neither so illiberal nor so opposed to reform as was the Church in many parts of Spanish America, a fact that must be given weight in any attempt to explain why Brazil has experienced less violence than have its neighbors. But there were two other equally important considerations favoring the military over the Church as the unifying force: its officers, like the civilian statesmen of the early republic, were more committed to material progress than were the churchmen, and both the officers and civilian politicians were influenced by Comtian-Spencerian doctrines, which the Church actively opposed. Two conclusions follow from this interpretation: first, the armed forces, in the absence of an acceptable alternative institution, had simply inherited the moderating role that was left without a claimant when Pedro was deposed; second, although the armed forces did not play the moderating role with the same sureness and detachment that Pedro had for so long, they probably did a better job than the Church could have in balancing the parties, the positivists and anti-positivists, the republicans and the monarchists, and the regions and the nation.

Between 1894, when the control of the republic was passed

on to civilians, and 1930, when the Vargas dictatorship was initiated, the record of the Brazilian armed forces, except in the presidential elections of 1922, appears in a generally respectable light when compared with either that of the national civilian leadership or the armed forces of Spanish America. It is true, however, that senior officers, throughout the era, accepted the basic tenets of a narrow oligarchy that kept Brazil shackled economically to agricultural commodities produced in limited areas by a relatively few individuals.

Oligarchical government left economic and social matters largely to take care of themselves. It showed a general lack of imagination in molding opinion and policy relating to commerce, industry, transportation, and power. It deprived the nation of effective leadership in the field of education. It did little or nothing to incorporate over a million immigrants into the body politic. It permitted provincialism to flourish; Brazil remained divided into a half dozen regions, each with its particular way of life and each possessed of a collective mentality compounded of geographical, racial, and cultural inheritances and experiences. Political parties and political machines, in which personal greed vied with local greed, reflected this sectionalism. The middle sectors, small in numbers and disorganized, gave no evidence of possessing leadership qualities that might have compelled the elite-military alliance to share political power with them.

But the Brazilian armed forces managed to create and preserve a relatively favorable image of themselves even while contributing to the maintenance of the status quo by backing the somewhat unimaginative if not morally decadent oligarchy. They did this by (1) helping to open the hinterlands and to develop the country technologically, (2) supporting a positive national foreign policy, (3) avoiding serious clashes with urban labor, and (4) taking from time to time a progressive stand, as for example in 1922–24, when junior officers gave revolutionary expression to stirrings of social unrest and demands for a modification of institutional patterns.

No military establishment today, far less a generation ago,

has contributed as much to the technological and scientific development of a Latin American republic as have the Brazilian military. And the Brazilian military is the only one in all of Latin America that could at any time justifiably claim technological superiority over the civilian sector. The reason almost certainly is that Brazilian forces have the longest tradition of technical training. Before 1814 Brazil had both a Royal Naval Academy and a Royal Military Academy, both staffed by professors from Portugal and both providing eight-year courses. Up to 1874, when the Polytechnical Institute was established, the Military Academy supplied both civil and military enginers for the empire. Even after the founding of the Polytechnical Institute, the Military Academy continued to train the major share of Brazilian engineers, a role it performed until approximately the end of World War I. The Naval Academy provided its cadets with the equivalent scientific training, but naval officers were not used so generally in the civilian area.

Much of Brazil was still unexplored when, before the end of the century, a growing number of army engineers began to carve trails and string telegraph lines toward the nation's distant and still ill-defined frontiers, and to compile scientific data on the republic's interior provinces. Army engineers, who ordinarily would have gone unheralded, won national acclaim as cartographers and naturalists of Brazil's frontier. Their maps filled the archives of the Instituto Histórico e Geográfico Brasileiro. Their natural history specimens overflowed the museums of the coastal cities. General Cândido Rondon, who went into the interior as a young army engineer in 1892 and spent much of the next forty years there, became one of Brazil's distinguished and beloved scientists, an expert in botany, zoology, geography, and ethnology of the hinterland. But in the eyes of his countrymen General Rondon's true greatness lay in his success in bringing the Indian into "our civilization" by means of a rational Indian policy. Brazilians continue to reap great satisfaction and the army reflected credit from the way that the General, who was himself part Indian, established and maintained friendly relations with primitive tribes. Rondon, who had become a legend before his death in 1958, did not permit his men to use firearms against the Indians, even when attacked, or to remove anything from the Indian villages. This policy cost the lives of an undetermined number of Brazilian soldiers, but the Indian tribes in Brazil's interior, it is pointed out, were spared the gunfire that the Indians of the Great Plains of the United States experienced.

Back in the settled coastal area, meanwhile, army engineers were charged with constructing roads, railroads, port installations, and factories built to produce anything conceivably related to defense. The navy charted the waters of Brazil's coastline, provided the best drydock facilities available in the country, and, in certain instances, assumed responsibility for moving people and products into frontier areas like the Amazon basin, a task that was unattractive to commercial operators.

The armed forces' preoccupation with perfecting the technical area reflected, on the one hand, their positivist training, which qualified them to deal more successfully with material things than with the human element, and on the other, the need they felt to catch up with rapidly developing Argentina, which they viewed as a potential enemy. The armed forces' record was impressive, not only because they possessed technical skills, but because they had the support of powerful civilian leaders. As was observed above, many prominent politicians of the republic were positivist-oriented. They favored material development of the nation not only because it squared with their philosophical underpinnings but also because railroads, port facilities, power plants, factories, and urban modernization served to conceal, in part, the fact that as statesmen they lacked both the prestige and the administrative experience to cope with Brazil's basic social problems. Those same statesmen who supported technological development also urged an aggressive foreign policy because it, too, distracted attention from internal issues that were going unattended.

Brazil is said to have more neighbors than any sovereign state with the exception of the U.S.S.R. In the face of a fast-rising national spirit and the need to win some sort of public commendation, the men who inherited Pedro's government determined to resolve existing boundary disputes with their neighbors. By 1910 a series of agreements affecting territorial limits were reached with France regarding French Guiana, with Great Britain over British Guiana, and with Venezuela, Colombia, Ecuador, Peru, Bolivia, Uruguay, and Argentina. In only one of those disputes, the one with Great Britain, did Brazil receive less than she claimed; and in only one, that with Bolivia over the Acre Territory, did Brazilian troops become directly involved. Although troops were required only sparingly, Brazil prepared for such eventualities. The army was modernized. An obligatory military service law was passed in 1908 and in the same year Brazil, to the great consternation of Argentina, placed orders with Great Britain for several war vessels, including two dreadnoughts. And, despite the limited use of troops, there appears to be no question that Brazil's military power was in part responsible for its diplomatic successes during this period, which Brazilians refer to as their "expansionist era" (rejecting any suggestion that it might just as appropriately be called their "imperialistic age"). By serving the nation on its far-flung frontiers and by providing the strength to support a successful foreign policy, the armed forces enhanced the already favorable public image they enjoyed. The armies in several of the Spanish American republics were at this time playing similar nationalistic roles, which was how they attained a stature in the eyes of the public that most of them had not had since the Independence era. The Brazilian and Spanish American experience suggests, therefore, that to ride waves of nationalism is one of the surer means for the military to arouse public approval.

The Brazilian military establishment as a responsible public institution also profited from the fact that it was able to avoid the kind of violent confrontation with urban industrialized labor that before 1920 cost the armed forces of Argentina, Chile, and Mexico so dearly in public esteem. This fortuitous circumstance—for so it was as far as the armed forces were concerned—resulted, it would seem, more from the docility of the Brazilian laborer than from any predetermined governmental or military policy or unusual foresight on the part of the entrepreneurs or the armed forces officers.

Brazilian labor was docile for a number of reasons. Brazil turned to industry and mining very slowly as compared to Argentina, Uruguay, Chile, and Mexico, and as a consequence it had, in relation to size, a much smaller industrial proletariat than any of them. As late as 1920, for example, Brazil had less than 275,000 industrial workers in a total population of over 26 million. Their sheer lack of numbers alone, therefore, presumably would have tended to discourage the workers from assuming a posture that might have invited the industrial class to call on a government and army dedicated to the preservation of private capital. There were other factors. Numerically small as was the industrial labor force, it was distributed in more than 12,000 plants spread over four states: São Paulo, Rio de Janeiro, Minas Gerais, and Pernambuco, plus the Federal District. Given existing means of communication, this alone would have made labor unity next to impossible. A vast majority of the plants, moreover, were family-owned, and paternalism dominated the thinking of the proprietors just as surely as it did that of the owners of the plantations whence most of the pre-1930 generations of industrial workers came. This latter point provides two keys to understanding the Brazilian industrial worker: he was a one-time farm hand rather than a professional laborer, and he was ordinarily content to keep his relations with his employer on a personal basis such as he had grown up with in the country. Neither of these important characteristics made him good material for the anarcho-syndicalist organizers who were responsible for most of the radicalism that sooner or later led to conflicts between labor and the armed forces. Those organizers achieved their greatest successes in Latin America among laborers conditioned to work for large, impersonal, and, often, foreign-owned organizations, as for example, mining operations in Mexico and Chile and meat-packing companies in Argentina.

By the late 1930's, when Brazil finally had to deal seriously with the growing body of workers demanding a greater role in society, the anarcho-syndicalist movement had all but disappeared in Latin America and laborers either had formed or were in the process of forming political alliances with the emergent middle-sector parties. And the Brazilian civilian and military leadership knew that labor was "politically safe" as long as it remained aligned with the middle sectors and was kept beholden to the ruling groups. Consequently, when Vargas determined to bring the workers more fully into the political life of the nation, the armed forces did not raise serious objections.

Junior and senior officers won a reputation for being modern and liberally progressive when they worked together for the abolition of slavery and the overthrow of the empire. When they revolted at Copacabana fortress in Rio de Janeiro in 1922 and in São Paulo in 1924, junior officers again moved into the vanguard of those seeking to upset the traditional social-economic order, but on those two occasions they were opposed by their superiors, who remained allied with the old ruling aristocracy.

The Copacabana revolt was quixotic in the extreme. Only a handful of officers, all but one or two of whom were quite young, were involved. They had no special program or particular ideology, other than that the armed forces should help to regenerate the nation, which was being badly managed. They did not desire military rule or a change in republican institutions. They protested the abuse of those institutions and wanted them protected. With pieces of the Brazilian flag over their hearts and "to our deaths to help save Brazil" on their lips, the last eighteen revolutionaries (Eduardo Gomes, twice candidate for the presidency after World War II, is the only living survivor) marched out of the fort and into the fire of entrenched loyal troops. However, their actions, which at the time were passed off as vague protests against the corruption and stagnation of the power elite, found somewhat more concrete expression a few years later. And their ideas, reformulated by more mature minds, provided the ideological core of the revolt of 1930, which marked the end of the "Old Republic."

The São Paulo uprising of 1924, known in history as the Tenente (Lieutenant) Revolt, further affirmed the fact that there were elements in the army whose social-economic thinking was in advance of the dominant civilian leadership. The *tenente* revolutionaries demanded minimum salaries for laborers and regulation of work for women and children, but they were unsympathetic to anarcho-syndicalism. They approved limited capitalism and democratic liberalism but favored state ownership of natural resources. They opposed the latifundia system, which they associated with economic backwardness and rigidity. They held that government was a benevolent authority and that the armed forces had a redemptive role to fulfill. They believed further that the government should be expanded, the better to protect the common man, and that government should also be the principal agent in forming an integrated Brazilian nationality and in developing the nation's vast interior. They pushed Brazilian nationalism into new frontiers, to the deep concern of their superiors and the civilian elite, whose profound conviction that Brazil's welfare and coffee were inseparable made them at heart internationalists. The *tenente* program, commonly referred to as *tenentismo,* thus combined modernization and progressivism in the social-economic area with pseudo-scientific rationalization and authoritarianism in the political sphere. In evolving such a program the *tenentes* were reflecting simultaneously the thinking of the middle- and lower-sector elements from which they came, their technical military training, and the tradition of regimentation in their profession.

The 1924 revolt lasted only a few weeks and many of the young officers were forced into exile, but *tenentismo* survived and was popularized during the 5,000-mile march of the Coluna Invicta (Invincible Column) led by Luiz Carlos Prestes, in the backlands in defiance of the best efforts of the Brazilian army. But more important, *tenentismo* was made to symbolize both protest and self-sacrifice in the public mind. Before

Prestes crossed over into Bolivia, convinced that the rural population was not yet ready to be aroused, *tenentismo,* despite its authoritarian content, had attracted many civilian, middle-sector adherents. They held in common with the young officers the conviction that the ruling elite, associated as it was with the large estates, monoculture, "imperialism," and corrupt electoral machines, was incapable of injecting new life into the nation. It was this civilian middle-sector backing that kept *tenentismo* alive and then made it the ideological substance of the Liberal Alliance formed in 1930 to combat the political monopoly of the elite, particularly the elite of São Paulo. And when the Liberal Alliance chose to revolt after it was "cheated" of victory in the presidential election of 1930, many of the *tenentes* who had remained in exile returned to direct the military campaigns.

When rebel bands took to the field and it became apparent that the sympathies of the public were overwhelmingly on the side of the revolutionaries, senior officers of the regular forces determined to remove the legal regime and turn the government over provisionally to Getulio Vargas, in whose name the civil wars were being carried on. Since the senior officers had vigorously opposed reincorporating the *tenentes* into the army and had in fact kept them in exile for several years, and since the evidence strongly suggests that the military leadership originally had been content to accept the electoral returns as they were reported by the reactionary and corrupt civilian element with whom the armed forces had cooperated throughout most of the post–World War I years, one must search elsewhere for the explanation of the armed forces' response in this situation. Proceeding from the possible to the probable, the arguments seem to run somewhat as follows: (1) The officers felt that, with the country returned to peace, they could take over the movement. (2) There was nothing in Vargas's background to suggest that he posed a serious threat to the status quo, and the armed forces therefore trusted him with power. (3) If Vargas and his closest advisers, who included some *tenentes,* had been interested in violent reform, they could have been countered by the many intellectuals who were in the Liberal Alliance not because of an interest in radical change but because they wanted to see the administration of the republic reformed. (4) The officers reasoned that in view of the public sympathy for the rebels, putting down the revolt and sustaining the old group in power would not be worth the price, if it could be accomplished at all. (5) The officers recognized that the struggle for power had permitted a vacuum to form, and in their assumed role as "arbiters of the nation's destiny in the social convulsions which disturbed normal Brazilian life" they were obliged to return the country to the rule of law, and this could be done safely and effectively only by giving power to the rebels.

Of the five propositions set forth above, only the last two need elaboration; the first one cannot be sustained in view of the apolitical role the national armed forces played before and immediately following the revolt, and the possibilities presented in the second and third are in fact embodied in and superseded by the last proposition. If the officers based their decision on the fourth proposition, they were acting in accordance with good Brazilian military tradition. The evidence overwhelmingly supports the conclusion that before 1930, as well as since then, the Brazilian armed forces in this century have sought consciously to avoid moves that would provoke bitter popular resistance. They have not always succeeded, but their record is good, and it is better than in any Spanish American republic except Uruguay.

If their decision was based upon the thought contained in proposition five—that the armed forces were determined to exercise a moderating power, as Pedro had done during the empire—then the officers were reaffirming what was the armed forces' most strongly held political tenet. As far as they were concerned the civilians had failed to resolve their differences and the country was faced with the question of "legality," which they felt obliged to decide in the interest of restoring order.

As recently as August 1962, during the dispute between

the executive and legislative branches of the government over the return to the presidential system, highly placed armed forces officials stated that the services might eventually be compelled to arbitrate the dispute but that in the meantime they would not prejudice the democratic process by taking sides, nor should their loyalty to the President, which was both proper and normal, be construed as prevailing over their loyalty to the government as a whole.[6] They were saying to the civilians what the armed forces have said many times in Brazil: "Settle your differences without exhausting yourselves in division or we will settle them for you." In 1960 one of the half-dozen top Brazilian army officers told this author that the armed services would have to play the role of "guardians of the constitution" for the next twenty years at least.

The revolution in 1930 propelled the armed forces into the center of Brazilian politics and the locus of power has resided in them ever since. Getulio Vargas, during his fifteen-year dictatorship, was never able to extricate himself from their influence. Since 1945, when the dictatorship was terminated, the president has had to have his *"dispositivo militar,"* a group of officers who "guarantee him." The record of the officers has been spotty. On several occasions they have seemed to play well the role they have assumed. On other occasions they have taxed the patience of those civilians who looked to the armed forces to guarantee the democratic process. More significantly, perhaps, within the last decade the representatives of the armed forces again have become increasingly prone to take public positions on policy conflicts rather than being content to arbitrate the differences that arise from civilian debate.

During the 1930's and early 1940's the armed forces drained the reservoir of good will they had filled by participating in the overthrow of the old regime. Vargas briefly catered to the *tenentes* who swarmed into administrative posts without reference to their capabilities or experience, but many of them had

---

[6] *Visão* (August 17, 1962), p. 15.

deserted him by 1932 and supported the São Paulo revolt. The dictator, meanwhile, appeased the regular officers by spending recklessly on guns, armored vehicles, airplanes, and naval vessels. When the São Paulo revolt broke out in 1932, the main body of the armed forces remained loyal to the government, but large numbers of officers individually deserted to the rebel forces. Shortly after the uprising was suppressed, a scattering of officers and non-coms became involved in the abortive communist revolt of 1935, which was staged in an effort to seize control of the army preparatory to taking over the entire government. In that revolt the pro-communist forces relied almost entirely upon the regular forces for their fire power. The anniversary of the *putsch* is observed each year and serves to strengthen the military's aversion to communism; army officers who served in action against the communist attempt are entitled to a special one-rank promotion upon retirement. Two years after the revolt, and partly as a reaction against communism, both the regular forces and the *tenente* contingent, represented by Cordeiro de Farias, Juarez Távora, and Gomes, among others, did not raise their voices against Vargas when he decreed the "Estado Novo," which was in essence a neo-fascist corporate state with much of its fascist paraphernalia, including a "new nationalism" borrowed from the Old World. Then the armed forces sat back as the dictator redeemed his pledge of a "political renovation" by imposing severe curbs on civilian political activities.

By the outbreak of World War II some officers close to Vargas, such as Góes Monteiro, had become fascinated by nazism and fascism and they tried, without success, to dissuade the dictator, who had earlier been disposed rather favorably toward Germany and Italy, from aligning Brazil with the West. But once in the war, the prestige of the services soared as Brazilian troops became the first from Latin America to fight in Europe, and by the war's end not only had the Brazilian military come of age as a fighting force but its leadership was clearly pro-democratic. Meanwhile, the officers' nationalistic aspirations were satisfied somewhat by United States commit-

ments to provide machinery, capital, and technicians for the
construction of an integrated iron and steel plant at Volta Redonda following Brazil's leasing of land for airstrips along the
"Hump." There were striking manifestations of the new military mind during the half-decade after the end of the war.
In October 1945, officers, reflecting the general repugnance of
the Western World to totalitarianism following the defeat of
Germany and Italy, forced Vargas into retirement when it appeared that he might renege on his promise to hold general
elections. Then they turned the government over to Chief Justice Linhares of the Supreme Court, who ordered that the election be held as scheduled.

The public, uncertain of what had occurred during the
Vargas dictatorship, instinctively turned to the military. Both
major parties named armed forces generals to head their presidential tickets and at the polls the public voted the colorless and
unimaginative Eurico Dutra into office. The General's administration devoted itself to taking the nation's pulse as it returned to the democratic system. The armed forces tended to
withdraw from public view, and their representatives remained
undecided as to the meaning of the vastly broadened political
base as indicated by the extended electorate and the strong
showing of the communists, who captured approximately 10
per cent of the vote in the 1945 and 1947 elections.[7]

There was a recrudescence of military politics in 1950, and
since then the armed forces have at ever-shortening intervals
served notice that they consider themselves "the court of final
political resort." Vargas had to have the tacit consent of the
military in order to return to power through presidential elections in 1950. In 1953 some officers, in spite of strong opposition from their colleagues, intervened openly in political affairs
for the first time since 1945 and in February 1954 forced the
dismissal of Vargas's Minister of Labor João Goulart, who had
been appealing demagogically to labor. And after an air force
officer was accidentally shot in what appears to have been an

----

[7] There was a 400 per cent increase in the number of qualified voters
between 1930 and 1945.

attempt masterminded by members of Vargas's bodyguard on the life of Vargas-baiting Carlos Lacerda, editor of *Tribuna da imprensa,* and now conservative, publicity-seeking governor of Guanabara state, dominant groups in the three services demanded Vargas's immediate withdrawal from government. Rather than accede to their ultimatum, the President committed suicide on August 24. (1954)

Although civilians were permitted to head the government between Vargas's death and the election and inauguration of a new president, the armed forces were in complete control despite the fact that they failed in their demands for a single candidate. After the election in which Juscelino Kubitschek, the presidential candidate of the Social Democratic Party (PSD), and João Goulart, the vice-presidential candidate of the Brazilian Workers' Party (PTB), were victorious, an army-led "preventive coup" or "anti-coup"—strongly opposed by a large majority of navy and air force officers and an important group of army officers—guaranteed that Kubitschek would be inaugurated. Five officers served in Kubitschek's cabinet and during his presidency, Brazil spent more funds on the armed forces than on all public development programs, despite the fact that massive development programs were the hallmark of his administration.

Both the PSD and PTB nominated Marshal Henrique Texeira Lott as their presidential candidate in 1960. Goulart, who was named by the PTB to run for re-election as vice-president, in his acceptance speech said, "With Marshal Lott and [Minister of War] Marshal Denys, no one will fail to respect the will of the people," thereby inviting the armed forces to be the guarantors of the electoral process.

Marshal Lott was trounced in his bid for the presidency in 1960 by colorful, erratic Jânio Quadros,[8] just as General Juarez Távora had been beaten by Kubitschek in 1955 and General Eduardo Gomes by Vargas in 1950. But the public's rejection of Lott as presidential material no more deterred the mili-

---

[8] Quadros received 5,576,040 votes, which was a 48 per cent plurality in a three-way race. He defeated Lott by approximately 1.5 million votes.

tary than had the setbacks suffered by Juarez Távora and Gomes.[9] Refusal of the armed forces to support his demands for broader powers was apparently one of the factors that led President Quadros to submit his resignation unexpectedly in August 1961, less than seven months after his inauguration. Thereupon the three top-ranking military men—one from each of the services—in Quadros's last cabinet moved quickly to prevent Vice-President Goulart, who was at the time on a state visit in the Far East, from returning to Brazil and fulfilling his constitutional duties. The ministers soon found themselves in a minority. The National Security Council, made up of high-ranking military and civilian officials, issued a statement disassociating itself from the anti-Goulart manifesto of the service ministers, the general public voiced its disapproval, and the commander of the Third Army, in an act which served to emphasize the growing dissatisfaction within officer ranks, declared for Goulart. When the ministers found themselves without widespread support, they first wavered and they then drew back from plunging the country into civil war. In good Brazilian fashion a compromise followed which converted the country from a presidential to a parliamentary system with a severely circumscribed Goulart as president. But Goulart was not satisfied and began immediately to campaign for a return to the presidential system. The differing public statements of the officers during the debate on the issue not only called attention once again to the serious rivalry between the various branches of the armed services and within the army; it gave further grounds for believing that the Brazilian armed forces since 1954 have been moving in the direction that their Spanish American counterparts have historically pursued.[10] It is too early to guess whether this trend will be followed to its

[9] There was bitter opposition to Lott's candidacy in the air force and the navy, and the army was far from united in support of him.

[10] It should be recalled that while the Brazilian armed forces have acted less responsibly in recent years, the military in many of the Spanish American countries have become somewhat more responsible, hence the gap between the Brazilian forces and their Spanish American counterparts has narrowed noticeably.

logical conclusion before an increasing lack of military agreement on vital issues destroys the military's capacity to continue its traditional role as the moderator of constitutional processes.

The armed forces' influence over policy formulation has been further enhanced through numerous individual officers holding elective and appointive positions at the national, state, and municipal levels. The extent to which these officers are distributed in government is suggested by a document prepared at the request of the author by an armed forces officer who must go unnamed, but who may be considered highly reliable. The document, dated May 20, 1959, begins as follows: "The number of Brazilian military now in the fields you mention must be in the hundreds.[11] There are no lists of such personnel available, but I will name as many of the more important ones as I can readily recall." According to the list that follows, officers were then holding the following key positions in national agencies related to industrial development: Minister of Transportation and Public Works; Director-General, National Mail and Telegraph Service; Executive Commission, National Post and Telegraph Planning; President, Radio Technical Commission; President, Merchant Marine Commission; Administrator, Leopoldina Railway Company (state-owned); President, National Petroleum Council; President, National Steel Company; President, National Alkali Company; President, National Petroleum Company; Superintendent, National Oil Tanker Fleet; Director General, Civil Aviation; Secretary General, National Coordinating Council of Food Supply; President, National Executive Commission for Coal Production Planning; Director, Food Supply Service; Chairman, National Price Control Board; President, National Commission on Nuclear Energy; President, National Transportation Council; "plus many more, particularly in Petrobras, the National Petroleum Company." In the National Legislature of the government there were two generals, one admiral, and one colonel,

---

[11] I have another source for September 1961 that fixes at 1,100 the number of officers on detached duty and holding civilian positions.

"plus at least twenty others who have not been active in the armed forces recently." At the state level a general was governor of Pará, a colonel was governor of Bahia, and two colonels held the highest political positions in the Territories of Rondônia and Fernando da Noronha, "plus an estimated fifty or more who are serving as state Directors of Public Safety and Public Works, etc." In the Federal District, a general and a colonel were respectively Chief and Assistant Chief of Police and a colonel was Fire Chief, "plus an estimated twenty-five more armed forces officers in police and fire units." The informant adds, "The police chiefs of all major cities are ex-colonels or generals." Although the source declined to estimate the number of ex-armed forces officers in private industry, he did observe, "I am sure that there are a great many, particularly in the engineering field."

In response to a question regarding why officers held positions in the civilian area, he wrote, "The main reason for so many military men accepting non-military positions is financial. . . . In most of the governmental positions listed above, an officer can draw one-half of his active-duty service pay in addition to the generally higher non-military governmental salary. Furthermore, he receives half credit applied to his army service for the time spent in jobs which have been decreed by the president to be 'of military interest.' The main reasons for the selection of officers for such positions, in my opinion, are their generally higher educational level, their administrative ability, and their honesty."

Other than the impact that nazism and fascism had on the armed forces and on Brazil in general, the military's changing conception of its responsibilities in non-military fields since 1930 can be explained in terms of the profound but uneven transformation that the republic has undergone. In turn, the developments most directly affecting the military mind lie within three major areas: (1) regionalism, (2) the rise of competing social-economic groups, and (3) the emergence of a perverted nationalism with a distinct economic bias.

Regionalism represents, as it has historically, a formidable obstacle to Brazil's development. When Vargas came to power in 1930 the republic gave the impression of seemingly infinite space fragmented into a number of distinct areas, each consciously seeking maximum self-sufficiency rather than coordinated growth through national unity. Since then, improved transportation, mass media of communication, and large-scale internal migration have contributed somewhat to the breakdown of sectional peculiarities. But at the same time uneven economic development of the regions has served to keep alive animosities that weaken the nation. Plagued by drought, critical shortages of transportation, power, and industry, its sugar, cocoa, and vegetable oil undersold on the world markets, the "Hump" has been too weak economically to respond to the relatively feeble assistance provided at first from Rio de Janeiro and now from Brasilia. The great Amazon drainage basin has not lived up to expectations. It may be a sleeping giant—a term often applied to the republic as a whole—which will have to await still further advances in technology and science before it will yield up its resources. It remains to be seen if the new national capital at Brasilia can serve as a hub from which will radiate the roads and economic stimuli required to develop the largely unexploited, temperate hinterland. Only the center-south has prospered; its three states, São Paulo, Guanabara, and Rio de Janeiro, produce over 50 per cent of the national income and pay over 60 per cent of the revenues collected by the national government. Paraná, Rio Grande do Sul, and Minas Gerais, also in the center-south, are expanding rapidly.

The armed forces become involved when provincialism is reflected politically, as when representatives of the economically advanced states oppose broad programs that their constituents would have to finance, and thereby make it difficult to get a clear-cut consensus on broad issues of public policy. In such circumstances the armed forces, national in scope as they are, and charged as they are with the nation's defense, do not feel obliged to stand aside indefinitely in favor of politicians whose thinking does not transcend issues of interest to their patrons. On such occasions the officers conceive of their role as "consolidators in a federation beset by regionalism." Furthermore, a disproportionate number of officers, as in the case of Spanish America, have come from the lesser-developed areas of the country, the areas that have felt most the need for federal assistance. Thus it was that officers during the 1930's favored Vargas in his successful effort to curb the autonomy of the states; today they support federal financing of development projects, such as for roads and power, that contribute to over-all national development. The national outlook of the armed forces ordinarily places them politically closer to the president of the country, who is elected by popular vote and who is more likely to hold a national point of view, than to legislators, who find it difficult to resist local pressures.

Still, it is apparent that the social, regional, and economic divergencies which characterize Brazilian society are reflected in the military establishment, and there is some evidence that military personnel tend to group themselves more or less unconsciously along regional lines and to maintain some of their natural ties with the regions from which they come. As long as regionalism continues to be a factor in Brazilian society, tendencies toward division along regional lines may be expected to continue in the armed forces, although almost certainly on a decreasing scale.

The ideological crosscurrents resulting from the emergence of industrialists and urban laborers as politically competing groups after 1930 were of interest to the Brazilian military from the first and had become an overriding concern by 1950. Prior to Vargas's seizure of the government, the latifundia oligarchy, occasionally assisted by the mercantile oligarchy with whom they often had family ties, held a firm monopoly on political power. Aspirants to power who reached their goal were automatically absorbed into the oligarchy-controlled Republican Party. The uprisings of 1922 and 1924, the Prestes Column, the Liberal Alliance, and the Revolution of 1930 were all forerunners of the struggle that had been waged by the new groups against the latifundia oligarchy, who, through their control of state and municipal government, continued to exercise power at the national level far out of proportion to their numbers or to their total contribution to the economy. The unpredictability of the armed forces in this heated struggle has served to make Brazil one of the most politically complex countries of the Western Hemisphere.

The armed forces were able to develop cordial relations with the rising industrial community while remaining on good terms with the landed elements. Reflecting their historical relationship with the agricultural sector, the armed forces were reluctant to support rapid industrial expansion during the early years of the Vargas dictatorship. However, by the outbreak of World War II, the officers had discarded, in principle, their historic willingness to rely upon foreign sources for war matériel in favor of a policy calling for an industrial buildup at home, in the hope that domestic industry might eventually satisfy all of the nation's military and civilian requirements. But the rate of expansion that the armed forces favored after World War II was such that it could not be met by private Brazilian capital, and as an alternative the armed forces urged direct state participation in basic industries such as railroads, electric power, petroleum, and steel, "the backbone of contemporary civilization."

The military's advocacy of state intervention in the economic sector might have led to a conflict of interest with the industrialists, but two considerations operated to prevent such an occurrence. In the first place, Brazilian private industrial capital always had been attracted to the production and distribution of consumer goods rather than to the basic industries which, as a consequence, had been neglected or had been left largely to foreign capital. Thus when the armed forces called upon the state to assume responsibility for developing the basic industries, the officers were nowhere treading upon the interests of local private capital. In the second place, the moneyed class simply did not have the investment capital needed to finance the rapid expansion of heavy industry, which was, of course, very much the situation that existed throughout Spanish America.

The armed forces welcomed industrial expansion, but they have been deeply distrustful, for the most part, of the rapidly growing and increasingly articulate urban labor forces that have been an inevitable by-product of industrial growth. When Vargas first came to power the labor force was numerically small, weakly organized, and politically ineffective. The dictator, conscious of the privileged group's attitude toward the workers, paid little attention to them during his early years in office, and they in turn were unresponsive to his occasional gestures of good will. But when the institution of the neo-fascist Estado Novo in 1938 cost him support among the middle and upper classes, he opportunistically set out to capture labor's backing with promises of better wages, shorter hours, more jobs, and by appealing to their latent nationalism. The *tenentes* applauded the dictator's decision, but officers of the regular armed forces looked askance at the maneuver. By the end of the war Vargas had made the proletariat an indispensable element of social cooperation, and labor was firmly tied to and dependent on the government. The dictator's ouster produced stirrings of labor discontent, but the workers did not dare challenge the armed forces' action.

By 1950 there were approximately five million urban workers of all kinds, most of whom were crowded in the half-dozen largest cities. They were generally underpaid and underfed, as were workers elsewhere in Latin America. They were politically unsophisticated because their leaders and irresponsible politicians had consciously kept them that way. But despite their political immaturity they had come to realize that politics was a means of getting what they wanted, and as they qualified for the vote the electorate swelled quickly to twelve million. The new voters were easily appealed to by demagogues, including students, who were in revolt against the established order. As voters they noisily but with little violence demanded more of the comforts and benefits that the privileged elements took for granted. They gave bread, shoes, and freedom precedence over God, country, and family.

It was the clamor of the urban masses and the proliferation of politicians demagogically soliciting their votes that brought the military back into politics in 1950. Their response to what they viewed as a threat to the status quo was to make Vargas's return to the presidency contingent upon guarantees by him that he would not attempt to overstep the constitution by going directly to the masses for support. That was what Vargas, who had won election as "the father of the poor," in effect did in 1953 when he assigned Goulart to bring about a rapid resurgence of popular support for the government, with reckless promises to the workers. Early in 1954 the armed forces determined that Vargas could not be trusted and as "defenders of the constitution" they drew up a memorandum of grievances against the administration. Thereafter the officers were relentless in their attacks upon the administration and finally drove the President to take his own life.

Vargas's death marked the beginning of a new era in relations between the armed forces and labor. Up to that moment, despite occasional indications of radicalism in the Clube Militar (Officers' Club), the military, for all intents and purposes, had presented a united front against the workers. Since then an ever-growing number of officers, most notably in the army, have aligned themselves with political elements who favor incorporating the workers more fully into the body politic.

At least until 1960 Marshal Henrique Lott was the principal spokesman for those officers who were prepared to grant the masses a greater political role. Lott came into public prominence when, as Minister of War, he gave unstinting support to Café Filho, Vargas's successor in office, for his policy of refusing to interfere in the electoral process or to prevent the election of a Vargas-type president. When officers representing the air force, navy, and more conservative elements of the army and civilian groups threatened to prevent the inauguration of Kubitschek, who had won election as the heir of Vargas, Lott engineered the "anti-coup" or "preventive coup" to assure that Kubitschek would be permitted to take office. The Minister's action had a two-fold impact. It produced wounds in the military that had not healed eight years later, and it initiated the courtship of labor by powerful and perhaps dominant elements in the army.

Lott, who had resigned as War Minister to run for the presidency in 1960, was replaced by Conservative Marshal Odilio Denys. After Jânio Quadros's landslide presidential victory over Lott, Denys was joined in the cabinet by equally conservative navy and air force ministers. When Quadros resigned the presidency in August 1961, it was this triumvirate of officers who, in violation of the constitution, sought to prevent labor-backed, leftist-leaning Vice-President Goulart from becoming President. The air force and navy stood firm behind the ministers, but the army split and those favoring constitutionality were sufficiently strong that the ministers backed down rather than risk the possible consequences of resorting to force in order to see that their directives were carried out. Thus in a clear test of strength—the second in six years—the Brazilian army by its actions refuted the oft-repeated allegation that the military in Latin America is committed to the defense of the conservative position. And afterward they were consistent when they upheld the results of the plebiscite held on January 6, 1963, that by a five-to-one margin favored a return to the presidential system.

As of early 1963 it appeared that the army's response to the growing power of the masses had resulted from a conviction that those groups must be given a greater voice in government. Lott and certain other officers may have acted opportunistically or demagogically in their desire to achieve political recognition, but such a charge could not be leveled at the armed forces as a whole. Officers had accepted with equanimity the people's mandate when they voted for Quadros rather than Lott. They had refrained from taking advantage of the extreme instability resulting from the severe deterioration of the nation's economy and the ineffectiveness of the parliamentary system to assume direct control of the government. Still, one could hardly think that the opposition elements in the armed forces would remain content with their respective roles. Civilian politics were becoming progressively complex as students injected themselves more forcefully into the political picture and poverty-stricken, politically immature rural workers clamored for recognition. Privileged groups were wondering if they had been pushed to the point where they must strike back or surrender. Officers were wearying of standing by as the nation marked time; some of them would favor using the armed forces to renovate the country, much as the *tenentes* had proposed to do four decades earlier. Within all of the more politically conscious groups there was an increasing feeling that Brazil had not lived up to expectations. Short-run disappointments were reinforcing more profound self-doubts and anxieties to produce an ever-sharpening sense of hostility toward politicians as a class. In many a Latin American republic, where weak governments mean a strong military, such a combination of circumstances, at least until recently, would have constituted an open invitation to intervention by the armed forces on their own account. In Brazil tradition argued against such a development, but it was apparent that if its officers were to continue on the course that they had pursued since Vargas's death—a course which involved them more and more in policy conflicts and less and less with legality—intervention on their own behalf sooner or later would become a necessity which no amount of civilian façade could conceal. There was no question but that the Brazilian armed forces had been moving in the direction of their Spanish American counterparts. The only question was whether or not over the short range the victorious element would have popular opinion on its side, as in 1889 and 1930, or whether conservative elements would triumph over the popular will, as happened in 1954.

The course that the army follows in all probability will be determined in the Clube Militar, a recreational and mutual benefit society comprised of a majority of Brazilian army officers. Established in 1887 in an atmosphere of crisis, as a direct result of the military's desire to express itself on the issues of slavery and republicanism, the Clube historically has provided a forum for debates on political issues between army factions. It was closed temporarily by President Pessôa (1919–22), when its president, Marshal Hermes da Fonseca, recommended that military units stationed in Pernambuco ignore presidential orders relating to an internal security matter in that state. Later the Clube was a hotbed of *tenentismo*. It was kept under a fairly tight rein during the Vargas dictatorship, but since the early 1950's it has reflected the crosscurrents of social and political thought found in the army. Debate in the Clube becomes particularly heated during the elections, which are held biennially (in even years) and are usually contested by two slates of candidates, one of which ordinarily represents the views of the War Minister, while the other is likely to speak for the opposition. On occasion a successful candidate may claim to be apolitical, but in most instances the election is fought out and the outcome determined by views of the candidates on matters of national policy rather than army welfare. The War Minister's candidate, ordinarily an officer with a general's rank, is usually but not invariably successful. The Clube thus has served at least two purposes. Watched closely by the Brazilian press and politicians, it is at all times a microcosm of the attitudes and antagonisms of the various factions within the officer corps, and it provides a sounding board for the opposition, usually made up of younger officers of field command rank. Serving these functions as it does, the Clube tends to discourage the formation in the Brazilian army of the "secret" organizations that have been so commonplace and disruptive in the armies of Spanish America.

Nationalism, the third of the developments affecting the military's conception of its non-military role, has been the most significant addition to the ideological field since 1930. Brazil's major political ideology for over a decade, nationalism has now become institutionalized. But in its current social appeals and economic-political emphasis, this nationalism is a far cry from the type inherited from "the old regime." Three decades ago nationalism was practically a monopoly of a few intellectuals, who were interested in it primarily as an abstraction. And by the outbreak of the war, Vargas, taking his cue from the nazis and fascists and with encouragement from the *tenentes,* had usurped the ideology from the intellectuals and assigned civilian bureaucrats to give it a concreteness which would be meaningful to the urban masses and as such could be translated into political capital.

Since the war nationalism has undergone three major modifications, more or less simultaneously. First, as a sense of personal identification with the country, it has become generalized to the point where it is felt by individuals belonging to all sectors of society. This in turn has given the Brazilian people a sense of destiny, and they have come to think of their country as a future world power. Second, nationalism has been given a sharpened economic focus, and as such has become the central rallying point for all those who feel that the nation has not lived up to its potential. Third, the hard core of nationalism's support has passed from the civilian bureaucrats to the armed forces, and they have been primarily responsible for its institutionalization.

The military became the depository of nationalism largely by default. The elite groups, constrained as they were by regional obligations and still unable to think about things not related to the coffee market, remained essentially internationalists. They looked for closer ties with the United States, at a time when the submerged peoples of Africa and Asia were insisting upon their political and economic emancipation. The communists, who would have been logical contenders for the role of nationalist leaders, were outlawed as the cold war became hotter. Labor, as noted above, remained under the domination of the state. Thus only the armed forces possessed the necessary qualifications. Their organization, as has been pointed out, was national in scope and they had primary responsibility for national defense. Officers had associated themselves with local industry during the war and claimed the iron and steel plant at Volta Redonda as their brainchild. They were trusted by the industrial community. They needed only an issue, and they were given one when the cries of the underdeveloped areas made protection of natural resources a national obligation of the first order. The officers took control of Petrobras, the national oil monopoly, and made it the symbol of the republic's determination to become economically independent.

Until 1955 Brazilian nationalism was of a mild variety. It involved primarily identifying the individual with the nation and as such it might have been termed patriotism. It seldom manifested the xenophobic or anti-American characteristics associated with nationalism in certain other countries of the developing world. Public opinion and national legislation favorable to the more nationalistic elements in the industrial community and the armed forces were countered by quite close relations between the governments and the armed forces of Brazil and the United States. The nature of Brazilian nationalism during this phase of its development is explained by the fact that it was regulated by the armed forces.

Since 1955 a number of developments have lent themselves to a somewhat more xenophobic, anti-American type of nationalism. As was discussed above, there has grown up in the armed forces an element that is prepared to give the radical masses a greater share in government. The World War II generation of officers, who had a close attachment to the United States, is rapidly being supplanted by a new generation of officers who have not formed such an attachment and who are less inclined than their superiors to associate themselves with the United States. The rapid rise of the prestige of the U.S.S.R. following its launching of the first satellite in 1957, and the subsequent success of Fidel Castro, with Soviet support, in withstanding the pressures applied from the United States, have encouraged the growth of neutralism vis-à-vis the East-West conflict. Neutralism, a by-product of nationalism, may have become more important than the nationalist ideology itself. In early 1964 it was still too soon to determine for sure whether or not the armed forces would influence neutralism to the same extent that they had influenced nationalism, but the probability was that they would not, simply because the students and the rural masses, as well as traditional pressure groups, were insisting that they also share the demagogic political capital that neutralism promised.

VIII

THE PUBLIC IMAGE OF THE
BRAZILIAN MILITARY

ALTHOUGH SCHOLARLY publications and the press in the
United States have often criticized the military forces of Latin
America in general, they have usually treated the Brazilian
armed forces cordially. The late Clarence H. Haring, a professor of Latin American history at Harvard University writing in the mid-1950's, observed that "since 1930 the army, in
spite of recent vagaries, has on the whole thrown its weight
on the side of the democratic government."[1] Alan K. Manchester of Duke University, an authority on Latin America
and a long-time resident of Brazil, left no doubt about his
opinion of the Brazilian armed forces when he wrote, in 1955:
"That the nation has been able to survive the incredibly rapid
transition to industrialization without discarding its basic political structure is due in no small part to the army. Under the
leadership of the General Staff the army has been the stabilizing factor which has stopped the political pendulum from
swinging too far from the center. It terminated the [Vargas]
dictatorship when the need for the regime was over and stood
aside while the civilian leaders laid the foundations for a real
democracy. It stepped in again when the political leadership
swung too far to the opposite extreme. It has played a conservative, stabilizing role since its rise to decisive influence in
1930."[2]

[1] *Empire in Brazil, A New World Experiment with Monarchy*
(Cambridge, Mass., 1958), p. 171.
[2] "Brazil in Transition," *South Atlantic Quarterly*, LIV (April
1955), 175.

The economist Morton S. Baratz, writing about the same time as Manchester, declared: "Time and again the military men have led the resistance against aggressive politicians who have appeared bent on subverting or destroying the Republic. It is equally significant that on each of such occasions the army has eschewed golden opportunities to seize power in its own name and to establish a military dictatorship."[3] A professor of economics in a major United States university, who taught in Brazil for three years, explained in an interview with the author in São Paulo in 1960 that the influence of the armed forces in state-owned agencies has been possible because "Brazil has a demoralized civil service," and "military morale is better than that of the civilian sector."

Leslie Lipson, a political scientist at the University of California, has written: "The armed forces have not lacked influence in civic affairs, but their actions have generally been restrained and have often assisted the constitutional regime. The Army helped to stabilize the infant republic in the 1890's and was instrumental in procuring Vargas's resignation in 1945. Along with the Air Force, it contributed to the events that led to his downfall and suicide in 1954 after the Interregnum. For the most part the generals have stayed in the background, buttressing the civilian authorities as occasion required."[4] Charles Morazé, in his *Les trois âges du Brésil: essai de politique* (1954), spoke of the "cult of virtue incarnated in the Army" during the early years of the republic.

The press in the United States has been equally friendly. Herbert L. Matthews, a Latin American expert for the *New York Times* and no friend of the Latin American military, declared in 1954: "Brazil has one of the most honorable records in Latin America so far as its military are concerned. The Army helped Vargas in 1930 and forced him out in 1945, but the officers never tried to take power."[5] On the occasion of

[3] "The Crisis in Brazil," *Social Research*, XXII (1955), 347–361.
[4] "Brazil," *Encyclopaedia Britannica* (Chicago, 1961).
[5] "Brazil in Travail," *Foreign Policy Bulletin*, XXXIV (December 1954), 47.

Marshal Lott's "preventive putsch" of 1955, which was by Lott's own admission extra-constitutional, the *New York Times* editorialized: "The lightning coup . . . was praiseworthy because its intention was to enforce a democratic electoral decision and to uphold the constitution. Only twice in the last thirty years has the military intervened and each time it was to enforce constitutionality, not to overthrow it, as is normally the case in Latin America. On neither of those occasions did the commanding officers of the armed forces take any power themselves, although they could have, and the same was true yesterday."[6] A few months later the *Christian Science Monitor* noted approvingly that "The [Brazilian] military have long considered themselves the 'elite' . . . removing governments they consider dangerous or incapable, but always handing direction back to the civilians."[7]

Reputable Brazilian novelists, playwrights, and poets may well have attacked the armed forces for interference in the civilian areas, but except for an occasional passage in the humanistic review *Anhembi,* such attacks seem to be quite rare. Neither Erico Verissimo, one of Brazil's most illustrious contemporary novelists, in his cleverly written *Brazilian Literature, an Outline* (1945), nor Samuel Putnam, in his brilliantly interpretive *Marvelous Journey: A Survey of Four Centuries of Brazilian Writing* (1948), mentions a single work concerned with the Brazilian milieu since 1870 that suggests an author's serious concern with militarism in his own country.[8] On the basis of those two surveys and others that treat Brazil in the larger context of Latin American literature, it appears safe to say that Brazil has had no critics of the military of the stature of Mariano Azuela, Gregorio López y Fuentes, Rómulo Gallegos, Jorge Icaza, or Ciro Alegría.

Brazilian scholars, too, have either held their fire on the

---

[6] *New York Times,* November 12, 1955, p. 18.

[7] *Christian Science Monitor,* March 3, 1956.

[8] At the time he wrote *Brazilian Literature,* however, Verissimo was personally apprehensive about the use of political power by the military and felt that the proclamation of the republic under army auspices had set a dangerous precedent.

military or presented them in a favorable light. Neither Fernando de Azevedo in his *A cultura brasileira* (1943) nor Pedro Calmon in his numerous studies of Brazil's social evolution found occasion to criticize the military's participation in the political life of the republic. João Ribeiro Fernandes's secondary textbook *História do Brasil* went through twelve editions between 1900 and 1929 without criticizing the political role of the armed forces. José Mario Bello's *História da República* (third edition, 1956) occasionally takes the military to task but in no way gives the impression that officers should have forsaken politics. Moreover, the editors of the Brazilian government and history section of the *Handbook of Latin American Studies,* a bibliographical guide prepared under the auspices of the Hispanic Foundation of the Library of Congress, which has appeared annually since 1936, as of 1961 had not listed a single scholarly study, and only two political tracts, of an antimilitary nature.

The Brazilian armed forces, moreover, can point to considerable comment in their favor from novelists, poets, scholars, and the local press. Alfredo d'Escragnolle, Viscount of Taunay, perhaps Brazil's ablest writer of the 19th century, was the first of many Brazilian novelists who, after the Paraguayan War, helped to create a favorable image of the military. Like Ricardo Palma of Peru, who found his military heroes in the awful defeat that his country suffered at the hands of Chile, Taunay chose courage in adversity as the theme of his *A retirada da Laguna*; in brilliant descriptive passages he praised the dignity and glory of a Brazilian army corps, which, harassed by the enemy and plagued by hunger, cholera, exhaustion, and torrential rains, avoided annihilation as it withdrew northward for six weeks after being driven from the Paraguayan outpost of Laguna. In appreciation of Taunay's efforts, the Brazilian army named an annual literary award in his honor.

Roughly a half a century after the retreat from Laguna another military venture caught the imagination of the Brazilian literary community. Its hero was Luiz Carlos Prestes, a long-time leader of the Communist Party in Brazil but in the mid-1920's a young army engineer in revolt against his seniors. He won lasting fame after the suppression of the *tenente* revolt of 1924, when his "Invincible Column," marching from Rio Grande do Sul to Bahia, fought off the regular armed forces sent against him. Forgetting that he was in fact an outlaw, common men left their homes and jobs to join him, and men of letters poured out praise and poems in recognition of his revolt against tradition.

Between the retreat from Laguna and the creation of Prestes's army, Brazil was stunned by a "rebellion" at Canudos, located in the remote interior of the state of Bahia, and the headquarters for the mystic Antônio Maciel and his followers, who were drawn from all sectors of the backlands population. The "rebellion" was kept alive throughout most of 1896 and 1897, with three army expeditions suffering defeat before a fourth succeeded. Euclides da Cunha narrated the episode in *Os sertões* (1902), which is generally acknowledged to be Brazil's literary masterpiece of all time.[9] In da Cunha's account the military came off more or less where they began. The author, by profession a military engineer, was highly critical of the gross incompetence of the army, but he also recognized that the officers and men were doing their duty in upholding the republic and constitutional authority against a group of dedicated but misguided fanatics. The government did not fare so well at his hands, for he was first of all a nationalist and he had little patience with the Brazilian administrators in Rio de Janeiro who chose to use force against the benighted people of the interior rather than take measures to incorporate them more fully into the Brazilian nation.

Shortly after the "Canudos affair" the armed forces acquired one of their more illustrious (if not one of their firmest) intellectual supporters, the poet Olavo dos Guimarães Bilac, one of Brazil's most distinguished men of letters. Bilac had serious reservations about the armed forces, but he also recognized that they represented one of the few institutions that

[9] Translated by Samuel Putnam and published as *Rebellion in the Backlands* (Chicago, 1944).

could contribute meaningfully to national unification and education. It was his ambivalence toward the armed forces that make his observations so interesting and pertinent. His faith in the armed forces gave him courage to support a strong military, but his doubts drove him to advocate an army in which only the officers would be professional; the conscripts, he thought, should be chosen by lot, with those fortunate enough to be selected to be given the rudiments of education and made to feel a part of the nation. With great sincerity he recalled that as a child the achievements of Brazilian troops had filled him with reverence and that later as a man he had seen the swords of soldiers defend the slaves and contribute to the abolition movement. Then, he said to the military, "I encountered you anew the morning of November 15 [the day the imperial house was overthrown in 1889] and saw you in all your bravery and beauty. . . . It was thus I have loved you." But with equal sincerity he admonished, "If at times my love for you has diminished, it is because I have loved you more as soldiers than as politicians."[10] Elsewhere he cautiously balanced his praise for those officers who were giving their lives to the opening of Brazil's hinterland by lecturing other officers who became involved in issues he thought should be left to civilians. Bilac was in sum a friendly critic, a far cry from his contemporary, González Prada across the Andes in Peru, who had nothing but contempt for the man in uniform.

Most Brazilian scholars have seemed to give the military the advantage of every doubt. The standard works on the military by Leopoldo de Freitas (1911), Gustavo Barrosa (1935), J. P. Magalhaes (1946), and Theodorico Lopes and Gentil Torres (1945) range from very sympathetic to frankly laudatory. João Pandía Calogeras's secondary textbook *Formacão histórica do Brasil* (first edition, 1930, fifth edition, 1957) was decidedly favorable to the military in general and raised Marshal Caxias to heroic heights.[11] Calogeras wrote: "It has been

[10] From *A defesa nacional* (Rio de Janeiro, 1917), pp. 136–37.
[11] Translated and edited by Percy Alvin Martin and published as *A History of Brazil* (Chapel Hill, N.C., 1939).

the sad lot of the Brazilian Army never to have been understood by the civilians and especially by the political parties.
Safe in their homes, or installed in comfortable berths in the
administration or parliament, these self-appointed critics have
been prone to discuss, prove, or accuse, the actions of soldiers,
whose self-sacrifice and achievement they are unable to measure or even fully to comprehend." In praise of Caxias's action
during the Paraguayan War, historian Calogeras noted that
"The General was tireless in carrying out his duties, and did
not allow himself a moment of repose. He was in personal
command of an army of 50,000 men. . . . He undertook
reconnaissance himself, and was to be found in the thick of the
battle like a young officer. At the bridge of Itororó . . .
though an old man . . . weakened by ill health, he emulated
the heroic action of Bonaparte at Arcole and, sword in hand,
led his troops across the bridge swept by shrapnel, after three
generals had been laid low by deadly, even mortal, wounds."[12]

The sociologist Gilberto Freyre, who won international
recognition for his *Casa-Grande & senzala*, in his two-volume
Ordem e progresso (1959), which covers approximately the
first three decades of the republic, presents a decidedly friendly
view of the armed forces. To him the army of the early republic
performed the moderating function formerly exercised by the
Crown and protected the nation from being sacrificed to party
ambitions and regional interests. In an earlier work, *Nacão e
exército* (1949), Freyre, although he did not say so explicitly,
obviously conceived of the military as an institution concerned
with the preservation of Brazil's traditional values and equally
concerned that the politicians should not be allowed to thwart
popular aspirations for economic and social progress.

Generally speaking, the Brazilian "democratic press" has
been willing to go at least as far as intellectuals and scholars in
sanctioning the military's participation in politics. The attitude of the press between 1953, when the armed forces began
to exert great pressure on Vargas, and early 1956, when Kubit-

[12] *A History of Brazil* (Martin translation), pp. 229–30.

schek was inaugurated, serves to emphasize this point.[13] Later, the conservative newspaper *O Estado de S. Paulo*, with the largest circulation in Brazil, on October 9, 1955, criticized the armed forces not for having acted politically but only for not having acted with sufficient decisiveness. In a discussion of an article appearing in the *Review of the Military Club*, in which the author justified the armed forces' political role, the *Estado de S. Paulo* called the article "a useless effort, since who in this country is not profoundly convinced of all that is asserted here?" It continued: "If enlightened public opinion differs in any measure from what the author alleges in defense of his class [the military], it is precisely in respect to the excessive legalism that that class has demonstrated in the last two interventions [against Vargas in 1945 and 1954] in which it has, against its will, been obliged to involve itself." The newspaper then went on to accuse the armed forces "of not having understood the true mission that destiny had committed to them, the magnitude of the evil it was their duty to overthrow, and, more particularly, the importance of the operation they were called upon to perform. Imbued with the false respect for the law and demonstrating a legalistic fetishism incompatible with the gravity of the situation, they did not dare cut deeply enough to remove the gangrene which had invaded the nation."[14] Finally, in December 1955 the deputy Carlos Lacerda (as of 1963 governor of the state of Guanabara), "editor-in-exile" of the newspaper *Tribuna da imprensa,* in an interview in New York, called for a military coup that would set aside the results of the election that brought Vargas's protégé, Kubitschek, to the presidency.

Brazilian artists, for all intents and purposes, have completely ignored the extra-military activities of the officers. An examination of perhaps a thousand prints, by no less than a hundred artists, appearing in the architecture and art review

[13] The *New York Times* reported on October 2, 1954, that the Brazilian press had been "virtually unanimous" in applauding the army's high command in bringing pressure to bear on President Vargas during the debate on the minimum wage law.

[14] *Estado de S. Paulo,* October 9, 1955.

Habitat did not reveal a single piece of art that reproached officers for their interference in civilian politics or for collusion with corrupt politicians, although in the early 1930's an occasional artist would chide officers for having the pretensions of the *nouveau riche*. Cândido Portinari, Brazil's best-known artist, left no doubt of his horror of war in his painting *Guerra e Paz* (later presented to the United Nations by the Brazilian government), but it is believed that he never attacked the armed forces and their officers in his work. Nor is there anti-military art in the leading museums of São Paulo and Rio de Janeiro. Thus the conclusion must be that just as Brazil has not yet had in the field of literature an Azuela, a López y Fuentes, a Gallegos, or an Icaza, neither has it had in the field of art a Rivera, a Siqueiros, or an Orozco to decorate public buildings with representations of disgusting, debased militarists.

Nor has the Brazilian movie industry chosen to depict the military unfavorably. Considerable correspondence and interviewing failed to turn up any instance in which a Brazilian newsreel, short subject, or feature film presented the military or an officer in a role that might reflect unfavorably upon the armed forces.[15] Quite the contrary has probably been the case. A highly placed executive in the movie division of the state of São Paulo maintained that "the military and armed forces officers are always shown as being patriotic. If a soldier or a sailor starts out badly he is reformed before the end." He added that the military are seldom shown in newsreels because "they have little public appeal." And in response to a question regarding the public reception of newsreel releases on the military, a ranking officer of the United States Embassy in Rio de Janeiro in a letter of March 31, 1960, wrote: "We do not know of any cases in which a newsreel story about the Brazilian military forces has been criticized by any theater audience in recent years. On the contrary, newsreel stories, such as that of the

---

[15] The inept representatives of law and order in the widely acclaimed motion picture "O cangaceiro" were state militiamen or police, not members of the regular armed forces.

Brazilian paratroopers participating in the maneuvers in Panama, and the many short subjects made by private producers in Brazil for theatrical release, are always well received and certainly reflect credit on the Brazilian military."

The relative lack of interest shown by the men of letters in the military has been reflected by the legislators. Nowhere does one find evidence that more than a few elected officials of Brazilian government have ever sought to deprive the armed forces of the political prerogatives that they assumed upon the overthrow of Pedro II. Article XIV of the constitution of 1891, the first one referring to the armed forces, made the land and naval forces permanent national institutions, charged not only with the defense of the country abroad but with the maintenance of domestic laws. The Article had the dual effect of guaranteeing that the regular forces would not be dissolved in favor of the national guard and of making the military ultimately responsible for public order. Subsequent articles in the 1891 constitution (except for one that took punishment of officers out of the hands of civilian officials), were essentially the same as those in the contemporary constitutions of the Spanish American republics. The role of the armed forces was not affected by the constitutions of 1934 and 1937, except that their responsibilities were spelled out in somewhat greater detail than in the 1891 charter. Finally, the 1946 constitution, currently in force, reaffirmed the services as permanent national institutions under the supreme authority of the president "within the limits of the law." The last phrase, in effect, conferred upon the War Ministers the privilege of denying final authority to the President should they believe he had exceeded the limits of the law. Currently, no constitution in Latin America except that of Honduras gives the military greater discretionary power. But it is equally true that between World War II and 1960 no other armed service in a major Latin American republic was more committed to constitutional government.

The current Brazilian view of the nation's military establishment conforms rather closely to the historical view recorded above. One does not find in Brazil today the extreme positions that are commonplace in many of the Spanish American republics. Outside of the universities and the intellectual left, the vehemently anti-military individual is so rare in Brazil that he speaks for almost no one but himself, while those who are "neutral" or pro-military make clear that their good will is dependent upon the continued acceptable conduct of the armed forces. As might be expected in such an atmosphere, there are in Brazil important areas of civilian consensus on the military; these areas will be examined below before the areas in dispute are discussed.

It is agreed that the services are generally well received in all parts of the country. The Jesuit Father Beltrão, one of Brazil's most respected and learned churchmen, made this point by recalling that the Church once shifted the Day of the Feast from February 12 to Independence Day, September 7, in the hopes that more Catholics would turn out for the observance on a national holiday; but quite the reverse proved to be the case, because the masses went to the military parades rather than to the churches. As a consequence the next year the day was shifted again, this time to May 11. An ex-communist employed by a São Paulo newspaper was sure that "The army is respected everywhere, although probably less so in São Paulo than elsewhere." A labor leader observed, "The workers everywhere like the army, but not the police. The army does not interfere in social conflicts, but the police do." An army general attached to the chief of staff believed that to the extent that there was opposition to the military, it came almost entirely from intellectuals who "think that we are competitors, and they have some reason for thinking so."

Almost as if by common consent, when Brazilians feel compelled to bring charges against the military, they do so against the services as national institutions rather than against individual officers. This is understandable. Brazilian officers have conducted themselves reasonably well both professionally and in relations with the general public, and they have performed their duties faithfully if not always with high competence. Their handling of conscripts and non-commissioned officers, drawn almost wholly from the lower classes, has been commendable compared with the harsh practices in most neighboring republics. Nor have the officers as a group been corrupt, lascivious, vulgar, and abusive, as they have been all too often in Mexico, Peru, Bolivia, and Venezuela. And in comparison with the arrogant plantation-owning "colonels," so described vividly by Freyre, Jorge Amado, and others, the officers' norms of conduct and respect for national institutions must be considered civilized and socially responsible.

Civilians in general approve of the officers' status in society. Historically, officers have come primarily either from the lesser developed regions of the republic or from the dynamic state of Rio Grande do Sul, which has a long history of domestic warfare and fighting against neighboring republics. Their families have belonged to the rural middle- and lower middle-income groups. At present the trend in Brazil, as elsewhere in Latin America, is to dip deeper into the social strata for officers. This simultaneously confirms the view that "formerly the aristocrats could control the country without controlling the armed forces" and the observation of a young woman, a professor of history in a Rio de Janeiro university, that "today the younger officers understand the problems of the masses from having experienced them." It also means that the most economically productive areas of the country have relatively little direct influence over the armed forces.

All levels of society concur that armed forces officers tend to rise socially. "A high ranking officer has access to all social levels," according to one businessman. A labor organizer observed: "In the eyes of the working man, being a colonel is like being a baron in Europe." However, another labor leader, in answer to a question designed to elicit responses on the social status of the officers, declared: "There are no inferior or superior classes. We do not recognize classes. We accept categories of work and the military does theirs well." The officers themselves feel that the armed forces have provided them with an opportunity to improve their status, and they have few complaints about the approval they receive from civilians.

The social advancement made by officers would seem to

result not only from the public respect they enjoy, but from the level of education they can claim. It is widely accepted that at least until World War II officers received the best scientific training available in Brazil, with the exception of the instruction provided in the privately run MacKenzie School in São Paulo, which for several decades has had the most difficult entrance requirements of any educational institution in Brazil. Yet today the training received by cadets compares well with that available to civilians in the public institutions of higher learning. A São Paulo union leader, for example, was sure that "officers receive brilliant training" and that the Escola Superior de Guerra (Superior War College) is set up to provide officers with unusual promise or political connections with advanced training in the sciences and social sciences. Thus senior grade officers are often quite well informed about contemporary domestic and world problems and are better prepared than most civilians to discuss the acute problems confronting the Brazilian government. This should not be taken to imply that there are not many civilians who are as competent as are the armed forces officers to cope with the social and economic strains resulting from rapid change; it means rather that many officers are at ease in discussing problems of interest to informed civilians, and also, perhaps incidentally, that they possess the sort of skills and knowledge which, if properly channeled, could speed up the rate of growth in the civilian sector.

The salaries that officers receive on active duty and the income from their retirement plans give them greater economic security than the average Brazilian civilian of comparable education and experience. Today the officer's prospects for security, combined with his relatively high level of academic training, make it possible for him to marry into the urban middle sectors, just as formerly the prestige of the uniform in the rural areas opened the doors to membership in the landholding groups. Also, there are ordinarily no barriers to one of his sons preparing for a profession that guarantees middle-sector status, or one of his daughters marrying freely into the professions.

His wife does not fare so well. As in Spanish America, intellectuals tend to rate the officers socially above their wives. "Some officers are all right, but their wives! They are both unsophisticated and uninformed. We prefer not to entertain them because they have nothing in common with us. I have trouble getting my friends to sit next to them at the table," remarked one lady professor in Rio de Janeiro, who claimed to be interested in understanding "the military mind."

Brazilians are sure, and with some reason, that the navy is the most aristocratic of the three services and that the army "represents the country better and is more progressive-minded." This judgment springs from two considerations: The navy has a certain prestige because it has ordinarily managed to remain out of the limelight, and because naval officers as a group are "whiter" than army and air force officers. According to a Catholic priest, "In Brazil there are two fortresses of the old families, the navy and *Itamarati* (the Foreign Office).[16] Navy officers freely acknowledge that their service has been racially discriminatory. The cash required to cover the expenses of the "navy trousseau" (uniforms, swords, and so forth), levied on cadets before graduation and paid for by their parents, tended to restrict candidates to families of considerable wealth. Families also had to finance the education of their sons in "exclusive" preparatory schools, which were thought to enhance greatly the chances of being accepted as a cadet. Although the navy, at least until recently, openly discriminated against the lower classes, historically it was also particularly determined to prevent Negroes from becoming officers. The official position that thus far Negroes have not been able to meet the "standard of training and initiative" required is not taken seriously. The public is more inclined to accept such statements as "the psychological tests that the navy requires make Negroes feel that they are not wanted." In 1962

[16] It should be noted that the Foreign Office has in recent years dipped into the middle sector for personnel, but it has also continued to give examinations only in Rio de Janeiro, an effective means of discouraging low-income families of the provinces from seeking admission.

middle-grade naval officers assured the author that no Negro had ever graduated from the Naval Academy, a startling bit of information in view of the fact that there are millions of Brazilians who are pure or nearly pure Negro and non-negroid Brazilians are quick to maintain that their nation is free from prejudice based upon race. But the Negro is slowly breaking the naval color barrier. A high official in the Naval Academy in 1960 estimated that "Since 1956 we have accepted about ten mulattoes." One admiral said: "Oh yes, we have Negro officers. They are doctors and dentists and that sort of thing. They do not fill obvious positions, like that of a commanding officer at sea." Such a situation need not have much significance in itself, but when taken in conjunction with the widely repeated observation that the army is the most democratic service and that in a showdown in the services the masses would be on the side of the army, the navy's reputation for being aristocratic does affect its public image adversely.[17] Many naval officers freely acknowledge this, and the feeling undoubtedly affects their thinking in times of political crisis.

Differences in civilian opinion about the armed forces spring chiefly from three questions: (1) Can the nation afford to maintain such a costly institution? (2) Should the officers be so active in the state-owned or controlled social and economic institutions and agencies? (3) Has Brazil reached sufficient political maturity for civilians to run the government without the benefit of the moderating role that the military has played in varying degrees ever since the founding of the republic?

In recent years the armed forces have received about 30 per cent of the total national budget and have placed an undetermined but heavy strain upon the republic's very limited foreign exchange earnings.[18] Those who object to such expenditures

---

[17] Brazilians have been less inclined than Argentines to admit first- and second-generation nationals to officer rank in the services, although some representatives of the newcomers, including the Japanese, are to be found in the officer corps.

[18] A large part of the foreign exchange used by the armed forces is spent on fuel for airplanes and ships and on repairs for existing equipment.

have argued from one basic assumption: that Brazil is not in danger of attack from its neighbors, and that in case of war involving the United States and the U.S.S.R., Brazil's possible military contribution would be nil. To this group, which includes a sizable contingent of intellectuals, the military is a parasite, sucking the life blood away from the health and welfare services, from industry, and from education. Particularly offensive to this element are the officers who receive assignments abroad, where they are paid in hard currency and are able to bring home, customs free, automobiles, household goods, watches, liquor, and electrical gadgets.

Others, most of them strongly nationalistic, believe that the nation must maintain an impressive military establishment in order to achieve the international prestige its size and population warrant. They are anxious for Brazil to rush forward in its drive to become a world power, which, on the basis of the 20th century-experience of Western Europe and the United States, they equate with industrial and military might. They are ready to pay dearly for a military establishment that would command international recognition. This explains why some intellectuals who might normally oppose the military in general, and heavy military expenditures in particular, accept them as "the price of future world prestige." It also explains in part why the Brazilian armed forces, who are themselves more nationalistic than the civilian elements as a whole, have cooperated with the United States-sponsored anti-submarine warfare campaign throughout the Hemisphere and why Brazilian officers, with official approval, have from time to time proposed that Brazil be made the southern anchor of an alliance involving the total defense of the Atlantic. Brazil's military cooperation at the international level may and probably will decline over the short run as a result of the republic's increasingly "neutralist position," but by the same token the nation's new international policy should in the normal course of events lead to an increase rather than a reduction of the nation's military might.

Excluding the workers, who, on the basis of the responses of their leaders, do not have strong views one way or another, and university students, who do, and are almost unanimously opposed, Brazilians appear to divide quite evenly on the question of using officers at policy making levels in state-controlled welfare and economic agencies. Those who believe that officers should not be used as widely as they have been, contend that officers do not have better qualifications than civilians. In the words of a Rio de Janeiro journalist: "The capability of officers is a subject of discussion." A literary critic declared that "officers hold important posts because they use the phrases 'in the national interest' for every purpose." The rector of a private school believed that "appointments are political." And the editor of a review, borrowing from Gaetano Salvemini, said despairingly: "Generals think they can do anything. Tell one that he was going to have a baby and he would go confidently to bed." But neither the review editor or others who firmly opposed the military on this score had any complaint against General Edmundo Macedo Soares, who headed the Volta Redonda steel plant from its founding until 1959. "The whole of Brazil loves him," according to a Rio de Janeiro university professor decidedly opposed to the military interference in the civilian area; and "Edmundo Macedo Soares is an exception," was the view of a journalist. The normal response was, "Macedo Soares? He is more a civilian than an officer."

Those who justify or at least condone the employment of officers in government institutions and agencies do so on grounds other than the technical and administrative competence of military men. Some accept without enthusiasm the argument that many of the positions held by officers are in activities in one way or another related to national defense, and that the military therefore has a legitimate professional interest in them. Persons with this point of view invariably cited examples of areas critical to national defense: transportation, mass communications, civil aviation, merchant shipping, and, almost without fail, the government oil monopoly. Others hold that well-trained civilians ordinarily will not accept appointments at salaries the government is empowered to offer, and that as a result, the armed forces have the best reservoir of personnel available to the state. Still others believe that Presidents Vargas and Kubitschek, both of whom depended heavily on the armed forces and were largely responsible for instituting the practice discussed here, felt that officers were more loyal, and would follow orders better, than civilians. Businessmen in particular are aware that high-level government positions outside the services give officers an opportunity to increase their income while continuing to earn credit toward retirement. An occasional individual welcomed the use of officers because "they are conscious of the communist threat," and are on the lookout for communist infiltration in the agencies in which they exercise influence. The most common reply of all, however, was something like this : "In the eyes of the public the armed forces are a guarantee of relative honesty." The officers themselves believe that they are employed in government because they have the necessary technical and administrative skills or because the assignments they receive are too hot for politicians to accept. One naval officer asked, "What individual with political ambitions would allow himself to be named the Director of the Leopoldina Railroad? It is a financial mess, and little can be done to reduce the strain on personnel and equipment that results in periodic accidents and a heavy loss of life." The total impression that was received from the discussion of the extra-military activities of the officers was that the public regards the officers at least as highly as it does civilian bureaucrats, whom many believe are incompetent and often dishonest.

There are, naturally, Brazilians who disapprove of the active social-political role that the armed forces have played. They are few, however, and they argue in general rather than in specific terms and often seem to contradict themselves by approving the role that the armed forces have played since 1889. A young lady professor in a Rio de Janeiro university, for example, insisted that the military "should turn the country over to the civilians," but she approved the army's decision in 1889 because the republic "was coming anyway"; she did not consider the civilian-military struggle during the presidential election of 1910 important because there was "no real issue in terms of liberalism and conservatism"; she felt that between 1922 and 1924 the *tenentes* were ahead of the civilians in their thinking on liberalism and in their idealism; she did not believe that the military played a major role in the revolution of 1930; she wished that in 1945 the armed forces had removed Vargas "on grounds other than corruption (which was not, of course, the basis of the armed forces' decision); she regretted that when the armed forces moved against Vargas in 1954 they created "the impression that corruption made his government valueless, which was not true"; and she defended Lott's "anti-coup" in 1955 because "it was in the interests of popular government." Likewise, an air force officer who insisted that the military were too actively engaged in extra-military affairs, when asked what his position as a soldier would have been at key moments in the history of civil-military relations, replied that he would have supported the overthrow of the empire; fought on the side of the *tenentes*; favored the removal of Washington Luiz in favor of Vargas in 1930; approved the ouster of Vargas in 1945 and and again in 1954 [he actually participated in the 1954 action against Vargas]; and opposed Marshal Lott's "counter-coup" in 1955 on the grounds that it was unconstitutional. His choices, except the last one, were the ones that the average liberal, progressive, nationalistic Brazilian intellectual probably would have made.

The majority view of those who accept or actually promote military intervention in civilian politics derives from two convictions. They are that "without the stabilizing influence of the armed forces there would be constant political crises," and that "the military do not want anything for themselves and thus are the best qualified to play the part of political common denominators." The minority view is that officers should regulate politics because it will restrain the growth of popular forces. This is the attitude of the group that poses the most serious threat to Brazilian political evolution along democratic lines. Their thinking fails to give due consideration to the profound transformation Brazil has undergone. With seeming disregard for the "democratic" role the armed forces played in the difficult months between Vargas's suicide and the inauguration of Kubitschek and again at the moment Quadros abdicated, the minority talks and acts as if the military is still committed to social and economic conservatism. But even if they are presently correct in their estimate, which is very doubtful, they are wrong about the younger officers, the decision-makers of the coming decade, who will be far more sympathetic than the present generation of senior officers to the demands of the historically oppressed masses. This minority group of civilians, then, is in effect urging the prolongation of a political situation which, if it remains, will in the foreseeable future inevitably operate to their disadvantage. Also, this minority presumes that because the armed forces have been able to moderate civilian differences in the past they will succeed in doing so in the future. This view fails to appreciate fully that in the past when officers have served as political moderators, they dealt with antagonisms between civilian groups who had different political objectives but who were agreed on primary social and economic issues. This situation no longer obtains. As new social groups have become politically active, the political arena has been crowded with representatives of widely differing social and economic strata, some of whom show a strong disposition to obtain their objectives by force if they cannot obtain them otherwise.

Finally, the minority assumes that because in the past when the armed forces have moved to moderate political disputes they have done so under the leadership of responsible officers, they will do so in the future. But the truth is that some officers, in order to increase their potential political influence, have solicited the support of non-commissioned officers. It is too early to predict the eventual outcome of this development, but it may be that a Pandora's box has been opened and that a new era of civil-military relations has actually begun—one in which sergeants, first in alliance with commissioned officers and later, conceivably, on their own account, will hold the balance of political power.

IX

RETROSPECT AND PROSPECT

THIS CHAPTER reviews the historical evolution of the Latin American armed forces and their behavior today in extra-military fields; then, taking into consideration the changing social-economic character of both Latin America and the armed forces, it speculates on the probable responses of the military to developments that may be expected during the next ten to twenty-five years.

While in Spanish America militarism is a cultural residue of the Wars of Independence and the subsequent disorders, in Brazil it derives from the uncertainties arising from the abolition of slavery in 1888 and the overthrow of the empire in 1889. Independence in Spanish America was not achieved by the exertion of the will of the masses, but by the decisions of isolated groups. Before it was everywhere secured, individualism and local pride had taken precedence over nationalism, and popular sovereignty proved insufficient to promote a general consensus. Then, when the constitutions of the new republics failed to command universal allegiance, bitter disputes arose between the intellectual theorists of the cities and the oligarchs of the countryside; these were arguments about the legitimacy of power, about who should command positions of authority and about what orders they should be entitled to give. The landed aristocrats established their supremacy, but not before they had plunged the republics into a quarter of a century of chaos; in this period, force was made a prominent part of the political process, constitutions were respected more in theory than in practice, and the armed forces assumed the pivotal position in the balance of power.

The sword and the rifle became weapons of politics as generals and would-be generals exploited the general discontent. Public and private armies became a necessity to the functioning of society; they were the only instruments by which power could be secured and held, and they made the revolutions that became the remedy for bad government and the means by which changes of officials were commonly effected. The public armies, their ranks filled with ill-armed, ill-trained, and docile peasants, were organized along defensive lines. They were led by rapacious men who moved in and out of the military at will, men swayed more by personal ambition than by patriotism. Not unusually such armies were a source of violence rather than a deterrent to it. Private armies were little more than makeshift bands composed of mounted peons and gauchos, which owed their success to being mobile forces in an essentially immobile society. These armies were led by *caudillos*, who, until the end of the nineteenth century, were generally the holders of local political power, men with military and political talents who often exhibited both the authoritarianism of the colonial period and the anarchism of the republican era. As long as these militarists and *caudillos* were competing for power, life in Spanish America was tortured and uncertain, continually buffeted by the forces of democratic action, the injustices of the aristocracy, and the abuses of unlimited power.

In this situation, the ruling aristocracy tended to unite around those who commanded public and private armies. But few men with the skills and talents needed to provide leadership during periods of violence and confusion also possessed the qualities of leadership needed to stabilize and develop the new nations in periods of calm. Some of the officers and most of the *caudillos* were members of the elite, and those who were not aspired to acceptance by the oligarchy, and they accordingly cooperated with the elites in the preservation of established institutions and class interests against encroachments by the landless masses. It is not surprising that such officers were systematically absorbed by the civilian ruling oligarchies or that the dictatorships they established became the refuge of social groups associated with reaction. Under such circumstances aristocratic families felt no compulsion to put their sons in the armed forces and those from the aristocracy who actually became officers usually did so with political rewards in mind. Only in Brazil did militarism fail to obtain a hold before the middle of the century—although it is true that in Chile a responsible oligarchy had curbed the nation's armed forces after the promulgation of the constitution of 1833.

By about 1850, the leaders of the Spanish American republics despaired of finding political solutions to their problems and began to search for economic solutions to them. In Brazil, which had been stable, and in those countries that achieved a reasonable degree of order and stability (such as Mexico, Chile, Uruguay, and Argentina), monumental material changes followed. Workers, technicians, and capital poured in from abroad and made possible a technological revolution. To their traditional political and cultural functions, cities added industrial and commercial activities, and their populations expanded spectacularly. The urban middle sectors grew, industrialists emerged as a new group, and social relationships were forced out of their colonial mold. An enormously expanded volume of international trade provided the states with valuable new tax resources. The governments used their economic strength to encroach upon individuals and to consolidate their own power. But the legacy of the past remained, as it still does in many of the republics, and almost uniformly the further one moved away from the capital cities the more pervasive became the influence of traditional customs and institutions.

Much like the republics themselves, the armed forces of Latin America after 1850 began to change while retaining much from their violent past. In the new climate, the services were first of all instruments of force that brought the semblance of order necessary for real economic growth. Later, taking their cues from the Chileans, who were the first to bring in military advisers from abroad, several of the republics began a process of professionalization, with the armies ordinarily under the guidance of German or French personnel and the navies receiving instruction from British officers. Before World War I professionalization had not made significant strides except in Chile, Argentina, and Brazil, but three of its potential effects were already discernible. First, it tended to divorce officers from the civilian population, which was where democratic aspirations, however weakly sustained, were generally incubated. Second, the armed forces increasingly represented continuity in areas lacking developed bureaucratic and civil service organizations. And third, the technological and managerial orientation that professionalization offered the officers made it easier for them to accept the shift of power from the old rural elites to the new urban alliances that began in Latin America shortly after the turn of the century.

On the other hand, professionalization before 1915 had no impact in certain important areas. For one thing, the armed forces showed no greater reluctance than formerly to serve politicians as instruments of coercion against civilians. Also, except in Brazil, where officers contributed significantly to technological development, natural science, and development of the hinterland, the training that the new professional soldier received still did little to prepare him to contribute constructively to civilian life. And nowhere had professionalism led officers to transfer their loyalty away from audacious leaders to the military as an institution; when they looked to politics, they continued to look to a "leader," and not toward doctrines.

Professionalization was the outgrowth of an emergent nationalism stimulated by misapprehensions over the long-range impact of demographic and technological growth and fear of territorial designs on the republics by outside powers. Support of nationalistic foreign policies, which served as a unifying force in the republics, in most instances gave the military their first opportunity since Independence to associate themselves with a popular ideal. The Brazilian army, in particular, was an integrating force at the national level and an instrument of foreign policy. This new role of the armed forces had the effect of making military careers attractive to more serious and dedicated young men, who came for the most part from small provincial towns hardly affected by the transformations so evident in the larger cities. Also, it was under the impulse of nationalism, and the accompanying desire to have military establishments capable of backing up progressive foreign policies, that conscription finally gained almost universal acceptance in the republics.

Prior to World War I, modernization of the military had broader implications than did professionalization. Modernization was closely related to the expansion of international trade and the resultant growth of tax revenues. Before the outbreak of war in Europe, the military forces in all of the more advanced republics of Latin America, except Mexico, had achieved or were on the way to achieving an arms monopoly at the expense of the regional *caudillos,* whose private fortunes were no longer sufficient to permit them to compete with the state in the armaments race. The "warlords" were thus ultimately restrained not by professionalization and military management but by their inability to buy modern military weapons and matériel.

The consequences of the monopoly of force, where actually attained, and hence of violence, were immediate and profound. By destroying the smaller centers of power, central governments indirectly set free the people historically oppressed by their *caciques.* For the first time the entire community was made dependent upon the central government. With the military *caudillos* removed from the power struggles, the generals were assured of playing a dominant role, on one side or another, in any revolutionary contest. The arms revolution, consequently, may be considered as having made the national forces a great source of strength to the state, but not necessarily to the parliamentary form of government.

In the early stages professionalization and modernization did not significantly alter the armed forces' political role. Down to World War I, officer politics remained endemic in most of the republics. Mass armies formed to suppress revolutions persisted in making revolutions themselves. Smaller republics appeared to be subnations dominated by superarmies. Armies were often little more than political parties without platforms or ideological strength.[1] But it is also true that under favorable circumstances they sometimes did provide the framework within which political growth could take place. Most often the officers, rising rapidly in rank and knowing only brief periods of subordination, were political independents who acted without regard for the institution of which they were theoretically a part. Only a few such officers could make a revolution, but once they began to march every uncommitted officer was forced to decide whether or not to resist. A military career was thus a precarious one, and the junior officers appeared much more disorderly than they actually were. Most of the common soldiers continued to be so illiterate and politically apathetic that they did not figure in the calculations of their officers or in the plans of civilian revolutionary elements.

Since World War I the degree of material change and the extent of social disorder in the several republics have been the primary determinants in the evolution of the Latin American military establishments. Consequently, in backward countries like Haiti, Nicaragua, and Paraguay, where the concept of government as a prize to be won still persists, the armed forces, although now possessing relatively modern armament, function very much as they did in the nineteenth century. Such military establishments can hardly be considered national, since pay, promotion, and retirement are subject to the whims of the currently dominant "leader" on whose personal behalf the officers act until such time as it seems appropriate to unseat him. On the other hand, in the advanced countries like Argentina, Chile, Brazil, and Mexico, and also in lesser developed Colombia, professionalization and institutionalization,

---

[1] The army of Francisco Solano López was probably the only important exception. Under him Paraguay became a prototalitarian society. His Indian troops were long conditioned by servitude under the Jesuits; and like Hitler, Solano López injected the race issue into his struggle in order to arouse his "pure Guaraní" against the "monkey" Brazilians with Negro blood. See Alfred Vagts, *A History of Militarism* (Greenwich edition, 1959), p. 470.

gh far from complete, have developed sufficiently to have
sive effect on the composition and attitudes of armed
officers.

_ .ofessionalization has had the double effect of drawing
cadets from a wider range of social-economic groups and of
making officers less competent to exercise civilian rule. Except in Argentina, Chile, and recently Mexico, economically
retarded small towns serving essentially rural areas continue
to be a major source of officer material, although men from
other areas and social groups are entering the officer corps at
an accelerating rate. It is a direct result of professionalization
that one such group is the sons of officers; in some of the more
developed countries, they constitute 25 per cent or more of the
officer corps, and this appears to be creating, for the first time
in Latin America, a basis for the growth of a typical military
caste.

In Argentina and Chile, both countries with large immigrant populations, first and second generation nationals have
become officers because of the security and prestige that the
armed forces promise to persons seeking acceptance in new
societies. More recently, offspring of the urban lower-middle
sectors and artisans and upper-level working groups, benefiting from more and better public education, have been qualifying in growing numbers for the military academies. If this
development continues, which seems likely, it will mean that
the industrial-commercial bourgeoisie in Latin America will be
surrendering control of the armed forces, which are maintained
by their taxes, to groups more radical than themselves; this will
be the reverse of what happened in 19th century France, where
control of the armed forces was left by the bourgeoisie to the
politically conservative "old aristocracy."

Historically, the Latin American armed forces have provided one of the few avenues of social advancement, a situation that officers freely acknowledge. Thus it has been that up
to the present the average officer has entered a military academy in the full expectation that his social status would improve
following graduation. This in fact has occurred; officers receive salaries and retirement compensations at least equivalent

to and usually greater than those received by civilians of equal education and experience.

Officers and their families are accepted, although at times reluctantly, as having middle-sector status, except that wives of officers find it difficult to win more than superficial acceptance in certain social circles in which their husbands move freely and comfortably. Officers are cognizant of this ostracism and may in fact encourage it by their willingness to appear in public without their wives and to talk much more freely in public about the accomplishments of their children than about their wives. The children of officers have the same educational advantages as do the children of middle-sector families. They find the same kinds of employment, are accepted in the same professions, and both sons and daughters, when they do not marry service juniors, marry teachers, bureaucrats, and professionals, in much the same way as the children of middle-sector civilians.

Social-economic background, social status, and professional experience have combined to give officers, as a group, characteristics that influence their thinking when they intrude in civilian politics. They are, for example, superpatriots. They are more pro-Catholic and more anti-communist than the civilian middle sectors from which the politicians are customarily recruited. They are non-propertied, although they may have some ties with the landholding elements through relatives. They know something of agrarian economics, and aspire to own land. They come from families that know almost nothing about the workings of corporate industry. They are essentially bureaucrats, which, along with their non-propertied status and lack of acquaintance with large-scale, impersonal industry, has encouraged them to give ready approval to state intervention in the industrial economy when domestic private capital has not been forthcoming in sufficient amounts. This is in sharp contrast with the attitude of officers in the United States, who generally disapprove of the idea of a managed economy.[2] Knowing the advantages of modernization and technological

[2] See Morris Janowitz, *The Professional Soldier* (Glencoe, Ill., 1960), p. 246.

development, they are often divided between values absorbed in their youth and new values that encourage them to associate themselves with groups anxious for rapid change.

Professionalization and institutionalization have not as yet served to discourage the armed forces from attempting to exercise social control at the national level. In most of the republics, including even large and populous Brazil, the military generally continues to maintain that their transcendental duty is loyalty to the nation, and that this may from time to time entail a duty to be disloyal to the incumbent government. This in effect means that they reserve the right to support the constitution while refusing to support politicians. Professionalization and institutionalization, however, have served to alter the methods by which officers seek their objectives, which are in fact often quite personal or ideological.

Particularly since World War II when "direct intervention" has appeared to be called for, officers have increasingly substituted the junta of government for the heroic leader to whom the armed forces historically surrendered any claims to power or privilege on institutional grounds. Above all else, the junta, which ordinarily contains representatives of each branch of the services, suggests that as institutionalization takes place, loyalty of man to man will be slowly transformed into organic solidarity and a collectivist concept, reflecting the growth of a mass consciousness, will be substituted for the traditional individualistic one. This change in thinking has already gone far enough to place severe restraints on the retired officers who would like to dabble in conspiracy because, being off the active lists, they can no longer speak for the group.

Juntas have seldom held power for as long as the traditional military dictators, and they have not made successful statesmen of officers. Whether trying to hold back the process of change or seeking to profit from social ferment, junta members as a rule have been notoriously incompetent as administrators of public affairs. Nor have they been very successful in promoting technological development. Except in Argentina after the overthrow of Perón, in Venezuela following the oust-

ing of Pérez Jiménez, and in Colombia following the removal
of Rojas Pinilla, juntas have nowhere commanded more than
passing commendation, and the juntas that replaced Perón,
Pérez Jiménez, and Rojas were popular not for their efficiency
or what they stood for, but for what they were against. The
typical junta has stifled public debate and, subject to the taming
effect of politics, they have not supported daring or even new
approaches to the problems they have inherited from civilian
leaders. They have displayed a basic distrust of the civilians
upon whom they must depend to mobilize popular support,
probably because officers have had limited contact with the
new interest groups, such as organized labor. They have been
inclined toward ruinous financial policies and economic programs that favor production of consumer goods at the expense
of such basic requirements as transportation and power.

Unlike the leaders of the past, who could speak pragmati-
cally of nationalism and "cleaning up the mess," many of the
more recent generation of the military *jefes* and junta members
have felt compelled to support ideologies. Thus far they have
tended to favor a political conservatism with fascistic over-
tones. Their conservatism offers a narrow range of alternatives and is free of parliamentary control, and has been made
workable in Latin America by improved mass communications,
the centralization of industry, and modern technology. But the
same set of circumstances can serve military dictators like
Pérez Jiménez and Batista, who, seeking some degree of public
approval and wishing to give their regimes a plebiscitarian
aspect, did not hesitate to make accommodations with the communists.

However, in the more advanced republics, where the increasing political interests of the masses have served to create
more popularly based governments in which the military has
less freedom of action, officers have shown a growing preference for more subtle means than force to influence government.
They now seem to prefer to pick an occasion to checkmate
civilian officials and then withdraw and bide their time. This
tactic serves them well in at least two ways: it makes civilians

appear ultimately responsible for actions over which they may have minimal control, and it permits the military to influence decision making without forcing them to test their own conclusions by actually exercising power.

Especially since World War II, the armed forces have been able to influence policy formulation by holding directorships in many of the numerous and powerful public agencies created as states have extended their functions. Officers have received these assignments for a variety of reasons, some of them valid, but they have not been appointed to key positions because they have possessed technical or administrative skills that are not available in the civilian sector. Brazil affords the only exception; there, at least until recently, the armed forces did possess skills more or less equal to those possessed by civilians available for government service.

The armed forces' generally nonviolent response to the shift of power from the traditional elite to the urban middle sectors—whose economic policies were compatible with the organizational needs of the military—and subsequently their ready cooperation with the middle-sector leadership stand as landmarks in their historical evolution. Those developments are the best evidence that the armed forces are responding to radical changes in the civilian environment. In the more progressive republics, the middle sectors and the armed forces are now so closely aligned that the economic and social conservatism of the officers is that of the middle sectors. Furthermore, as officers come increasingly from the cities the tensions that have arisen between the military, once overwhelmingly from the rural areas, and civilian authorities, who have been strictly urban groups, will tend to subside.

On the basis of the military's acquiescence to the political rise of the middle sectors and the increasing number of officers of proletarian background, it would seem that within a decade or two the armed forces may be inclined to accept the working classes, with whom they are currently learning to live; this will be especially probable when labor leaders can attain influence within the constitutional framework of government. There is absolutely nothing in the evolution of the Latin American armed forces to suggest that they can any longer be trusted to be the stronghold of tradition or that they will for much longer "hold off the mob power of the left." Those persons in and out of Latin America who fail to appreciate this face a rude awakening, as do those abroad who fail to understand that no group from which potential officers currently are being recruited has close ties with any foreign power.

Given their continuing determination to perform or influence decision-making functions even though they have generally lacked the administrative skills that can be easily and profitably transferred to the civilian areas, there would be little to recommend the military were it not that force and corruption remain parts of the political process in Latin America. Since this is the case, the armed forces cannot be judged by absolute standards, but, it would seem, should be evaluated in comparison with the groups with whom they "compete." By this measurement they do not fare badly. To date they have been more responsible than either the police or the armies raised by ideological parties, and there has been relatively little to choose from between the regular armed forces and the national guards, which, given the opportunity, tend to assume the same relative position in the power structure as do the regular forces under ordinary circumstances. The question of corruption becomes particularly important as the chances to practice financial dishonesty accrue with the creation of each new state-controlled institution or agency. The public is satisfied that the officers who direct the institutes and agencies are less corrupt than the civilians to whom the assignments would otherwise go.

Looking to the future, at least a dozen basic developments are currently operating against the military's present stature in civilian affairs. Channels for the orderly transfer of government power are beginning to work and the locale of supreme authority is being established. Further advances in either of these areas will tend to narrow the field of political action for the armed forces. The political vacuums that historically have formed whenever the hold of a charismatic leader has been loosened, and into which the armed forces have been wont to rush, will be created less frequently as political parties become strong and provide the basis for greater political continuity. Mass communications will weaken provincialism and tend to strengthen the central authority, which promises reduced opportunities for the armed forces to plunge into politics in order "to save the nation." Civilians certainly will improve their technical and administrative capabilities, and as they do so any real or imagined advantage in entrusting the task of modernization to the armed forces will be eliminated permanently. Children of officers, because they have educational advantages not enjoyed by the majority, may be expected to fill an increasing number of the appointive and elective government offices, which means that the interests of officers will be well represented without their forceful intervention in the civilian area. Also, it may be anticipated that the voters will continue to view with caution officers who offer themselves for elective positions. Even in those republics where the public image of the military is generally favorable, officers have not shown a strong voter appeal. In Brazil, for example, army officers who in 1950 and 1955 sought the presidency with strong party support were badly defeated, and in 1960 Marshal Henrique Lott, heading the ticket of Brazil's largest single party (the PSD) was crushed in the landslide victory of the erratic Jânio Quadros.

As the masses become ever more politicized and learn more about how to make revolutions, the cost in lives of suppressing popular uprisings can be expected to rise to a level where the armed forces will be reluctant to extract it either in the interest of civilian groups or on their own behalf. Trade unions already have the power to paralyze national life by resorting to partial or general strikes, and as economic functions become more specialized, the strike will become an even more effective instrument with which to counter the armed might of the military. Taken together, the greater political activity of the masses and the use of the strike will sooner or later add a vitally important dimension to politics, and when that occurs it may well reduce the political effectiveness of officers. Historically they have attained their greatest influence when the masses have been apathetic, the trade unions feeble or few, and the officers themselves free to perform the relatively simple function of providing the balance of power between groups competing for political power but in essential agreement on social-economic objectives. The emergence of the working groups, furthermore, will tend to take communication between ruler and ruled out of the political marketplace, where officers have operated most advantageously, and make it depend upon the political informer or agent, whom the officers are only beginning to understand.

Greater professionalization can be predicted with considerable assurance. As it occurs there will be a tendency for officers to rise in rank and reach senior positions so late in life that they will have lost their political ambitions and will have learned to obey as well as to command. Professionalization as well as population expansion and the increasing complexity of government will serve to make the military more impersonal. To the extent that these developments take place, officers will have greater opportunities to reach decision-making positions without being known to politicians or indebted to them, with the result that those who prefer to confine themselves to soldiering will ordinarily find it easier than at present to do so.

The police forces in Latin America, which are generally highly centralized bodies, will in all probability eventually become professional and modern as well. They may not only serve as a counterpoise to the regular armed forces, but by carrying on their duties more responsibly and efficiently may reduce the need of the military as a second-line police force, a role that has traditionally given them vast influence in civilian matters. Finally, international organizations, if they continue to improve their machinery for resolving differences between nations and for moderating electoral disputes, will tarnish the often self-projected image of the armed forces as defenders of nations and the only impartial arbiters of political differences.

Impressive as are the forces that may be expected to reduce greatly the military's influence in civilian life, developments favoring a continuation of the military's present role will probably remain dominant for another ten to twenty-five years. International values and Hemisphere concepts practically guarantee the armed forces a major role in their respective societies. The military as an institution is more powerful in the world today than it has ever been in civilized history, and the most powerful nations are considered to be those with the strongest military establishments. The leaders of Latin America are quite aware of these truisms; they argue that if their nations are to enjoy freedom from outside pressures and respect in the community of nations they must not become "skeletons without armor." At the Hemisphere level, the military establishments are now and will continue to be symbols of national sovereignty as long as capacity for self-defense, by military means if necessary, is central to the modern concept of sovereignty. Armies are considered decisive forces in the regional balance of power. The importance given them is manifest in civic functions, where the armed forces have displaced the Catholic Church as symbols of social unity. In the major countries of Latin America, only the Mexican leaders seemingly feel secure enough in their international relations that they do not need military displays to convince their people and themselves that their nation has international respect. As long as international prestige and security at home are associated with military might there will be little or no popular support for cuts in armaments. The opposite can in fact be demonstrated by the popularity among working groups of Perón's inflated military pronouncements and by the broad popular support of Castro's machine in Cuba.

The followers of Perón and now of Castro were swayed to frenzied approval of military expansion by appeals to national greatness and to the need for defense against outside powers. Agricultural elements, and perhaps eventually the growing industrial sector, will be moved to support the armed forces for more concrete reasons. In every country in Latin America a major share of the armed forces budget goes for salaries, food, and clothing. The "bean and rice farmers" are thus the civilians who tend to benefit most from military expenditures. In Brazil, for example, 70 per cent of the armed forces budget is devoted to pay and allowances, including pay for retired personnel. Even more impressive is the fact that at the beginning of this decade the Brazilian armed forces were spending 88 per cent of their combined budgets for maintenance and only 12 per cent for improvements. This illustrates how closely even the most modern Latin American military establishments are tied to basic domestic production.

While it is easy to exaggerate the tie between the military and the industrial community, it is reasonable to theorize that at least two considerations may in the future strengthen that tie in Latin America. As industrial development occurs the republics will improve their abilities to modernize their armed forces with profit to local manufacturers, who as a result may come to welcome "war scares" if not war itself. And once the services can be equipped locally they will cease to compete with industrialists for foreign exchange, which will almost certainly continue to be scarce. In Europe the complexities of modern warfare and preparedness against sudden attack have caused civilians and the military to understand one another somewhat better than before. It is quite conceivable that in Latin America, where the public has seldom owed its survival to the armed forces, industry will perform a similar role in bringing about a new understanding.

The need to conserve irreplaceable natural resources, to promote industry, and to keep workers at their jobs has provided a firm basis for economic nationalism throughout much of Latin America. Armed forces officers charged with the defense of their countries will be vitally interested in the protection of natural resources and of those sectors of the economy, such as transportation and power, which are in any way important to national defense. And nearly every officer or army that chooses to become directly involved in politics, in order to gain some claim to popular support for an administration, will be tempted to win the backing of industrial workers through nationalistic legislation. The Brazilian armed forces have already moved in the direction of economic nationalism; in the 1950's they took the lead in successfully preventing foreign capital from participating directly in the development of Brazil's petroleum industry.

The social and economic revolution now in progress in all parts of Latin America is bound to accelerate regardless of any domestic or international policies designed to halt it or slow it down. The social upheaval will keep societies in disequilibrium and will bring to the surface people who in their restlessness and insecurity will welcome ideologies requiring total commitment. The armed forces, in circumstances in which frustration and disappointment over national development have often left politicians plagued with anxieties and self-doubt, may become increasingly confident of their ability "to clean up the mess." If and when such situations arise, the armed forces may choose to provide, as did Hitler and Mussolini, the security that is being sought by so many. In any event, since the armed forces will probably remain for some time the only agency capable of countermanding rampant demagoguery, they will appear different to the states of Latin America than they do to states with great national social cohesion.

It will be possible for the armed forces to profit in at least three ways from dips in the generally upward trend of economic activity. Economic deterioration, if it is severe enough, will tend to invite military intervention that will have popular approval. The armed forces may also function as a substitute for rapid industrialization by providing employment in sluggish economies, as the civilian bureaucracy has historically done. Or, finally, in periods of slowdown or depression officers would be a logical choice to direct "make-work agencies" resembling, perhaps, the Civilian Conservation Corps in the United States in the 1930's. The role of this type of agency will probably become more important in Latin America as cities grow and city dwellers loosen their ties with their families in the villages, to whom they have traditionally fled when urban unemployment has been most severe.

A successful civil service could be a most important deterrent to the military, but the prospects of creating such organizations are not bright for the near future. Except, perhaps, in Uruguay, the civilian bureaucrats as a group are ill-trained and notoriously incompetent. They have in general raised the historical art of avoiding work to new heights of sophistication. At least 40 per cent of the Brazilian government's expenditures go for wages for civil servants, compared with 14 per cent in the United States. The services rendered by U.S. bureaucrats are so superior to those provided by their Brazilian counterparts that comparison becomes ridiculous. It bears repeating that, except in Venezuela, civilians to whom I talked were of the opinion that army officers were more honest than civilian bureaucrats. Thus until responsible civil services emerge, the armed forces as coherent groups of men often will be as competent as any other group concerned with national policy. Furthermore, for the next decade or more, they will on occasion be the most reliable institution to ensure political continuity in their countries. They will, in certain instances, stand as a bulwark of order and security in otherwise anarchical societies; at other times, if they were to follow a policy of nonintervention in the civilian area, it would mean the preservation of an unsatisfactory status quo.

There are at least four additional reasons why it must be anticipated that the armed forces will continue to have a major voice in civilian affairs. (1) Militarism flourishes more in peacetime than in war. Latin America almost certainly will be at peace, and consequently it can be forecast that in the years ahead, as traditionally, the pressure of military planning will not be so demanding as to deprive officers of the time needed to engage in politics. (2) Even when the armed forces do withdraw from the stage, everyone will be aware that the undercover threat of violence remains a key component of military influence. This negative aspect is bound to give the armed forces considerable weight in decision making. (3) The appeal of the military academies will continue to be strong among the lower-middle sectors and the working groups in the absence of well-developed systems of aid for higher education. (4) The major guarantee against militarism will be the growth of civilian political practices that will accommodate the divergent dynamic interests in each country. The Latin American republics have been moving in this direction, but progress has been slow. There is little reason to expect that the goal will finally be attained under the guidance of the increasingly unimaginative leaders of the present generation.

If the arguments of this volume have been sound, the military in the several Latin American republics not only cannot be talked or written out of existence, but they will continue to have "a spoon in every soup," or so it must be assumed. Latin American societies thus are in a sense confronted with an accomplished fact. Faced with such a situation, they could throw up their hands in despair and say to the officers, "Do what you will not let us do." That would be dramatic, and conceivably effective in certain instances. Or, knowing that they are moving rapidly into an era of profound social disorder and that Western representative democracy no longer has a monopoly in this Hemisphere, the public can maintain their armies as deterrents against extremist-provoked violence but at the same time work to convert them into more socially constructive institutions. That would not be so heroic but it would certainly be realistic, and Latin Americans will probably have to be more realistic than they ordinarily have been if they are to survive the onslaught of extremists from both the right and the left.

In 1960 I returned from Latin America confident that a vast majority of articulate citizens were prepared to accept the second alternative and that they had been thinking seriously about how to maintain their armed forces within their organizational framework while transforming them into effective instruments of social progress. For example, in discussing the military relations of the United States with Latin America, at least a half dozen individuals volunteered statements to this effect: "If the United States feels obliged to encourage our armed forces, why doesn't it also train and equip them to build roads?" I was no less convinced that many armed forces officers were deeply sensitive to the unfavorable aspects of their public image and would be amenable to developing new relationships with the civilian sector, if such measures would help to justify their existence. In short, I satisfied myself that the military could be induced to take on worthwhile civilian assignments, as they actually had been doing on a limited scale for several decades, which would not impair their professional prestige or their security. Shortly before I reached this conclusion the Defense Department in Washington became seriously interested in the concept, and was preparing to give it world-wide implementation. Washington uses the term "civic action" for what it has in mind, and since that term has gained currency, I adopt it here. But I hasten to add that while United States assistance will often speed up specific undertakings—as it has, for example, in Guatemala and Ecuador—it is in no sense essential to the success of the type of activities I suggest below. When foreign aid is provided, great precautions must be taken lest the pattern of the army supplying public assistance be reproduced, which could widen rather than narrow the gap between the officer corps and civilian government and society.

At the outset it should be made clear that civic action, as I conceive of it, is not an operation from which a Latin American people will get the absolute maximum of service for its dollar; but it is an operation that will give it something, and at times a good deal, for its money. The effectiveness of civic action rests on a number of assumptions. (1) The skills possessed by the military, as noted above, are not such as to give officers premium value in urban environments; their skills are needed most outside the major population centers. (2) Noncommissioned officers, regulars, and conscripts need not spend a full eight-hour day every day in order to fulfill their constitutional duties as military men, and can spare some time for civic action. (3) Military personnel provide a control group for experimental purposes. (4) The military, by concentrating their posts near major population centers, have contributed to the already too-rapid urbanization movement by giving conscripts from the villages the psychological security necessary to adapt to urban living. (5) The abuse of civilians by soldiers can be stopped if the punishments are made sufficiently severe. Nothing can overcome the harm of bad troop behavior; a stolen duck or a thoughtless jeep driver can do irreparable damage. (6) The regular services—notably the army, but in the case of Venezuela the combined army and national guard—will be responsible for the suppression of insurrections, which must be expected to increase. Their chances of successfully carrying out their missions will be enhanced if by contributing to the improvement of conditions in the rural areas, soldiers first gain the confidence of the peasants. This is essential, for peasants, in the last analysis, are the only ones who can provide the military intelligence necessary to combat widespread rebellion successfully.

These premises suggest that intensified or new efforts should be made in certain specific areas of military activity. In the first place, the education of conscripts must be improved. An estimated 300,000 conscripts are called up each year in Latin America for periods of six months or more; at least two-thirds of them are illiterate when they report for duty, and an even larger share have only the vaguest notion of being a part of the nation. The armed forces should do more than they have thus far by way of instructing the conscripts in the official national language and introducing them to national symbols, national heroes, and perhaps, even national objectives, particularly as they pertain to the rural areas. If the proper effort were made, it should be possible to go beyond language and nationalism and help the conscript understand that events follow from human decisions and not only chance and fortune, that he stands in some definite relationship to the national community, and that he is, or can be, of political importance in society.

It has been observed that military personnel can mend water mains better than they can manage civilians, and the Latin American experience supports that view. Only a handful of the tens of thousands of villages in Latin America have water mains to mend, and most of them lack even the most rudimentary sanitary facilities. Lieutenants and their men should help villagers obtain potable water and show them how to overcome their basic sanitation problems, in much the same way that some members of the United States Peace Corps are doing. There is probably no better or cheaper way for the armed forces of Latin America to win the confidence of rural people.

Many of the republics have huge public domains (60 per cent of Honduras, for example, is government-owned) and now for the first time large numbers of people are indicating a willingness, or are being driven by population pressures, to break away from their villages and migrate. The armed forces can contribute in several ways to the redistribution of populations. By offering direct assistance, as the military in Bolivia and Brazil are actually doing, they can promote colonization by civilians and can encourage conscripts, when they have completed their tour of duty, to settle on frontiers where they might serve as "stabilizers." Engineering battalions could build access roads, which would assure prospective settlers that they could maintain contact with established communities and that they could expect to move their products to market cheaply and rapidly. Such roads might also help bind the nations together, as did the roads and canals built by United States Army Engineers in the 19th century. Soldiers might also help farmers to clear new land, as the Philippine army did at the height of the fight to suppress the Huks. Even if officers may not be able to run iron and steel plants efficiently, they have or can be given the technical skills needed to direct the building of some bridges, the draining of some swamps, and the construction of some dams. It is estimated that approximately 20 per cent of the Brazilian armed forces budget is spent on such civilian enterprises, and in recent years the army engineers have been responsible for most of the road building in the northeast, the central states, and the Amazon Valley.

Companies of soldiers, if strategically located, could serve as forest fire brigades and build fire breaks in their spare moments. Perhaps more important, soldiers should probably take the lead in managing the vast forestation or reforestation programs, as they are in Brazil and Venezuela. It will take millions of trees to halt the erosion of hillsides in Mexico. The topsoil of thousands of square miles of Brazil is being washed into the sea for lack of ground cover. In Ecuador, Peru, and Bolivia, the area threatened by erosion grows annually, while the manpower needed to save the land sits in army barracks or marches up and down in front of them.

Most of the republics have done practically nothing in nutritional experimentation. They know almost nothing about the reaction of the human body at differing elevations and temperatures to the basic foodstuffs of the various countries. Republics such as Ecuador and Peru could quarter troops at elevations ranging from sea level upwards to 16,000 feet and use them as human guinea pigs. Nutritional studies carried out under controlled conditions could make a major contribution to the national welfare of most of the republics.

It may naturally be asked why civilians couldn't do a better job than the military in the areas mentioned. The answer has several sides. One is that civilian bureaucrats have generally displayed little interest in isolating and resolving the problems of peasants or in winning their respect. The armed forces, on the other hand, have several factors favoring them: the military is national in scope, and has drawn conscripts and officers from all classes and areas; soldiers can be shifted about with relative ease; and officers have far more experience than civilian bureaucrats in working with peasants. Furthermore, and this is probably the key to the situation, village life is totally repugnant to the average civilian bureaucrat, who is city bred and trained. He and his family would look upon a prolonged assignment in a rural area as tantamount to banishment from civilization. The conclusion must be that soldiers would in most cases be the only effective intermediaries between the government and the rural masses during periods of emergency.

Finally, politicians, labor leaders, and businessmen in Latin America must decide whether they are going to work to maintain their favored positions or whether they are going to shoulder some of the responsibility for trying to satisfy the minimum aspirations of the emerging working groups. Were it not for the armed forces, the moment of decision in many cases would already have passed. The armed forces are undergoing a social-economic and professional transformation that portends misfortune for those who assume that men in uniform will always provide a bulwark behind which the politicians, labor leaders, and businessmen can put off making their choice indefinitely.

BIBLIOGRAPHY

BIBLIOGRAPHY

*This Bibliography is divided to correspond with the chapters
of the volume. Official publications are ordinarily not annotated;
those by individuals and private agencies in general are, unless the
titles appear to be self-explanatory. With a few exceptions, titles
mentioned in the sections of the text dealing with the public image
of the military are not listed.*

GENERAL WORKS

Almond, Gabriel A. and James S. Coleman, eds. *The Politics of
the Developing Areas.* Princeton, 1960.—Excellent compara-
tive politics. One chapter, by George I. Blanksten, is devoted
to Latin America.

American Universities Field Staff. *List of Publications: 1961–
1962.* New York, 1963.—The *List* contains bibliographical references to four reports on Brazil by Frank Bonilla; three general reports, one on Argentina, and one on Argentina and Chile
by K. H. Silvert; and thirteen reports on Bolivia and Peru by
Richard W. Patch. All of the reports are pertinent because they
deal with current and lively problems and because some of them
contain interesting sidelights on the military.

Andrzejewski, Stanislaw. *Military Organization and Society.*
London, 1954.—In many respects the most exciting of the theoretical studies of the armed forces and militarism.

Carr, A. R. M. "Spain: Rule by Generals," in Michael Howard,
ed., *Soldiers and Governments. Nine Studies in Civil-Military
Relations.* London, 1957, pp. 135–48.

Chaney, Homer Campbell, Jr. "The Mexican–United States War
as Seen by Mexican Intellectuals, 1846–1956." Unpublished
doctoral dissertation, Stanford University, 1959.—Extremely
valuable for studying changing attitudes toward the armed
forces.

Chapman, Mary Patricia. "Yankeephobia: an Analysis of the
Anti-United States Bias of Certain Spanish South American

Intellectuals (1898–1928)." Unpublished doctoral dissertation, Stanford University, 1950.—Good background material for the period of rising political nationalism.

Christensen, Asher N., ed. *The Evolution of Latin American Government.* New York, 1951.—Contains several articles that are pertinent to the study of the military.

Coester, Alfred. *The Literary History of Spanish America.* 2d edition, New York, 1941.—A most valuable survey.

Daalder, Hans. *The Role of the Military in the Emerging Countries.* The Hague, 1962.—A short essay that seeks to examine objectively the positive and negative aspects of the military in development and administration.

Davis, Harold Eugene, ed. *Government and Politics in Latin America.* New York, 1958.—A good selection of articles dealing with political dynamics in Latin America.

Delgado, Luis Humberto. *El militarismo en el Perú, 1821–1930.* Lima, 1930.—The author strongly favors officers over politicians.

Díaz A., Julio. *Historia del ejército de Bolivia, 1825–1932.* La Paz, 1940.—The author, a colonel, shows considerable objectivity in discussing Bolivia's military defeats.

Ekirch, Arthur A. *The Civilian and the Military.* New York, 1956.—On the essentially antimilitary thinking in the U.S.

Finer, S. E. *The Man on Horseback, The Role of the Military in Politics.* New York, 1962.—The author's facts, as they relate to Latin America, are sometimes in error, but the analysis is interesting and thoughtful.

Fisher, Sydney Nettleton, ed. *The Military in the Middle East.* Columbus, Ohio, 1963.—Seven thoughtful essays that stress the role of the military in society and government.

Germani, Gino, and Kalman Silvert. "Politics, Social Structure and Military Intervention in Latin America," *Archives européennes de sociologie,* II, No. 1 (1961), 62–81.—This article came to my attention after my manuscript went to press. The authors construct topologies which they use to correlate military action and the general state of social and economic development. Their conclusions in many cases are quite similar to the ones I arrived at independently, using distinctly different methods.

Gibson, William Marion. *The Constitutions of Colombia.* Durham, N.C., 1948.

Gutteridge, William. *Armed Forces in New States.* London, 1962.—Concerned primarily with Africa, but Part I, which deals with functions of the armed forces in new states and their social and political roles, is relevant to the Latin American situation.

Hallgarten, George W. F. *Why Dictators; the Causes and Forms of Tyrannical Rule Since 600 B.C.* New York, 1954.—Attention is directed to Latin America as illustrative of some types of dictatorships.

Herring, Hubert. *A History of Latin America, from the Beginnings to the Present.* 2d ed. New York, 1961.—Comprehensive and excellently written.

"Historical Account of the Military College of Mexico." Manuscript, Washington, D.C., Columbus Memorial Library, Pan American Union, n.d.—A short, factual account.

"History of El Colegio Militar de Bolivia." Manuscript, Washington, D.C., Columbus Memorial Library, Pan American Union. n.d.—Brief and factual.

Howard, Michael, ed. *Soldiers and Governments; Nine Studies in Civil-Military Relations.* London, 1957.

Humphreys, Robin A. "Latin America, The Caudillo Tradition," in Michael Howard, ed., *Soldiers and Governments; Nine Studies in Civil-Military Relations.* London, 1957, pp. 149–56. Historical treatment.

Huntington, Samuel P. *The Soldier and the State; the Theory and Politics of Civil-Military Relations.* Cambridge, Mass., 1957.—Outstanding.

Janowitz, Morris. *The Professional Soldier, A Social and Political Portrait.* Glencoe, Ill., 1960.—Examines previously unexplored areas of military-civilian relations.

Johnson, John J., ed. *The Role of the Military in Underdeveloped Countries.* Princeton, 1962.—The volume contains chapters by Alba, Lieuwen, and Johnson on the Latin American military.

Latin America's Nationalistic Revolutions, special issue of the *Annals of the American Academy of Political and Social Science,* edited by Robert N. Burr, CCCXXXIV (March 1961).—Several articles that relate to the study of the military.

Lieuwen, Edwin. *Arms and Politics in Latin America.* New York, 1960.—This volume, the first in English to treat the Latin American armed forces in general terms, has received well-deserved recognition throughout the Western World. It is policy-oriented and in essence argues against United States support of the armed forces.

Linares Quintana, Segundo V. "The Etiology of Revolutions in Latin America," *Western Political Quarterly,* IV (June 1951), 254–67.—Holds that Spanish heritage, borrowed constitutions, and lack of political training account for many of Latin America's difficulties.

Millikan, Max F., and Donald L. M. Blackmer. *The Emerging Nations; Their Growth and United States Policy.* Boston,

1961.—Theoretical and policy-oriented. Latin America receives little attention, but many points relevant to it are taken up.

Millis, Walter. *Arms and Men; a Study of American Military History.* New York, 1956.—The author is a recognized authority on the U.S. military.

Mills, C. Wright. *The Power Elite.* New York, 1959.—A controversial study of the political influence of the armed forces in the United States.

Montes, Hugo, and Julio Orlandi. *Historia de la literatura chilena.* Santiago de Chile, 1955.—Good coverage.

Navarro, Pedro Juan. *Dictaduras de América.* Bogotá, 1936.— Impressions of some of Latin America's dictators.

Niedermayer, F. "Dictaduras de ayer y hoy en Ibero-América," *Latinoamérica* (Mexico), May 1, 1953, pp. 221–23.

Novoa de la Fuente, Luis. *Historia naval de Chile.* Valparaiso, 1944.—A text used in the Naval Academy.

Pauker, Guy J. "Notes on Non-Military Measures in Control of Insurgency." Santa Monica, Calif., The RAND Corporation, 1962, 12 pp.—Brief, thoughtful discussion of counter-insurgency measures used in the Philippines and Malaya.

Rapaport, David C. "Praetorianism: Government without Consensus." Unpublished doctoral dissertation, University of California (Berkeley), 1959.

Special Operations Research Office (The American University). *A Counterinsurgency Bibliography.* Washington, 1963.—English sources only.

———. "A Preliminary Bibliography on Studies of the Role of Military Establishments in Developing Nations." Mimeo. Washington, D.C., 1963.

Spell, Jefferson Rea. *Contemporary Spanish-American Fiction.* Chapel Hill, N.C., 1944.

United Nations, Department of Economic and Social Affairs. *Economic and Social Consequences of Disarmament.* New York, 1962.

United States, Department of State, Bureau of Intelligence and Research. *Studies in Progress or Recently Completed: Arms Control and Disarmament.* Washington, D.C., 1963.

Vagts, Alfred. *A History of Militarism.* New York, 1959.—Indispensable.

Valle, Rafael Heliodoro. *Historia de las ideas contemporáneas en Centro-América.* Mexico, 1960.—Chapter Two, "Democracia y Dictadura," containing quotes from a number of Central American writers on the subject of dictatorship, is especially useful.

CHAPTER I

Entries included in this section deal chiefly with the colonial period and the Wars of Independence.

Alamán, Lucas. *Historia de Méjico.* 5 vols. Mexico, 1849–52.— The conservative creole position and the anarchical period that followed the winning of independence.

Arnade, Charles W. *The Emergence of the Republic of Bolivia.* Gainesville, Florida, 1957.—Thorough treatment of a period of anarchy and violence.

Belaúnde, Víctor Andrés. *Bolívar and the Political Thought of the Spanish American Revolution.* Baltimore, 1938.

Bolívar, Simón. *Cartas del libertador, corrigidas conforme a los originales,* edited by Vicente Lecuna. 12 vols. Caracas, 1929– 59.

Bram, Joseph. *An Analysis of Inca Militarism.* Seattle, 1941.— The concern of the Inca leadership to protect civilians from the soldiers.

Bushnell, David. *The Santander Regime in Gran Colombia.* Newark, Del., 1954.—An excellent study that gives considerable attention to the role of the military immediately following independence.

Carro Martínez, Antonio. "El caudillismo americano," *Revista de estudios políticos,* May–June, 1957, pp. 139–63.—*Caudillismo* is made possible by the mentality of the people.

Colombia (Republic of Colombia, 1819–1831). Laws, statutes, etc. *Code of laws of the Republic of Colombia: containing the constitution and laws sanctioned by the First General Congress, in the sittings they held from the sixth of May to the fourteenth of October, 1821.* London, 1823.

George Washington University, Washington, D.C., Seminar Conference on Hispanic American Affairs. *South American Dictators during the First Century of Independence.* Vol. 5 of *Studies in Hispanic American Affairs,* edited by A. Curtis Wilgus. Washington, D.C., 1937.—Biographical. Good coverage.

Hidalgo, Daniel B. *El militarismo, sus causas y remedios.* Quito, 1913.—Holds Spain largely responsible for militarism but considers economic backwardness to be an important factor.

McAlister, Lyle N. *The "Fuero Militar" in New Spain, 1764–1800.* Gainesville, Fla., 1957.—A careful study of the rise of militarism in colonial Mexico.

Manning, William Ray. *Diplomatic Correspondence of the United States: Inter-American Affairs, 1831–1860.* 12 vols. Washington, D.C., 1932–39.—A basic set of documents for the period.

Masur, Gerhard. *Simón Bolívar*. Albuquerque, N.M., 1948.—The best single volume on the dictator.

Mitre, Bartolomé. *Historia de San Martín y la independencia argentina*. Buenos Aires, 1890.—A major biography of a major military figure.

O'Leary, Daniel F. *Bolívar y la emancipación de Sur-América; memorias del General O'Leary*. Translated by Simon B. O'Leary. 2 vols. Madrid, 1915.—Contains much material on civilian instability.

Restrepo, José Manuel. *Historia de la revolución de la República de Colombia en América Meridional*. 4 vols. Besançon, 1858.— A major source for the early history of Colombia.

Rojas, Ricardo. *San Martín, Knight of the Andes*. Translated by Herschel Brickell and Carlos Videla. Garden City, N.Y., 1945. —Almost mystical in its approach.

Santander, Francisco de Paula. *Cartas de Santander,* edited by Vicente Lecuna. 3 vols. Caracas, 1942.

Tannenbaum, Frank. "The Destiny of the Negro in the Western Hemisphere," *Political Science Quarterly*, LXI (1946), 1–41. —Discusses the Negro in the armies of liberation.

Worcester, Donald E. *Sea Power and Chilean Independence*. Gainesville, Fla., 1962.—Quite brief. Reviews much of the material covered earlier by Eugenio Pereira Salas.

CHAPTER II

The materials listed in this section generally stress developments during the period 1825–1850.

Alamán, Lucas. *Historia de Méjico.*—See entry under Chapter I.

Alberdi, Juan Bautista. *Estudios económicos; interpretación económica de la historia política argentina y sud-americana; con un estudio sobre las doctrinas sociológicas de Alberdi, por José Ingenieros*. Buenos Aires, 1916.—Contains good background material.

Basadre, Jorge. *La iniciación de la república*. Lima, 1929.—Indispensable for the early 19th century.

Blanco-Fombona, Rufino. *La evolución política y social de Hispano-América*. Madrid, 1911.—Pays considerable attention to the factors leading to civil wars.

Bushnell, David. *The Santander Regime in Gran Colombia.*—See entry under Chapter II.

Calderón de la Barca, Francis Erskine. *Life in Mexico During a Residence of Two Years in that Country*. 2 vols. Boston, 1843.

—Firsthand accounts of the turmoil in Mexico during the Santa Anna era.

Callcott, Wilfrid H. *Santa Anna: The Story of an Enigma Who Once Was Mexico.* Norman, Okla., 1936.—Describes the worst in the Mexican armed forces.

Carrancá y Trujillo, Raúl. *La evolución política de Iberoamérica.* Madrid, 1925.—The armed forces and *caudillismo* are treated in one chapter.

Carreño, Alberto M. *Jefes del ejército mexicano en 1847.* Mexico, 1914.

Chapman, Charles E. "The Age of the Caudillos: A Chapter in Hispanic American History," *Hispanic American Historical Review,* XII (August 1932), 281–300.—One of the earliest studies in English on the 19th-century *caudillo.*

Chile. Ministerio de Guerra. *Album gráfico del ejército. Centenaria de la independencia de Chile, 1810–1910.* Santiago de Chile, 1910.

Cotner, Thomas E. *The Military and Political Career of José Joaquín de Herrera, 1792–1854.* Austin, Tex., 1949.—A major contribution to the study of the Mexican military in the 19th century.

Gilmore, Robert L. "Federalism in Colombia, 1810–1848." Unpublished doctoral dissertation, University of California, 1949. —A first-rate treatment with considerable material on the military.

Great Britain, Foreign Office. *British and Foreign State Papers.* London, 1816–.—A most useful source for 19th-century official documents. Most of the material for the sections on the constitutions came from this set.

Humphreys, Robin A. *The Evolution of Modern Latin America.* London, 1946.—Chapter IV, "Democracy and Dictatorship," is particularly useful.

Jane, Cecil. *Liberty and Despotism in Spanish America.* Oxford, 1929.—Interpretative, with major emphasis on the 1825–30 period.

Konetzke, Richard. "Iberoamérica en la historia," *Cuadernos* (Paris), No. 36, May–June, 1959, pp. 47–50.—Deals with *caudillismo.*

Manning, William Ray. *Diplomatic Correspondence of the United States: Inter-American Affairs, 1831–1860.* 12 vols. Washington, D.C., 1932–39.—Absolutely essential.

Mora, José María Luis. *Méjico y sus revoluciones.* 3 vols. Paris, 1836.—The best contemporary account of Mexico after independence. Deals at considerable length with the military's role in the widespread anarchy that the republic experienced during its early years.

Morales Padrón, Francisco. "Dictaduras en Hispanoamérica," *Arbor,* XXIII (September–October, 1952), 1–19.—A good general survey with emphasis on the early 19th century.

Picón-Salas, Mariano, *et al. Venezuela independiente, 1810–1960.* Caracas, 1962.—Excellent on 19th-century *caudillismo* and anarchy.

Restrepo, José Manuel. *Historia de la revolución de la República de Colombia en América Meridional.* 4 vols. Besançon, 1858. —A major source for the anarchic quarter-century after independence.

Rippy, J. Fred. "Dictatorship in Latin America," in Guy S. Ford, ed., *Dictatorship in the Modern World.* Minneapolis, 1939.— Quite useful on 19th-century-style militarism.

CHAPTER III

The works included below were particularly useful in the preparation of the section covering the period 1850–1914.

Acosta, Cecilio. "Causas generales de las revoluciones en América Española," *Boletín de la Academia Nacional de la Historia* (Caracas), XX (April–June, 1937), 276–82.—An enumeration of factors contributing to political instability.

Alberto Rangel, Domingo. "Una interpretación de las dictaduras latinoamericanas," *Cuadernos americanos,* XIII (September–October, 1954), 33–42.—Stresses social factors.

Argentine Republic. Laws, statutes, etc. *Digesto de guerra . . . dictados hasta el 1° de octubre de 1909.* Buenos Aires, 1909.— A storehouse of rules, laws, and regulations. Also contains materials on foreign missions.

Argentine Republic. Laws, statutes, etc. *Justicia militar argentina; proyecto de código.* . . . Buenos Aires, 1914.

Ayarragaray, Lucas. *La anarquía argentina y el caudillismo.* 2d ed. Buenos Aires, 1925.—One of the best studies of Argentina for the period up to World War I.

Báez, Cecilio. *Ensayo sobre el doctor Francia y la dictadura en Sud-América.* Asunción, 1910.—A defense of Francia.

Baldrich, Coronel J. Amadeo. *Vida militar de Teniente General Donato Alvarez.* Buenos Aires, 1916.—Alvarez as told to Baldrich.

Beals, Carleton. *Porfirio Díaz, Dictator of Mexico.* A sustained attack on Díaz as president and on the military under his control.

Blanco-Fombona, Rufino. *La evolución política y social de Hispano-América.*—See entry under Chapter II.

Bryce, James. *South America: Observations and Impressions.* New York, 1912.

Bulnes, Francisco. *Las grandes mentiras de nuestra historia.* Paris, 1904.—Provocative treatment of Mexico after independence.

———. *The Whole Truth About Mexico.* Translated by Dora Scott. New York, 1916.—Good background material.

Bunge, Carlos O. *Nucstra América.* Barcelona, 1903.—A very thoughtful study of the problems that confronted Latin America during the 19th century.

Burr, Robert N. *The Stillborn Panama Congress: Power Politics and Chilean-Colombian Relations During the War of the Pacific.* Berkeley, 1962.—An important source for the use of power on the West Coast.

Bustamente Maceo, Gregorio. *Historia militar de El Salvador.* San Salvador, 1951. Accounts of battles engaged in by Salvadorean troops.

Carrancá y Trujillo, Raúl. *La evolución política de Iberoamérica.* —See entry under Chapter II.

Carreño, Alberto María. "El colegio militar de Chapultepec, 1847–1947," *Boletín de la Sociedad Mexicana de Geografía y Estadística,* LXVI (July–October, 1948), 25–92.—A recent Mexican version of the United States–Mexican War.

Chile, Academia de Guerra. *Reseña histórica, 1886–1936.* Santiago de Chile, 1936.—Official.

Chile, Ministerio de Guerra. *Album gráfico del ejército. . . .* — See entry under Chapter II.

Chiriboga Navarro, Angel Isaac. *Fuerzas morales en el ejército.* Quito, 1932.—Favorable account of the contribution of the armed forces. Contains considerable information on foreign missions.

Colombia (United States of Colombia, 1863–1885). Laws, statutes, etc. *Código militar expedido por el congreso de los Estados Unidos de Colombia de 1881.* Bogotá, 1881.

Cuevas, Gabriel. *El glorioso colegio militar mexicano en un siglo (1824–1924).* Mexico, 1937.

Cumberland, Charles Curtis. *Mexican Revolution: Genesis Under Madero.* Austin, Tex., 1952.—The political and military background to a major social revolution.

Epstein, Fritz T. "European Military Influences in Latin America." Unpublished manuscript in the Library of Congress, 1941. —Excellent treatment of foreign missions to Latin America.

280   *Bibliography*

Estrada, José Manuel. *Discursos: 1862–1890*. Buenos Aires, 1915.—Nationalism in 19th-century Argentina.

Flower, Elizabeth, "The Mexican Revolt Against Positivism," *Journal of the History of Ideas*, X, No. 1 (January 1949), 115–29.—Discusses the influence of positivism under the military dictator Díaz.

García, Leónidas. *El militarismo en Sud-América*. Quito, 1911–12.—Valuable for an early view of the subject.

García Calderón, Francisco. *Latin America: Its Rise and Progress*. Translated by Bernard Miall. New York, 1913.—Essential, both for background and for the author's thoughts on the armed forces.

García Cubas, Antonio. *Cuadro geográfico, estadístico, descriptivo e histórico de los Estados Unidos Mexicanos*. Mexico, 1884.—A chapter on the military breaks the army down into its various components.

Great Britain, Foreign Office. *British and Foreign State Papers*. —See entry under Chapter II.

Griffen, Charles C. "Regionalism's Role in Venezuelan Politics," *The Inter-American Quarterly*, III (October 1941), 21–35.—Points out that social as well as military problems plagued Venezuela throughout the 19th century.

Gutiérrez Santos, Daniel. *Historia militar de México, 1876–1914*. Mexico, 1955.—The author, a professor in the Escuela Superior de Guerra, limits himself to synthesizing what others have said. Of the four chapters in the book, the second, which deals with the campaigns against the Yaquis and the Mayas and the army's role in the Cananena and Río Blanco strikes, is of particular interest.

McGann, Thomas F. *Argentina, the United States, and the Inter-American System, 1880–1914*. Cambridge, Mass., 1957.—Chapters One through Six provide excellent background reading on the highly important 1880–1914 era.

Paz, Octavio. *The Labyrinth of Solitude*. Translated by Lysander Kemp. New York, 1961.—Good on 19th-century background, especially positivism.

Pérez, Enrique. "Chile y la cultura militar en la América Hispana," in *Hispania* (London), March 1, 1912, pp. 64–65.—Discusses Chile's contribution to military professionalization in Latin America.

Picón-Salas, Mariano, *et al. Venezuela independiente, 1810–1960*. —See entry under Chapter II.

Pierson, William W., Jr. "Foreign Influence on Venezuelan Political Thought, 1830–1930," *Hispanic American Historical Re-*

view, XV (February 1935), 3–42.—Contains extensive quotes from Arcaya relating to the military and society.

La Protesta. Buenos Aires.—An anarchist paper that appeared irregularly. Spot-checked for the 1880's and the first decade of the 20th century.

Rippy, J. Fred. "Dictatorship in Latin America," in Guy S. Ford, ed., Dictatorship in the Modern World. Minneapolis, 1939.— See entry under Chapter II.

Riva Palacio, Vicente. *México a través de los siglos.* 4 vols. Mexico, 1887–89.—An important source on Mexico until the time of Porfirio Díaz.

Santiago de Chile. Escuela militar de Chile. *Escuela militar de Chile, 1903.* Santiago de Chile, [1903?].—Photographs clearly indicate the German influence in the Chilean army.

Sarmiento, Domingo Faustino. *Facundo; ó, civilización i barbarie en las pampas arjentinas.* 4th ed. New York, 1868.—A classic on the problem of *caudillismo.*

Schiff, Warren. "German Military Penetration into Mexico During the Late Díaz Period," *Hispanic American Historical Review,* XXXIX (November 1959), 568–79.—Based on official documents.

Simmons, Merle Edwin. *The Mexican Corrido as a Source of Interpretive Study of Modern Mexico, 1870–1950.* Bloomington, Ill., 1957.—A major contribution. Many of the *corridos* reflect popular thinking on the military.

Telich, Marie Louise. "Manuel González Prada, The Social Content of his Writing." Unpublished master's thesis, Stanford University, 1955.—Shows a fine appreciation of one of Latin America's most controversial men of letters.

United States, Department of State. *Foreign Relations of the United States, 1861–.* (Until 1872, entitled *Messages and Documents.*)—Invaluable, particularly for the pre-World War I era. Contains numerous judgments on coups and military leaders.

Vallenilla Lanz, Laureano. *Cesarismo democrático.* Caracas, 1919. —A defense of strong government.

Warren, Harris Gaylord. *Paraguay, An Informal History.* Norman, Okla., 1949.—Solid coverage of military dominated Paraguay.

Wise, George S. *Caudillo, A Portrait of Antonio Guzmán Blanco.* New York, 1951.—Thin in spots and often redundant.

Zea, Leopoldo. *Dos etapas del pensamiento en Hispanoamérica: del romanticismo al positivismo.* Mexico, 1949.—Very good on positivism.

CHAPTERS IV, V, AND VI

This portion of the Bibliography contains works upon which I drew heavily in preparing the section on contemporary Spanish America.

Ahumada, A. *El ejército y la revolución del 5 de septiembre de 1924.* n.p., n.d.—Discusses in some detail the political activities of the Chilean armed forces during the critical months of 1924.

Alexander, Robert J. "The Army in Politics," in Harold Eugene Davis, ed., *Government and Politics in Latin America.* New York, 1958, pp. 147–65.

————. *The Bolivian National Revolution.* New Brunswick, N.J., 1958.—Friendly to the MNR in its long struggle against the oligarchy-oriented armed forces.

————. "Brazilian Tenentismo," *Hispanic American Historical Review,* XXXVI (May 1956), 229–42.—Examination of an indigenous, radical, nationalist movement within the military during the 1920's, certain leaders of which continue significantly to affect Brazilian national politics.

————. *The Perón Era.* New York, 1951.—Still useful as a study of Argentine military behavior.

Amaya, Laureano Orcenio. *El ejército: factor ponderable en el desenvolvimiento económico, social, y político de la nación.* Buenos Aires, 1949.—Favorable treatment of the armed forces, especially of the army.

Arcaya, Pedro Manuel. *Venezuela y su actual régimen.* Washington, D.C., 1935.—Friendly to the military dictator Juan Vicente Gómez.

Arciniegas, Germán. "La dictadura en Colombia," *Cuadernos americanos,* IX (January–February, 1950), 7–33.—The author largely avoids the military problem.

————. *The State of Latin America.* Translated by Harriet de Onís. New York, 1952.—The author is one of the strongest protagonists of democracy in Latin America.

Arellano Bonilla, Roberto. "Breve ensayo sobre el caso del militarismo en Honduras. Unpublished manuscript, 1960.—I am greatly indebted to Sr. Arellano Bonilla, who wrote the manuscript for me at my request.

Betancourt, Rómulo. *Posición y doctrina.* Caracas, 1959.—The author, President of Venezuela, argues at length for an apolitical military.

————. "El caso de Venezuela y el destino de la democracia en América," *Cuadernos americanos,* VIII (July–August, 1949),

27–66.—An attack upon the military following the overthrow of Rómulo Gallegos.

Blanksten, George I. "Caudillismo in Northwestern South America," *South Atlantic Quarterly,* LI (October 1952), 493–503.

——. *Ecuador: Constitutions and Caudillos.* Berkeley, 1951.— The armed forces are taken to task in this scholarly presentation.

——. *Perón's Argentina.* Chicago, 1953.—Valuable for its discussion of militarism and fascism in the Argentine military.

——. "Political Groups in Latin America," *American Political Science Review,* LIII (1959), 106–27.—Among other things, the author calls for more research on clique formation in the Latin American armed services.

——. "The Politics of Latin America," in Gabriel A. Almond and James S. Coleman, eds., *The Politics of the Developing Areas.* Princeton, 1960, pp. 455–528.—A partly new approach to an old problem. Provides a useful framework within which to study the political development of the area.

Blasco Ibáñez, Vicente. *El militarismo mejicano.* Valencia, 1920. —A man of letters considers the military problem. Good on the common soldiers and *soldaderas.*

Bustamente Maceo, Gregorio. *Historia militar de El Salvador.*— See entry under Chapter III.

Cabero, Alberto. *Chile y los chilenos.* 3d ed. Santiago de Chile, 1948.—Friendly to military, says Chileans make good soldiers.

La Calle. Quito.—Contains numerous articles and editorials on the military, sometimes favorable, sometimes critical. Issues for 1959 and 1960 were consulted.

Cárdenas, Lázaro. *Discurso pronunciado en el banquete que le ofrecieron los CC. jefes de zonas militares, el día 5 de septiembre de 1939.* Mexico, 1939.—Calls for an army subservient to the civilian government.

Carril, Bonifacio del. *Problemas de la revolución y la democracia.* Buenos Aires, 1956.—Four essays that deal with revolution and democracy in largely theoretical terms. Examples are drawn almost entirely from the Argentine experience.

Chile, Academia de Guerra. *Reseña histórica, 1886–1936.*—See entry under Chapter III.

Chile. Laws, statutes, etc. *Código de justicia militar.* 2d ed. Santiago de Chile, 1944.

Cline, Howard F. *Mexico: Revolution to Evolution 1940–1960.* London, 1962.—A short section is devoted to the military in this volume, which gives the 1950's detailed coverage.

——. *The United States and Mexico.* Cambridge, Mass., 1953.

—This fine volume is not superseded by the author's 1962 volume.

Colmo, Alfredo. *La revolución en la América Latina.* 2d ed. Buenos Aires, 1933.—A penetrating examination of the revolutions that swept over Latin America in 1930. The overthrow of Irigoyen is treated in detail.

Cossio del Pomar, Felipe. "Oligárquia y militarismo en el Perú," *Cuadernos,* LVII (February 1962), 27–31.—Examines cooperation between the military and the oligarchy.

Council on Foreign Relations. *Social Change in Latin America Today; Its Implications for United States Policy.* New York, 1960.—Several social anthropologists examine problems of U.S. relations with the people of Latin America.

Cumberland, Charles C. "Bases of Revolutions in the Caribbean," in A. Curtis Wilgus, ed., *The Caribbean: Its Political Problems.* Gainesville, Fla., 1956, pp. 89–109.

Derr, Virginia B. "The Rise of a Middle-Class Tradition in Mexican Art," *Journal of Inter-American Studies,* III (July 1961), 385–409.

Donoso, Ricardo. *Desarrollo político y social de Chile desde la Constitución de 1833.* Santiago de Chile, 1942.—Chapter VI, "Anarquía Militar," covers the years 1924–32.

Dulles, John W. F. *Yesterday in Mexico: A Chronicle of the Revolution, 1919–1936.* Austin, Tex., 1961.—Unusually useful for the behavior of the officer corps during the turbulent 1920's.

Ercilla. Santiago de Chile.—A first-rate weekly. During 1955 *Ercilla* ran a number of thoughtful articles on secret cliques in the Chilean armed forces.

Fitzgibbon, Russel H. "How Democratic is Latin America?" *Inter-American Economic Affairs,* IX (Spring, 1956), 65–77. —Civilian supremacy over the military is one of the criteria from which the degree of democracy is judged.

———. "Revolution: Western Hemisphere," *South Atlantic Quarterly,* LV, No. 3 (July 1956), 263–79.—Revolution is viewed in the total context of Latin America's 20th-century development.

———. "What Price Latin American Armies?" *Virginia Quarterly Review,* XXXVI (Autumn, 1960), 517–32.—Discusses some of the conditions under which officers withdraw from direct participation in decision-making.

Fluharty, Vernon Lee. *Dance of the Millions: Military Rule and the Social Revolution in Colombia 1930–1956.* Pittsburgh, 1957. —The author was perhaps overly impressed with the achievements of the Rojas Pinilla regime.

Goldwert, Marvin. "The Argentine Revolution of 1930: The Rise of Modern Militarism and Ultra-Nationalism in Argentina." Unpublished doctoral dissertation, University of Texas, 1962.—Quite thoughtful. Considerable attention is given to the Argentine military.

Gómez, R. A. *Government and Politics in Latin America*. New York, 1960.—Chapters Four and Six briefly treat violence and strong-man rule.

"Green Dragons and Gorillas," *The Economist* (September 26, 1959), pp. 1031–32.—Secret organizations within the Argentine military are treated briefly.

Gruening, Ernest Henry. *Mexico and Its Heritage*. New York, 1928.—Contains a devastating attack upon the Mexican military.

Hadley, Paul E. "Latin America: Retreat from Violence," *Western Political Quarterly*, XI (June 1958), 385–87.—Many of the conditions that historically have contributed to violence and militarism remain.

Helguera, J. León. "The Changing Role of the Military in Colombia," *Journal of Inter-American Studies*, III (July 1961), 351–58.—Factual rather than interpretative.

Holmes, Olive. "Army Challenge in Latin America," *Foreign Policy Reports*, XXV, No. 14 (December 1, 1949), 166–75.—Early recognition of the changing character of the military following World War II.

Iturriaga, José E. "El tirano en la América Latina," in *Jornadas* (Mexico City, Colegio de México, Centros de Estudios Sociales), No. 15 (1945).—Despotism, encouraged by imperialists, was headed in the direction of fascism.

Jaramillo Alvarado, Pío. *La guerra de conquista en América*. Guayaquil, 1941.—Largely a discussion of inter-American relations prior to World War II. Examines certain boundary disputes.

———. *El régimen totalitario en América*. Guayaquil, 1940.—Three essays written to the question of democracy or fascism in Latin America. Uses Brazil and Peru during the 1930's as examples.

Johnson, John J. *Political Change in Latin America, The Emergence of the Middle Sectors*. Stanford, 1958.—Provides background material on the societies in which professionalization has been most pronounced.

Lieuwen, Edwin. *Arms and Politics in Latin America*.—See entry under General Works.

———. "The Changing Role of The Military in Latin America,"

Journal of Inter-American Studies, III (October 1961), 559–70.

———. "The Military: A Revolutionary Force," in *Latin America's Nationalistic Revolutions,* special issue of the *Annals of the American Academy of Political and Social Science,* edited by Robert N. Burr, CCCXXXIV (March 1961), 30-40.

———. "Neo-Militarism in Latin America: The Kennedy Administration's Inadequate Response," *Inter-American Economic Affairs,* XVI (Spring, 1963), 11–19.—Recommends alternative courses of action, including greater emphasis upon civic action.

Linke, Lilo. *Ecuador, Country of Contrasts.* London, 1954.— Contains a brief section on the Ecuadorian military in the 20th century.

Liscano, Juan. "Sobre 'el señor presidente' y otras temas de la dictadura," *Cuadernos Americanos,* XVII (March–April, 1958), 63–75.—Mainly about the novel *El señor presidente.* Decidedly anti-military.

Lott, Leo B. "The 1952 Venezuelan Elections: A Lesson for 1957," *Western Political Quarterly,* X (September 1957), 541–58.—Covers much of the Pérez Jiménez military regime.

Lubertino, José. *La tragedia de las dictaduras latinoamericanas y cuatro problemas argentinas.* Buenos Aires, 1956.—Dictatorship and the problem of education.

McAlister, Lyle N. "Civil-Military Relations in Latin America," *Journal of Inter-American Studies,* III (July 1961), 341–50.— Brief but highly provocative evaluation.

Mañach, Jorge. *El militarismo en Cuba.* Havana, 1939.

Mancera Galleti, Angel. *Civilismo y militarismo.* Caracas, 1960.

Mansilla Cortes, José M. *Justicia al soldado.* Mexico, 1952.— Friendly treatment of the military's role in Mexico's continuing revolution.

Mariátegui, José Carlos. *Siete ensayos de interpretación de la realidad peruana.* Santiago de Chile, 1955.—A key background source.

Marín Balmaceda, Raúl. *La caída de un régimen; julio de 1931.* Santiago de Chile, 1933.—Reasonably objective account of the overthrow of Ibáñez in 1931.

Marín Balmaceda, Raúl, Francisco Huneeus, y Rafael L. Gumucio V. *No más: Tres artículos publicados en "El Diario Illustrado."* Santiago de Chile, 1932.—Holds the armed forces responsible for the unrest following the overthrow of Ibáñez.

Martz, John D. *Colombia — A Contemporary Political Survey.* Chapel Hill, N.C., 1962.—The Rojas Pinilla era is given extensive coverage.

Melfi, Domingo. *Dictadura y mansedumbre.* Santiago de Chile, 1931.—Seeks to define some of the moral and psychological aspects of the Ibáñez dictatorship in Chile.

Mexico, Secretaría de Gobernación. *Seis años de gobierno al servicio de México, 1934–1940.* Mexico, 1940.—Discusses military contributions to the civilian sector.

Molina, Enrique. *La revolución, los estudiantes, y la democracia.* Santiago de Chile, 1931.—Student activity in the overthrow of Ibáñez.

New York Times.—Used extensively for the period after 1953.

Oddone, Jacinto. *Historia del socialismo argentino.* 2 vols. Buenos Aires, 1934.—Basic for background.

Otero, Gustavo Adolfo. "Las clases sociales en la América Latina," *Filosofía, letras y ciencias de la educación* (Quito), XI (January–June, 1958), 164–95.—Some discussion of the military as a springboard to social advancement.

Owen, Frank. *Perón: His Rise and Fall.* London, 1957.—Contains a brief discussion of the army in Argentine life.

Pareja Diezcanseco, Alfredo. *Historia del Ecuador.* 2 vols. Quito, 1958.—The best general history of Ecuador.

Patch, Richard W. See *American Universities Field Staff Reports Service* for Bolivia and Peru, published during 1961–62. —See the entry under General Works.

Perón, Juan D. "Significado de la defensa nacional desde el punto de vista militar," in Universidad Nacional de La Plata, *Curso de cultura superior universitaria; Cátedra de defensa nacional.* La Plata, Argentina, 1945, pp. 50–79.—An address delivered on June 10, 1944, while Perón was Minister of War, strongly advocating industrialization, with state support if necessary, as requisite to an effective military establishment.

Pike, Fredrick B., ed. *Freedom and Reform in Latin America.* Notre Dame, Ind., 1959.—Useful background material.

Plaza Lasso, Galo. *The Problems of Democracy in Latin America.* Chapel Hill, N.C., 1955.—Friendly to the Ecuadorian military.

Potash, Robert A. "The Changing Role of the Military in Argentina," *Journal of Inter-American Studies,* III (October 1961), 571–78.—A preliminary work, to be followed by a major study of the Argentine armed forces.

Prado Vázquez, Guillermo. *La carrera de oficial (lo que es y lo que debe ser).* Santiago de Chile, 1952.—A colonel's plea for greater professionalization.

Prewett, Virginia. "The Mexican Army," *Foreign Affairs,* XIX, No. 3 (April 1941), 609–20.—The Mexican army after 1920 in terms of its fighting capabilities and its role in government.

Pujades, Pablo. *Dictadores americanos, al ocaso, el justicialismo de Perón.* Bogotá, 1958.—A strong attack on Perón, with a chapter on the fall of Pérez Jiménez. Author was optimistic that Latin America was nearing the end of the era of dictators.

Ramos, Jorge Abelardo. *Historia política del ejército argentino.* Buenos Aires, 1959.—Short but highly pertinent; compares the political behavior of the armed forces before and after 1930.

Rangel, Domingo Alberto. "Una interpretación de las dictaduras latinoamericanas," *Cuadernos americanos,* XIII (September–December, 1954), 33–42.—Contends that the military in much of Latin America came under fascist influence during the 1930's. Calls particular attention to the academy at Chorillos, Peru.

Rojas, Ricardo. *La guerra de las naciones.* Buenos Aires, 1924.— Concerned primarily with nationalism.

Romero, César Enrique. "Crisis del gobierno civil en América Latina?" *Revista de estudios políticos,* CXXII (March–April 1962), 227–32. — Contends that military influence in Latin America has grown over the last forty years.

Romero, José Luis. *A History of Argentine Political Thought.* Translated by Thomas F. McGann. Stanford, 1963.—Extremely valuable. Fascism in the Argentine army is given limited attention.

Romero Flores, Jesús, ed. *Anales históricos de la revolución mexicana: sus corridos.* Mexico, 1940.

Ross, Stanley R. "Some Observations on Military Coups in the Caribbean," in A. Curtis Wilgus, ed., *The Caribbean: Its Political Problems.* Gainesville, Fla., 1956, pp. 110–28.—Thoughtful. Has some interesting conclusions.

Rueda Vargas, Tomás. *El ejército nacional.* Bogotá, 1944.— Treats the military as a fighting force.

Sáez Morales, General Carlos. *Recuerdos de un soldado; el ejército y la política.* Santiago de Chile, 1933.—The role of the army during the Ibáñez dictatorship and the disturbed period following his overthrow.

Samaniego, Roque. *Nuestra problema militar.* Asunción, 1919.— The author, a major in the Paraguayan army, treats the problem in a favorable light.

Sanmartino, Ernesto. *La verdad sobre la situación argentina.* Montevideo, 1950.—One of the best studies of the military rule under Perón.

Sarobe, General José María. *Memorias sobre la revolución de 6 septiembre de 1930.* Buenos Aires, [1957].—Highly valuable account by a person who was in on the revolt three months before it was staged.

Schneider, Ronald M. *Communism in Guatemala 1944–1954.* New

York, 1959.—The army and the army officers in politics are carefully analyzed.

Scott, Robert E. *Mexican Government in Transition.* Urbana, Ill., 1959.—Good general study; the military is treated quite briefly.

Silva Herzog, Jesús. "Las juntas militares de gobierno," *Cuadernos americanos,* VIII (July–August, 1949), 7–13.—The author has little sympathy for the military.

———. "Reflexiones sobre las dictaduras," *Cuadernos americanos,* XI (July–August, 1952), 57–63.—Except in Argentina, the author finds a close relationship between United States recognition and military assistance and the survival of military dictatorships.

Silvert, Kalman H. "Economics, Democracy, and Honesty; an Assessment of the Frondizi Regime," *American Universities Field Staff Reports Service,* VII (April 10, 1960). 15 pp.—Astute analysis of Argentine military-civilian relations during the months preceding Frondizi's overthrow.

———. "Political Change in Latin America," in *The United States and Latin America.* The American Assembly, New York, 1959. —A very thoughtful discussion. The army is treated only incidentally.

———. *Reaction and Revolution in Latin America; the Conflict Society.* New Orleans, 1961.—Contains thoughtful chapters on contemporary Chile and Argentina.

———. Also see *American Universities Field Staff Reports Service* for Argentine and Chile, published during 1961–62.—See entry under General Works.

Simon, S. Fanny. "Anarchism and Anarcho-Syndicalism in South America," *Hispanic American Historical Review,* XXVI (February 1946), 38–59.—Useful for attitudes of the syndicalists toward social-economic problems.

Sotta, Hector Rodríguez de la. *Crisis política, económica y moral.* Santiago de Chile, 1932.—A conservative spokesman on the issues raised by the political unrest of 1932 in Chile. The military is not discussed.

Stokes, William S. *Honduras: An Area Study in Government.* Madison, Wis., 1950.—Useful for background information. The military is largely ignored.

———. *Latin American Politics.* New York, 1959.—Facts and figures are up to date.

———. "Violence as a Power Factor in Latin-American Politics," *Western Political Quarterly,* V (September 1952), 445–68.—Describes the anatomy of violence in Latin American politics.

Szulc, Tad. *Twilight of the Tyrants.* New York, 1959.—Optimistic that military dictatorships were on their way out.

Tannenbaum, Frank. "Agrarismo, Indianismo, y Nacionalismo," *Hispanic American Historical Review,* XXIII, No. 3 (August 1943), 394–423.—Relates *caudillismo* to social-economic environment.

———. "The Future of Democracy in Latin America," *Foreign Affairs,* XXXIII (April 1955), 429–44.—Treats the dilemma posed by the dream of representative democracy and the fact of revolution or dictatorship.

———. *Peace by Revolution; an Interpretation of Mexico.* New York, 1933.—Excellent discussion of the problems arising from the Revolution of 1910.

Terán, Juan B. *La salud de la América Española.* Paris, 1926.— Considerable attention is given to militarism and demagoguery.

Tucker, William P. *The Mexican Government.* Minneapolis, 1957.—Valuable as a general account; armed forces receive relatively little attention.

Turner, Darrina D. "The Changing Political Role of the Mexican Army, 1934–1940." Unpublished master's thesis, University of Florida, 1960.—Quite general.

United States Senate, Committee on Foreign Relations. *United States Latin American Relations,* 86th Congress, 2d session, Washington, D.C., 1960. Doc. No. 125.—The military figures prominently in some of the contributions.

Valdes, Renato. *Tres Cartas,* con un prólogo y un epílogo. Santiago de Chile, 1932.—Seeks to explain the Chilean military's behavior after 1910 and, in part, to justify the Ibáñez regime.

Vekemans, Rev. Roger, S.J. "Synthesis of a Socio-Economic Typology of the Latin American Countries." Washington, D.C., Pan American Union, mimeo., 1960.

Venezuela, Comandancia General del Ejército, *Revista del ejército.*—Issues for 1960–63 carry articles on proposals for the military's contribution to the civilian sector.

Whitaker, Arthur P. *Argentine Upheaval: Perón's Fall and the New Regime.* New York, 1956.—Useful for what it has to say about the Argentine armed forces immediately following the overthrow of Perón.

———. *Nationalism in Latin America.* Gainesville, Fla., 1962.— Useful background material.

———. *The United States and Argentina.* Cambridge, Mass., 1954.—Detailed coverage of the crucial Perón era.

Wyckoff, Theodore. "The Role of the Military in Contemporary

Latin American Politics," *The Western Political Quarterly,* XII (September 1960), 745–63.—Groups the republics according to the extent that the military are a factor in civilian affairs.

――――. "Tres modalidades del militarismo latino-americano," *Combate,* II (September–October, 1960), 7–15, and continued in *Combate,* III (January–February, 1961), 15–22.—These articles discuss the armed forces in terms of the extent to which they intrude in the civilian area.

CHAPTERS VII AND VIII

The materials in this section were used in preparing the chapters on Brazil.

Alencar Araripe, General Tristão de. *Tasso Fragoso: um pouco de história do nosso exército.* Rio de Janeiro, 1960.—Biography of one of Brazil's leading military figures. The volume covers the overthrow of the Empire through the 1930 revolt.

Almeida, Alusio de. *A revolução liberal de 1842.* Rio de Janeiro, 1944.—Scholarly study of one of the many revolts of the interregnum and Caxias's role in it.

Alves, Francisco M. Rodrigues. *Democracia corrumpida; ou, golpe de estado?* São Paulo, 1955.—Polemical. Argues that in Brazil only the military are capable of freeing the country from corruption and demagoguery brought on by universal suffrage.

Associação do quarto centenario do descobrimento do Brasil. *Livro do centenario (1500–1900).* 3 vols. Rio de Janeiro, 1900–1902.—Volume II contains a section on the history and organization of the defense establishment.

Baratz, Morton S. "The Crisis in Brazil," *Social Research,* XXII, (October 1955), 347–61.—Background of events preceding Vargas's suicide and a brief glimpse into the future of Brazil.

Barbosa, Ruy. *Contra o militarismo.* Rio de Janeiro, [1910?].—Written during the campaign of 1910 in which Ruy Barbosa lost to General Hermes da Fonseca.

Bardi, Pietro M. *Art Treasures of the São Paulo Museum and the Development of Art in Brazil.* Translated by John Drummond. New York, 1956.

Barroso, Gustavo. *História militar do Brasil.* São Paulo, 1935.—Claims to be the first general history of the Brazilian military in colonial and modern times. The volume is divided into two parts, the history of the organization of the army and accounts of "great military campaigns."

Bello, José María. *História da república.* 3d ed. São Paulo, 1956.
—The best single-volume history of Brazil as a republic.

————. "Panorama da república," in Jornal do Commercio, *Aspectos da formação e evolução do Brasil.* Rio de Janeiro, 1953, pp. 85–111.—Especially useful for a review of the empire and the regimes of Deodoro and Peixoto.

Biblioteca Militar. *A república brasileira.* Rio de Janeiro, 1939.— Commemorates the 50th anniversary of the overthrow of the empire. Close attention is paid to conditions leading up to the Army's decision to move against Pedro II.

Bilac, Olavo. *A defesa nacional.* Rio de Janeiro, 1917.—Nationalistic. Undertakes to show how the military might contribute to the strengthening of Brazil.

Bonilla, Frank. See *American Universities Field Staff Reports Service* for Brazil, published during 1961–62.—See entry under General Works.

Brazil, Comissão de Linhas Telegráficas Estrangeiras de Matto-Grosso ao Amazonas. Publication No. 42: *Conferencias realizadas nos dias 5, 7 e 9 de outubro de 1915.* Rio de Janeiro, 1916. —Useful for material on the military contribution to the civilian area.

Calogeras, João Pandiá. *A History of Brazil.* Translated and edited by Percy Alvin Martin. Chapel Hill, N.C., 1939.—The armed forces receive considerable favorable attention.

Carneiro, David. *O Paraná e a revolução federalista.* São Paulo, 1944.—Scholarly discussion of the interregnum.

Centro Latino-Americano de Pesquisas em Ciencias Sociais. *Boletim* (Rio de Janeiro).—Contains extremely good articles on social-political problems.

Cordeiro de Farias, Oswaldo. "O exército brasileiro na II Guerra Mundial." *Provincia de São Pedro,* No. 9 (June 1947), pp. 95–104.—Written from the military point of view.

Costa, Didio Iratym Affonso da. *Tamandaré, Almirante Joaquim, Marques Lisboa.* Rio de Janeiro, 1942.—Laudatory.

Cruz Costa, João. *O positivismo na república.* São Paulo, 1956. —Chapter IX deals with positivism and the military.

Dean, Robert W. "The Military in Politics in Brazil," Washington, mimeographed, 1963.—This paper, which stresses the last decade and a half of Brazilian politics, was written while the author was attending the National War College, and the opinions and conclusions expressed in it are his and do not necessarily represent the views of either the National War College or any other governmental agency.

Dias, Everardo. "O socialismo no Brasil," *Revista brasiliense,* No. 11 (May–June, 1957), pp. 70–89.—Covers the relationship between the military and the labor movement, 1922–24, and the ideology of the *tenentes*.

Freitas, Leopoldo de. *Historia militar do Brasil.* São Paulo, 1911. —May be considered an official version.

Freyre, Gilberto. *Nação e exército.* Rio de Janeiro, 1949.—Discusses the role of the armed forces in major events affecting their evolution. Argues that civilians can learn organization from the armed forces.

———. *New World in the Tropics.* New York, 1959.—Nationalistic.

———. *Ordem e progresso.* 2 vols. Rio de Janeiro, 1959.—A major contribution. Much attention is given to the social-economic background of the officers and the public image of the services.

Godinho, Wanor R. *Constituintes brasileiros de 1934.* Rio de Janeiro, 1934.—Biographical. Good source on the influence of the military in the constituent assembly.

Goycochêa, Castilhos. *O espírito militar na questão acreana.* Rio de Janeiro, 1941.—Largely a chronology of developments leading to the Acre dispute.

Guimarães da Costa, Samuel. *Formação democrática do exército brasileiro.* Rio de Janeiro, 1957.—Emphasis is on the late colonial period and early empire.

Haring, C. H. *Empire in Brazil: A New World Experiment with Monarchy.* Cambridge, Mass., 1958.—Numerous references to the armed forces reflect the author's awareness of the vital role that the officers played during the empire.

Jornal do Comercio (Rio de Janeiro). *Aspectos da formação e evolução do Brasil.* Rio de Janeiro, 1953.—Studies published in 1952 on the occasion of the newspaper's 125th anniversary. Various contributions relate to the military.

Klinger, General Bertoldo. *Parada e desfile; duma vida de voluntário do Brasil.* Rio de Janeiro, 1958.—The author, a general, supported the São Paulo revolt against Vargas. Pleads for greater professionalization of the armed forces.

Leitão de Carvalho, General Estevão. *Dever militar e política partidária.* São Paulo, 1959.—A thoughtful study by an army general. Particularly useful for the early 1920's and the 1930's.

Lima Júnior, Augusto de. *Crônica militar.* Belo Horizonte, 1960. —Historical account of the military in Minas Gerais.

Lobo da Silva, General Arthur. *O serviço de saúde do exército brasileiro.* Rio de Janeiro, 1958.—Historical. Contains numerous laws affecting the armed services.

Loewenstein, Karl. *Brazil Under Vargas.* New York, 1942.—Contains information on the military under Vargas, prior to World War II.

Lopes, Theodorico, and Gentil Torres. *Ministros da guerra do Brasil: 1808–1950.* Rio de Janeiro, 1950.—Largely biographical.

Machado, F. Zenha. *Os últimos dias do govêrno de Vargas.* Rio de Janeiro, 1955.—The armed forces and officers receive considerable treatment.

Maciel da Silva, Alfredo Pretextato. *Os generais do exército brasileiro, de 1822 a 1889.* Vol. I, 2d ed. Rio de Janeiro, 1940.— Biographical sketches prepared by an army officer.

Magalhães, João Batista. "As fôrças armadas e a construção nacional," in Jornal do Comercio, *Aspectos da formação e evolução do Brasil.* Rio de Janeiro, 1953, pp. 59–67.—Good on military contributions to the civilian sector.

———. "Historia da evolução militar do Brasil," *Quarto congreso de historia nacional, Anais,* VI (1950), 347–607.—More on the military in politics than would appear from the title.

Manchester, Alan. "Brazil in Transition," *South Atlantic Quarterly,* LIV (April 1955), 167–76.—Friendly to the military.

Mangabeira, Octavio. *A situação nacional.* Rio de Janeiro, 1956. —Discusses military-civilian relations following Vargas's suicide.

Matthews, Herbert L. "Brazil in Travail," *Foreign Policy Bulletin,* XXXIV (December 1954), 45–48.

Maul, Carlos. *O exército e a nacionalidade.* Rio de Janeiro, 1950. —More favorable attention to the military than to the emergence of a Brazilian nationality.

Melo, Olbiano de. *A marcha da revolução social no Brasil.* Rio de Janeiro, 1957.

Mirales, José de. *Historia militar do Brasil.* Rio de Janeiro, 1900. —Covers the years 1549–1762, giving decrees, orders, expenses, and a catalog of names.

Morazé, Charles. *Les trois âges du Brésil; essai de politique.* Paris, 1954.—One of the very best volumes on contemporary Brazil.

Oliveira, Xavier de. *O exército e o sertão.* Rio de Janeiro, 1932.

Oliveira Rodrigues, Raúl. *Um militar contra o militarismo; a vida de Saldanha da Gama.* Rio de Janeiro, 1959.—A friendly biography of Admiral Saldanha da Gama, who opposed army interference in civilian affairs during the early years of the republic.

Oliveira Vianna, Francisco José de. *Instituições políticas brasileiras.* 2 vols. São Paulo, 1949.—Contains useful material on the private armies and the "colonels" who led them in the interior of Brazil during the 19th century.

Paula Cidade, General F. de. *Cadetes e alunos militares através dos tempos*. Rio de Janeiro, 1961.—History of the military academies, with extensive excerpts from memoirs, reviews, and newspapers.

————. "As verdadeiras bases do poder militar," *Cultura política*, II (September 1942), 114–19.—Argues that industry is ultimately the source of military power.

Pereira da Silva, Gastão. *Constituintes de 46: dados biográficos*. Rio de Janeiro, 1947.—The military is given less attention than might be expected.

Pires, Pandia. *"Preto 29."* Rio de Janeiro, 1946.—Sensational pro-Vargas attack on the military on the occasion of Vargas's removal from office in 1945.

Ramos, Guerreiro. "A dinâmica da sociedade política no Brasil," *Revista brasileira de estudos políticos*, I (December 1956), 23–38.—An economic interpretation of Brazilian political life.

Rodrigues, Lysias A. *Formação da nacionalidade brasileira*. 2d ed. Rio de Janeiro, n.d.—Concerned primarily with the wars with Holland during the 17th century and their influence upon the formation of the Brazilian nationality.

Seabra Fagundes, M. *As fôrças armadas na constituição*. Rio de Janeiro, 1955.—Brief and factual.

Simmons, Charles W. "The Rise of the Brazilian Military Class, 1870–1890," *Mid-America*, XXXIX (January 1957), 227–38.—Brings together considerable material on an important period. There is nothing new by way of interpretation.

Simonsen, Roberto Cochrane. *A construcção dos quarteis para o exército*. São Paulo, 1931.—Defense of military barracks construction program. The author's company was one of the major contractors.

Sodré, Nelson Werneck. *Introdução à revolução brasileira*. Rio de Janeiro, 1958.—Considerable, and for the most part favorable, attention is given the armed forces.

Sousa, Octavio Tarquinio de. *Historia de dois golpes de estado*. Rio de Janeiro, 1939.—Covers the period from the overthrow of Pedro I to the majority of Pedro II.

Vargas, Getulio. *Dois Discursos*. Rio de Janeiro, 1940.—The dictator was friendly toward the military at the time these addresses were given.

Wildberger, Arnold. *Os presidentes da provincia da Bahía. Efectivos e interinos, 1824–1889*. Salvador, 1949.—Very useful biographical material.

Wyckoff, Theodore. "Brazilian Political Parties," *South Atlantic Quarterly*, LVI (Summer, 1957), 281–98.

INDEX

INDEX

Acre Territory, 200
Adams, John Quincy, 26
Africa, 47, 53, 132–33, 221; mentioned, 22, 26, 36, 151
Agrarian reform, 95, 146–48, 150
Agriculture, 21, 65, 96, 258–59; commercial, 43–44, 64, 95; in Brazil, 192, 197
Aguirre Cerda, Pedro, 98
Air forces, 110, 123–24, 136, 142, 210n
Airlines, 136, 139
Alba, Victor, 77
Alegría, Ciro, 154–56, 226
Alemán, Miguel, 5
Alfaro, Eloy, 70
Alliance for Progress, 146
Alpuche, Wenceslao, 28
Alvear, Marcelo T. de, 125
Alves de Lima y Silva, Luis. *See* Caxias, Duque de
Amado, Jorge, 235
Amalia, 60
Amazon basin, 146, 199, 213, 265
Anarcho-syndicalism, 66, 74–75, 201ff
Anarchy, 38, 62, 65
Andes, 107
Andrade e Silva, José BoníFácio de, 181–82
Angostura, 87
Antarctica, 129
"Anti-coup," 218, 242
Antiforeignism, 71, 100, 222. *See also* Nationalism
Anti-militarism, 88, 153–59
Anti-Personalist Radicals, 121
Aprista Party, 145
Aramburu, Pedro Eugenio, 167
Arbenz, Jacobo, 7, 127f
Argentina, 4, 6, 75, 99, 141; uprisings, 21f; literature, 28f, 81f,

84–85; constitutions, 30–31, 161; and La Plata, 51; officer privileges, 55, 103–4, 166f; technological development, 62–65, 77, 130f, 133, 138–39; and Chile, 67, 142; training and professionalization of military, 69ff, 102–3, 119, 136, 247, 249f; gross national product, 94; origin of officers, 108, 108n, 113, 113n; civil-militarism, 121–22; secret organizations, 125, 126n; military and landed elite, 149–50; and Brazil, 182, 185, 188, 199f, 238n; mentioned, 27, 79, 89, 126, 129, 143, 147, 201, 246. *See also* Buenos Aires; Perón Arica, 88
Arica, 88
Armies, private, 37, 51, 76, 245. *See also Caudillos*
Army, 137, 142, 170, 245f; in Cuba, 111f; of political parties, 126f; of Argentina, 141; of Brazil, 189, 193, 198–99, 218; mentioned, 110
Arosemena Monroy, Carlos Julio, 6, 169
Artigas, José, 27
Asia, 47, 53, 77, 221; Southeast, 44, 132–33; mentioned, 22, 26, 36
Assassinations, 4f
Atlantic, defense of, 239
Avila Camacho, Manuel, 158
Avilan, Francisco, 111
Ayacucho, Battle of, 22
Azevedo, Fernando de, 227
Azuela, Mariano, 148, 154, 226, 232

Bahia, 179, 189, 228
Banana production, 63n, 95, 148
Baquedano, Manuel, 86

Baratz, Morton S., 225
Barbosa, Ruy, 192–94
Barrios, Justo Rufino, 77–78
Batista y Zaldívar, Fulgencio, 5, 111, 135, 145, 253
Becker, Carl, 134
Belaúnde Terry, Fernando, 121
Belgrano, Manuel, 29, 85
Bello, Andrés, 59–60
Bello, José Maria, 227
Beltrão, Father, 234
Benefits, 31, 103–5, 165–67, 193, 236, 250–51; retirements plans, 7, 104, 128, 151, 166–67, 236, 250; *fueros*, 19, 80, 162
Bermúdez family, 111
Bernardes, Arthur, 194
Betancourt, Rómulo, 99, 103–4, 150; and Democratic Action Party, 120; his civilian administration, 130–31; mentioned, 9, 128
Bilac, Olavo dos Guimarães, 228–29
Blanco Fombona, Rufino, 82
Blest Gana, Alberto, 58
Bogotá, 20f
Bolívar, Simón: attitude toward civilians, 24; honored by republics, 29–30, 84, 159; and Peruvian constitution, 33; mentioned, 22, 25, 27, 61
Bolivia, 4, 95f, 99, 149, 265f; civil-military relations, 9, 9n, 126f; and Bolívar, 29–30; war with Chile, 51, 58f, 69, 83, 86, 88; training of officers, 70; civil-militarism, 120–21; secret organizations, 125; literacy rates, 135; and Brazil, 200; mentioned 20, 27, 102, 204, 235
Bolognesi, Francisco, 88
Bonaparte, Napoleon, 21, 24, 32, 178f, 230
Borges, Jorge Luis, 83
Bosch, Juan, 6
Boundary disputes, 67, 69
Boves, José Tomás, 22
Braganza, House of, 179–80
Brasilia, 213
Brazil, 8f, 191, 244, 261, 265f; military in politics, 6, 204–12, 217–20, 240–43, 256; technological development, 7, 95, 197–99, 215–16, 246; and La Plata, 51, 181f;

and positivism, 66; nationalism, 69, 203, 207–8, 220–23, 239, 259–60; gross national product, 94; civilian-military relations, 149, 177–78, 193, 234–35, 243; constitutions, 161, 233; colonial period, 178–81; independence, 180–82; uprisings, 183, 183n, 194–95, 202–4, 207, 214, 228; interregnum period, 183–84, 225; Catholic Church, 184f, 196; reign of Pedro II, 184–90; shift to republicanism, 192–94; labor, 200–202, 216–17; regionalism in, 213–14; secret organizations, 220; literature and art, 224–32; background and privileges of officers, 235–38, 248–50
Brazilian Workers' Party (PTB), 209
British Guiana, 200
Budget, military, 49–50, 238, 259
Buenos Aires, 19–21, 45, 51; University of, 103; armed forces drawn from, 108, 108n; mentioned, 46, 65, 96, 166
Bulnes, Francisco, 159
Bureaucracy, 73, 78, 115–16, 261

Cabero, Alberto, 160
Caciques, 45, 248
Caldera, Rafael, 120, 122
Calmon, Pedro, 227
Calogeras, João Pandía, 229–30
Campobello, Nellie, 154
Canudos rebellion, 228
Capital: foreign, 64ff, 98, 139f; private, 139f, 148, 215
Caracas, 7, 21, 107, 142, 165
Cárdenas, Lázaro, 98, 135, 158
Carlota Joaquina, Queen (Portugal), 180
Carrera, José Miguel, 85
Carúpano revolt, 111
Castillo, Ramón S., 122
Castillo Armas, Carlos, 5, 7
Castro, Fidel, 6, 222, 258; and the Sierra Maestra, 76n, 112; mentioned, 93, 145, 167
Catholicism and the Catholic Church, 16, 21, 73, 97, 109; Church-state issue, 44, 55, 179n, 183–85, 190; and art, 89, 158; and military, 113, 142, 190, 196, 251, 258; and education, 135–37,

169; in Ecuador, 168; mentioned, 19, 23, 47, 147, 234
Caudillos, 39–48 *passim,* 83, 179, 245; decline of, 76–77, 158, 248
Caxias, Duque de, 8, 186–88, 229f
Ceará revolt, 183n
Central America, 32–33, 63n, 78, 132. *See also individual countries*
Chapultepec, college of 70, 160n
Chile, 9, 65f, 99, 146f; industry, 7f, 131f, 139; uprisings, 21, 123 literature, 28, 58f, 81, 85–87; 1823 constitution, 32; civil-militarism, 50n; War of the Pacific, 51, 58f, 69, 83, 86, 88; technological devolopment, 62f, 77; education, 65n, 188; and Argentina, 67, 142; professionalization and training of officers, 69–71, 102, 110, 246–47, 249–50; gross national product, 94; officer privileges, 103–4, 165–67; military in, 108, 113, 169–70, 172; secret organizations, 125; landed elite, 149; military art, 158–59; military codes, 163, 163n; labor, 200f; mentioned, 15, 48, 50, 79, 89, 97, 116, 133
Chocano, José Santos, 15, 88
Christian Science Monitor, 226
Church-state issue, 44, 55, 179n, 183–85, 190
Cinco de Mayo, 85
Círculo Militar, 7, 173
Cities. *See* Urban centers
Civil guards, 50n, 120, 123, 127
Civil-military relations, 24–26, 73, 104, 116–17, 120–23, 187–88; military interference in civilian politics, 3–4, 10, 129–31, 168; protection from military interference, 32–34, 79f; and the *junta,* 113–14; comparison of bureaucracies, 115–16; in Brazil, 149, 177–78, 193, 234–35, 243; mentioned, 118, 163
Civil wars, 4, 8, 127
Classes, social, 20, 68, 75, 98. *See also* Elites; Labor; Middle sectors
Clube Militar (Officers' Club), 217, 219–20
Clubs, military, 193, 217, 219–20
Coester, Alfred, 86–87

Coffee, 63n, 95, 185, 221
Colegio Militar of Mexico, 53n
Colombia, 34f, 94f, 147, 253; uprisings, 4, 20f, 127, 183; officers and politics, 5, 9, 160; literature, 29; constitutions, 32f, 56–57, 80; professionalization, 70, 249; origin and privileges of officers, 104f, 107; education in, 136; and Brazil, 200; mentioned, 24, 27, 48, 89, 102, 116, 128, 149
Colonies, Spanish, 14–22, 27
Colorado Party (of Uruguay), 185
Coluna Invicta (Invincible Column), 203, 214, 228
Comercio, El, 121
Commerce. *See* Trade
Communications, 45–46, 77, 119, 213, 256
Communism, 5, 99, 101, 127; and armed forces, 143–46, 150, 160, 251; in Brazil, 207f, 227, 241
Comte, Auguste, 66, 189, 196. *See also* Positivism
Conquistadores, 13–16, 23
Conscription and conscripts, 22, 54, 71–72, 248, 263–65; in literature, 154f; in Brazil, 234–35; mentioned, 37, 82, 105
Conservatism, 42, 48, 99, 151, 191, 253
Constant, Benjamin, 190
Constitutionality, 37, 41, 47, 62, 97, 223
Constitutions, 32–35, 55, 244; controls over military, 56–57, 79–80, 161–63; Platt Amendment, 67; of Brazil, 233; mentioned, 4, 44, 50
Copacabana revolt, 202
Coronado, Martín, 82
Corridos, 81f
Corruption, in armed forces, 4, 55, 255
Cortés, Hernán, 14
Costa Rica, 8f, 127, 135f, 144; coffee industry, 63; civil-militarism, 120; middle-sector control, 149, 149n; mentioned, 102, 116
Creoles, 19f, 22, 180f
Cuba, 94f, 112, 143–44; Batista, 5, 111, 135, 145, 253; Platt Amendment, 67; Independence movement, 84, 159; literature, 86–87;

national guards, 126f; mentioned, 97, 149. *See also* Castro, Fidel

Cunha, Euclides da, 228

Del Rio Chaviano, Alberto, 112
Delgado, Luis Humberto, 89, 160
Democracy, 36f, 100f, 134
Democratic Action Party (Venezuela), 104, 120, 145
Denys, Odilio, 209, 218
Depression, 94, 98
Díaz, Julio Lozana, 120
Díaz, Porfirio, 66, 81, 86, 90; and modernization, 63, 78
Dictatorships, 3, 38, 56
Directorio del Gobierno Federal, 130
Dominican Republic, 6, 51, 95; declaration of independence, 19; Constitution of 1858, 80; mentioned, 128, 145
Drago, Gonzalo, 156–57
Dutra, Eurico, 208

Economic development, 61, 63–67, 77–79, 89, 246, 251–52. *See also* Technological change
Ecuador, 6, 56, 80, 124; constitutions, 4, 79, 162; uprisings, 21; industry, 45, 95, 131, 133, 138; training and benefits of officers, 70–72, 102, 104, 121, 166; origin of officers, 106f; families of officers, 110, 172; secret organizations, 125–26; and communism, 127; education, 136; nationalism in, 142, 148; literature, 155; good will toward military, 161, 167–69; military codes, 163; and Brazil, 200; erosion, 266; mentioned, 27, 128, 164–65
Education, 65, 106, 134–37, 192, 264. *See also* Military schools
El Salvador, 70, 80, 95; origin and training of officers, 102, 105, 107, 107n; mentioned, 128, 143, 149
Electoral process, 37, 98–99, 130, 169
Elites, 54, 68, 147, 149f, 244; attitude toward military, 52, 171; decrease in power of, 97, 254; in Brazil, 204, 221
Estado de S. Paulo, O, 231
Estado Novo, 207, 216

Europe, 26, 45, 61, 66, 207; mentioned, 40, 68, 89

Family, of officers, 151, 171–73, 236–37, 251
Farias, Cordeiro de, 207
Farrapos Revolt, 183
Fascism, 119, 125, 158, 207, 212, 253
Fazendeiros (landholders), 184
Federalist-centralist issue, 44, 54f, 179n, 183
Ferdinand VII (Spain), 180
Fernández, João Ribeiro, 227
Fidelistas, 99, 101, 127, 143
Filho, Café, 217
Flores, Juan José, 60
Fonseca, Hermes da, 193–94, 220
Fonseca, Manoel Deodoro da, 192–96
Foreign Office of Brazil, 237, 237n
Forestation, 266
Forme (Formación de Oficiales Revolucionarios Ecuadorianos), 126
France, 18, 21, 52, 64, 118; in Haiti, 20; Revolution, 21, 44, 181; and Mexico, 51, 81, 85–86; officer training in Latin America, 70, 246; and Brazil, 200; mentioned, 27, 32, 250
French Guiana, 200
Freyre, Gilberto, 177f, 230, 235
Frondizi, Arturo, 122, 167
Fuente de Acción Popular (FRAP), 152
Fueros (special privileges), 19, 80, 162

Gallegos, Rómulo, 120, 155ff, 226, 232
Gálvez, Manuel, 155n
García Moreno, Gabriel, 80
Gauchos, 41, 69
Generales de dedo, 81
Germany, 64, 182; military influence of, 69–70, 113, 246; and Argentina, 119, 141; mentioned, 207f
Goldwert, Marvin, 121–22
Gomes, Eduardo, 202, 207, 209f
Gómez, Juan Vicente, 114, 120
Gómez, Laureano, 160
González Prada, Manuel, 61, 83–84, 229

Goulart, João (Jango) 6, 208ff, 217f
Great Britain, 52, 64, 247; and Argentina, 19–20, 51, 85, 141; and Brazil, 180, 185, 200; mentioned, 18, 27
Gross domestic product, 7–8
Gross national product, 94
Grupo de Oficiales Unidos (GOU), 125
Guadalupe Victoria, 49
Guanabara, 209, 213
Guatemala, 5ff, 95, 127f; mentioned, 143, 263
Guayaquil, 45, 107, 165
Guerrillas, 127
Guzmán, Martín Luis, 156f
Guzmán Blanco, Antonio, 77

Habitat, 232
Hacendados, 17, 39, 54
Haiti, 51, 95, 105, 135; mentioned, 20, 249
Haring, Clarence H., 177f, 224
Hemisphere defense, 101, 144f, 239, 258
Henríquez, Camilo, 28
Hernández, José, 66, 82
Hidalgo, Bartolomé, 28
Hidalgo, Father Miguel, 28
Honduras, 5f, 138f, 141–42, 145–46; origin and training of officers, 102, 106f; civil guard, 120, 127; Constitution of 1957, 162–63, 233; mentioned, 158, 265

Ibáñez, Carlos, 117, 125, 150, 151n, 169
Icaza, Jorge, 155, 226, 232
Immigration, 64, 67, 250
Independence, Wars of, 20–28, 31, 78f, 244; mentioned, 47, 50, 52
Independence movement, 26, 43, 51, 55, 84; literary production, 28; and Cuba, 84, 159; and Brazil, 179; mentioned, 73, 200, 247
Independent Socialists (Argentina), 121
Indian Wars of the 1830's (Argentina), 55
Indians, 22, 42, 46, 145f; conquest of, 13–17; in Brazil, 178, 198–99; mentioned, 20, 49, 155, 171, 249n

Industry and industrialization, 7, 137–40, 258f; in Brazil, 8, 201, 208, 211–16, 222, 224; 1850–1914, 63–64, 67–68, 79n; in 20th century, 94–96; military and, 130–32, 150; mentioned, 246, 251. *See also* Modernization
Institutionalization, 113–14, 128, 141, 148, 220–21, 249–50, 252. *See also* Professionalization
Intellectuals, 21, 52, 65, 100–101, 153, 171
International Labor Office, 97
Inter-service and intra-service rivalries, 123–24, 126
Irigoyen, Hipólito, 121
Iron and steel, 94, 130–32, 138, 208, 222, 240
Italy, 64, 113, 119, 141; mentioned, 137, 207f
Itamaratí, 237, 237n
Iturbide, Augustín, 28f

Jefferson, Thomas, 20
John VI (Portugal), 181
Juárez, Benito, 5, 90
Juntas, 7, 113–17, 120, 145, 252–53
Jefes, 25, 39, 142, 253
Justo, Agustín P., 121

Kennedy, John F., 127
Koerner, Emil, 69–71
Kubitschek, Juscelino, 8, 241; election and inauguration, 209, 217–18, 230–31, 243

Labarca, Guillermo, 156
Labor, 94f, 171, 221; urban, 65f, 96–99, 201–2, 214, 216–17; and anarcho-syndicalism, 74–75; mentioned, 64, 68, 129
Labor organizations, 98, 145
Lacerda, Carlos, 209, 231
Lafinur, Juan C., 28–29
Laguna, retreat from, 227f
Land, 147–49. *See also* Agrarian reform; Agriculture
Landed elements, 56, 95, 147, 244. *See also* Elites
La Plata, 51, 178–183 *passim*, 186
Larrazábal, Wolfgang and Carlos, 111
Lastarría, José Victorino, 66
Latifundia system, 55, 203, 214–15
Le Bon, Gustave, 74

Lefèbvre, François Joseph, 24
Leo XIII, Pope, 68
Ley Juárez of 1855, 80
Liberal Alliance, 204f, 214
Liberals, 42, 48, 72, 127, 191f
Libertador, Al, 29
Liddell Hart, B. H., 177f
Lillo, Samuel, 85
Lima, 28f, 96, 105, 121
Linéa Recta, 125
Linhares, Chief Justice, 208
Lipson, Leslie, 225
Literacy rates, 134f
Literature, on military: of Independence era, 28–29; 1825–50, 58–61; 1950–1914, 81–89; 20th century, 153–57, 160–61; of Brazil, 224–230
Lizardi, Fernández de, 28, 58
Logia San Martín, 125
López, Francisco Solano, 249n
López de Santa Anna, Antonio. *See* Santa Anna
López y Fuentes, Gregorio, 154, 226, 232
Lott, Henrique Texeira: defeated for presidency, 209, 209n, 210n, 256; his "anti-coup," 217–18, 226, 242
Loveira, Carlos, 156f
Luca, Estebán de, 28
Luiz Pereira de Souza, Washington, 194, 242

McAlister, Lyle N., 19, 108n
Macedo Soares, Edmundo, 240
Maciel, Antônio, 228
MacKenzie School, 236
Madrid, José Fernández, 29
Manchester, Alan K., 224
Mancisidor, José, 156
Marines, 111
Mármol, José, 59f
Martí, José, 87
Martín Fierro, 66, 82
Martínez, Carlos Walker, 85
Masons, 125
Masur, Gerhard, 23
Mato Grosso, 185; revolt, 183n
Matthews, Herbert L., 225
Matta, Guillermo, 83, 85f
Maximilian I, 85–86
Mercenaries, 182
Merchant Marine, 136, 139
Mestizos, 15–17, 42, 105–6

Mexico, 4, 8f, 94, 99–100, 258; as New Spain, 15, 19; uprisings, 17, 21f, 68, 78, 183; army before 1850, 18, 49–50, 59; literature, art, and music, 28, 46, 81f, 154, 157–59; constitutions, 32f, 80, 97; war with U.S., 46, 51, 87, 90, 160n; and France, 51, 85; technological development, 63–64, 95, 182; professionalization, 70, 72, 102, 249–50; origin and benefits of officers, 105, 110, 132, 166f; education, 106, 135–36; PRI, 121, 128ff, 143, 158; landed elite, 149; erosion, 266; mentioned, 62, 66f, 74, 116, 200f, 235, 246, 248
Middle sectors, 66, 171, 246, 254; as origin of officers, 52, 78; and politics, 67f, 97–101, 143; control of government, 149–51, 158; in Brazil, 199, 204
Militarism, 39, 58, 75, 246; economics of, 164–65; mentioned, 6, 25, 81
Military code, 80, 104, 163
Military schools, 53–54, 102–3, 106ff, 262; of Mexico, 53, 87; of Brazil, 190, 198, 236, 238; mentioned, 3, 69ff, 77f, 113
Militias, 9, 32–33, 77; colonial, 18–20; mentioned, 9n, 188
Mills, C. Wright, 105
Minas Gerais, 183n, 185, 201, 213
Mining, 22, 63f, 201
Miranda, Francisco de, 20
Miro Quesada family, 121
Mitre, Bartolomé, 85
Modernization, 72, 148, 251–52, 256; of military, 75–78, 81, 115–16, 118, 248; mentioned, 62–63, 93, 203
Molina, J. J., 111
Molina, J. T., 111
Monteiro, Gões, 207
Mora, José María Luis, 59
Moraes Barros, Prudente de, 193
Morazé, Charles, 225
Morelos, José María, 28
Moscas, Las, 154
Movie industry, 232–33
Movimiento Nacionalista Revolucionario (MNR), 121
Mulattos, 16f, 42, 105–6

Nahmens, Oscar, 111
Napoleon I, 21, 24, 32, 178f, 230
National guards, 126f, 188, 264
Nationalism, 26, 140–42, 244; as political force, 67–69; economic, 67n, 79n, 259–60; Xenophobic, 71, 100, 222; and foreign policies, 78, 247–48; in Brazil, 200, 203, 207–8, 220–23, 239, 259–60; mentioned, 90, 113, 150, 153, 159f
Navy, 125, 142, 170, 247; of Venezuela, 103, 111; of Chile, 110, 123; of Argentina, 124, 130, 141; of Brazil, 185, 189, 193, 195, 199, 210n, 237
Negroes, 16f, 23, 42, 87; in Brazil, 189, 191n, 237–38, 249n
Netherlands, the, 18
Neutralism (Brazil), 222–23, 239
New Spain (Mexico), 15, 19
New York Times, 225f, 231
Nicaragua, 5, 42, 71, 138, 249
Niños Héroes, 87, 160, 160n

Obregón, Alvaro, 4, 159
Odría, Manuel, 5f
Officer benefits. *See* Benefits
Officers: origin of, 52, 61, 152, 235–36, 250; social background, 78, 106–13, 137, 171; racial, 105–6, 237f; non-commissioned, 116, 172, 234–35, 243; family of, 151, 171–73, 236–37, 251. *See also* Professionalization; Salaries
O'Higgins, Bernardo, 27, 85
Olmedo, José Joaquin de, 29, 59f
Organization of American States, 145
Orozco, José Clemente, 157–58, 232
Ortega, Francisco, 29
Osorio, Luis Enrique, 156f
Osorio, Oscar, 106

PRI (Mexico), 121, 128ff, 143, 158
PSD (Brazil), 209, 256
Páez, José Antonio, 22, 27–28, 31
Palma, Ricardo, 88, 227
Panama, 67, 95, 127; Rémon's assassination, 5, 5n; mentioned, 56, 233
Paraguay, 8, 22, 30, 249n; Constitution of 1844, 57, 162; racial

origin of officers, 105; mentioned, 71, 159
Paraguayan War, 184–88, 191n, 230; mentioned, 8, 155n, 227
Paraná, 213
Paraná River, 185
Partido Revolucionario Institucional (PRI), 121, 128ff, 143, 158
"Pastry War," 51
Payró, Roberto, 82
Paz Estenssoro, Victor, 120–21
Peasants, 68, 146–47, 245
Pedro I (Brazil), 180–86 *passim*
Pedro II (Brazil), 183–91 *passim*, 196, 233; mentioned, 192, 194, 205
Peixoto, Floriano, 193, 195–96
Pellegrini, Carlos, 64
Peñaranda, Enrique, 125
People of color, 15–17, 42, 74, 105–6, 237f, 249n. *See also* Indians; Negroes
Pérez Godoy, Ricardo, 145
Pérez Jiménez, Marcos, 131, 135f, 139, 172f; overthrow of, 5, 124–25, 253; and communists, 144–45
Pernambuco, 201, 220; uprisings in, 180f, 183n
Perón, Juan Domingo, 118, 127, 151, 151n; overthrow of, 5, 161, 252; and workers, 98; and Radepa, 125; anti-Perón faction, 128, 167; and education, 135f; industrial development, 139; and San Martín, 159; mentioned, 115, 117, 122, 258
Peronistas, 122, 139, 167
Pershing, John P., 159
Peru, 5ff, 34f, 49, 130, 149; literature and art, 27ff, 81, 88; 1823 Constitution, 33; War of the Pacific, 51, 58f, 69, 83, 86, 88; origins and training of officers, 70, 105; in late 19th century, 87, 89; industry, 95, 182; *junta*, 114, 145; civil-militarism, 121; education, 136; nationalism, 142; and Brazil, 200; erosion, 266; mentioned, 8, 20, 113, 165, 229, 235
Peruano, El, 145
Pessôa, Epitacio da Silva, 194, 220
Petrobras, 211, 222
Petroleum, 63, 138f, 260
Philippine Islands, 265

Picón Febres, Gonzalo, 82
Pizarro, Francisco, 14
Platt Amendment, 67
Plaza Lasso, Galo, 4–5, 161
Poetry, 28–29, 81, 86; of Brazil, 226, 228–29
Poinsett, Joel Roberts, 25–26
Police, 102, 126, 129, 162, 257
Politics, the military in, 9, 151, 169–70, 256; officer-statesman, 9, 54f, 117–19; 1825–50, 38, 54f, 60; 1850–1914, 72–74, 76; in Brazil, 204–12, 217–20, 240–43. *See also* Civil-military relations
Popular Radical Party (Argentina), 122
Portales, Diego, 50, 50n
Portinari, Cândido, 232
Portugal, 178–82
Portuguese America, 149, 177ff, 182
Positivism, 65–66, 76, 89–90, 189–90, 196, 199
Potash, Robert, 108, 108n, 113n, 126n
Prado, Manuel, 114, 130
Pratt, Arturo, 86
Press, 160; Brazilian, 224–26, 227, 230–31
Prestes, Luiz Carlos, 204, 227–28; his Column, 203, 214, 228
Privileges of officers, 19, 80, 162. *See also* Benefits
Professionalization, 115–17, 249–50, 252, 257; 1850–1914; 69–78 *passim*, 81, 246–48; and industrialization, 137–38, 141; mentioned, 148, 153. *See also* Military schools
Protesta, La, 75
Puebla, 18; victory at, 85
Puerto Cabello revolt, 111
Pumas, the (Por un Mañana Auspicioso), 125
Putnam, Samuel, 226
Putsch, military, 5, 207, 226
Pye, Lucian, 115

Quadros, Jânio, 6, 210, 243; victory over Lott, 209, 209n, 218, 256
Quintana Roo, Andrés, 29
Quito, 45, 165, 168; uprising in, 21; origin of officers, 105, 107

Races. *See* People of color
Radepa (Razón de Patria), 125
Ramírez, Pedro, 6, 122
Regionalism, 48, 54, 213–14
Reissig, Luis, 156f
Religion, 54–55. *See also* Catholicism and the Catholic Church
Remón, José Antonio, 5, 5n
Rerum Novarum, 68
Retirada da Laguna, A, 227
Retirement plans, 7, 104, 128, 151, 166–67, 236, 250
Revolutions. *See* Uprisings
Rio de Janeiro, 201f, 213, 232; Escola Militar, 190; mentioned, 185, 228
Rio Grande do Sul, 213, 228, 235; revolts, 183, 183n
Rivera, Diego, 157, 232
Rojas, Isaac, 122
Rojas Pinilla, Gustavo, 5f, 117, 136, 160, 253
Romero, Nicolás, 86
Rondon, Cândido, 198–99
Roosevelt, Theodore, 67
Rosas, Juan Manuel de, 54f, 60, 185
Rousseau, Jean Jacques, 21, 28, 181
Ruiz Cortines, Adolfo, 5
Rural areas, 17, 68, 96f, 116. *See also* Peasants

Salaries, 103, 132, 165, 193, 236, 250
Salvador, Humberto, 155
Salvador, José Fernández, 60
San Cristóbal, 107
San Martín, José de, 23, 25, 27, 84–85, 159
Sánchez, Francisco, 28
Santa Anna, Antonio López de, 48f, 67, 87, 90, 157
Santander, Francisco de Paula, 24
Santiago, 21, 96, 103, 169; mentioned, 86, 112, 142
São Paulo, 201, 204, 213, 234; revolts, 200f, 207; mentioned, 8, 185, 232
Sargento, El, 156
Sarmiento, Domingo Faustino, 66, 69, 85
Savio, Manuel N., 131
Scott, Winfield, 87
Secret organizations, 124–26, 126n, 220
Segura, Manuel Ascensio, 59

"Sergeants' Revolt," 111
Sertões, Os, 228
Seven Years' War, 18
Sierra, Justo, 46, 87
Sierra Maestra mountains, 76n, 112
Silvas americanus, 59
Simmons, Merle Edwin, 82
Sigueiros, David Alfaro, 157–58, 232
Slavery, 23, 185; in Brazil, 187–191 *passim,* 196, 202, 244
Social Christian Party (Venezuela), 109, 120
Social Darwinism, 66
Social Democratic Party (PSD), 209, 256
Somoza, Anastasio, 5
Song, 81f
Sosa Ríos, Ricardo, 111
Spain: conquest of Spanish America, 13–21; overthrow of control, 20–26, 34; and independence of colonies, 51, 180; immigration from, 64, 137; and Chile, 85–87; administration of colonies, 178–79; mentioned, 113, 159
Spanish America, 3, 244ff; conquest of, 13–20; 1825–50, 36, 43f, 47, 51f, 59f; 1850–1914, 62–70 *passim,* 74, 76f, 80–81; 20th century, 96, 101, 114–16, 123–28 *passim,* 134–43 *passim;* and Brazil, 178–191 *passim,* 194, 210, 210n, 216, 219
Spanish American War, 67
Spencer, Herbert, 189; his doctrines, 66, 196. *See also* Positivism
State interventionism, 139–40, 150
Strikes, 99, 256
Stroessner, Alfredo, 8
Sucre, Antonio José de, 22, 29–30, 159
Sugar, 95, 182, 213
Sun Yat-sen, 71

Tabernilla y Dolz, Francisco J., 111–12
Tabernilla y Palermo, Carlos M., Francisco H., and Marcelo, 112
Táchira, 107, 109
Taunay, Viscount of, 227
Távora, Juarez, 207, 209f

Taxes, 7, 20, 46, 139; revenues from, 55, 68, 248
Taylor, Zachary, 87
Technological change, 63–67, 77–79, 89, 115, 246; 251–52. *See also under individual countries*
Tenente (Lieutenant) Revolt, 194, 202f, 228
Tenentismo, 203–4, 206f, 216, 219f, 242
Terán, Enrique, 155
Tiempo, El, 160
Tocqueville, Alexis de, 36
Torres, Carlos Arturo, 83f
Torres Matos, Juan Francisco, 145
Toussaint L'Ouverture, Pierre Dominique, 20
Trade, 43, 55, 94–96, 246; international, 64, 67–68, 69, 94, 248
Trade unions, 256f
Transportation, 45, 63, 77, 94, 213; railroads, 63, 67, 131
Trujillo Molina, Rafael Leonidas, 6, 145, 159
Tupac Amaru, 20

Union of Soviet Socialist Republics, 101, 199, 222, 239. *See also* Communism
United States of America, 8, 66ff, 96, 260; its Constitution, 33, 57; war with Mexico, 46, 51, 87, 90, 160n; economic assistance, 61, 64; armed forces in, 124, 129, 142–43, 251; military assistance, 127, 262–63; embassies, 133, 232; and Argentina, 141, 167; and communism, 143–44; and Brazil, 207–8, 221–22, 239, 261; Peace Corps, 265; mentioned, 40, 63, 102, 129, 161, 166, 199
Uprisings, 3f, 5, 21ff, 36–37, 248–49, 256; in Mexico, 17, 21f, 68, 78, 183; in Chile, 21, 123; in Brazil, 183, 183n, 194–95, 202–4, 207, 214, 228; mentioned, 22, 111, 188, 245
Urban centers, 68, 97, 116, 147; in 19th century, 17–18, 21, 40, 42, 45; movement to, 64–65, 96, 261
Uriburu, José F., 121f
Uruguay, 9, 65, 99, 205, 261; and Brazil, 51, 185, 200; industry in, 63f, 77, 201; gross national prod-

uct, 94; political role of military, 102, 120, 136, 144; literary rates, 135; military and landed elite, 149; mentioned, 27, 65n, 79, 116, 246

Valdes, José C., 46
Vargas, Getulio, 194f, 197, 213f, 221; and workers, 98, 202, 215ff; influence of armed forces on, 204–9, 225, 230, 231n, 241f; mentioned, 219, 224f, 231, 243
Vasconcelos, José, 156f
Velasco, Luis Rodríguez, 86
Velasco Ibarra, José María, 121, 168
Venezuela, 7f, 94, 110f, 124, 149f; uprisings, 4, 21; training of officers, 70, 72, 102, 165; art and literature, 82, 159; agriculture, 95, 147; industry, 96, 138; politics, 99, 120; officer privileges, 103–4; origins of officers, 105ff, 109; civil-militarism, 122; and communism, 127; education, 135f; nationalism, 142; and Brazil, 200; reforestation, 266; mentioned, 27, 63, 113f, 235, 252–53, 261, 264
Verissimo, Erico, 226, 226n
Versailles, Treaty of, 97
Viduarre, Manuel Lorenzo de, 56
Villagrán, Carlos Cariola, 156
Villeda Morales, Ramón, 6
Viñas, David, 160
Violence, 58–62 *passim*, 74, 101f, 123; mentioned, 9, 38, 245, 248
Volta Redonda, 208, 222, 240

War of Jenkins' Ear, 18
War matériel, 71, 76
War of the Pacific (1879–83), 69, 83, 86, 88
Washington, George, 28f
Webb, Walter, 46–47
Welfare programs, 130
West Point, 53, 70
Wives. *See* Family, of officers
Workers. *See* Labor
World War I, 61ff, 167
World War II, 62

Ydígoras Fuentes, Miguel, 6